MEALS FOR EVERY OCCASION

Marshall Cavendish

Published by Marshall Cavendish
  Books Limited
58 Old Compton Street
London W1V 5PA

©Marshall Cavendish Limited 1976-1983

First printing 1979
Second printing 1983

Printed by Toppan, Hong Kong

ISBN 0 85685 710 6

INTRODUCTION

Cooking individual dishes for a meal can be an exciting challenge; cooking a selection of dishes together to make up an entire meal can be a nightmare. So there are those times when every cook, from the most experienced and inventive to the complete beginner, welcomes help and advice in constructing a complete, well-balanced and attractive menu.

Meals for Every Occasion has been designed to provide this assistance and just about every type of meal you are likely to cook, whether for family or friends is included—from a romantic dinner for two, through a summer barbecue and a delicious selection of ethnic meals to those memorable once-in-a-lifetime occasions such as an engagement party. Each recipe has easy step-by-step instructions and there are lots of full-colour illustrations to give you an idea of what the finished dish should look like. The recipes are divided into sensibly headed sections so that you can see at a glance where to find the kind of menu that you need. As a special feature there is a 'countdown' section which will enable you to plan not only the separate courses of the meal itself but also the shopping and preparation time so that you won't be too tired to enjoy the fruits of your efforts!

Meals for Every Occasion can guarantee not only perfect eating results but also a more confident, relaxed hostess who has both the time and inclination to enjoy her own meals and make such occasions, whether for the family or social, a great success.

CONTENTS

Menus from overseas

Party menus

Lunch Menus

A lunch with a difference for three

Here's a menu that gets away from the standard 'hors d'oeuvre, meat main course, pudding' syndrome. This time most of your protein comes from, and your money goes on, the first course: luxurious smoked trout. It is followed by an inexpensive but intriguing vegetable dish from the Mediterranean of stuffed peppers and, instead of a conventional pudding, there are sinful cream cakes to finish. This lunch is planned to feed that awkward number: a threesome.

Most of us automatically think in terms of a small starter, big main course and a sweet to finish, when planning for guests. Dinner parties, too, always seem to be planned for couples: four or six round the table. There are, however, many other occasions when you want to entertain friends or relatives to meals rather more special than the family's normal fare. If you are planning a dinner party, varying the normal programme is a simple way to get effect and to make the occasion memorable to your guests.

For a start, there is no reason why a dinner or lunch for guests has to have three courses. Big banquets often boast six or seven—hors d'oeuvre, soup, fish course, meat dish, sweet, cheeseboard and petits fours. Equally, many excellent meals consist of only two: meat course and dessert—Christmas dinner is a good example of this; a starter would leave no room for Christmas pudding. So don't feel bound by that magic three!

If you decide that three courses is what you want, there is no need to stick to the traditional pattern. One interesting deviation is to finish with a savoury instead of a dessert. Welsh rarebit, sardines on toast, mushrooms etc, are all favourites from before World War II: gentlemen used to enjoy them in their London clubs and the idea is well worth continuing. You could simply substitute the savoury for the sweet, or perhaps you could omit an hors d'oeuvre course altogether and start straight away with the meat dish (especially convenient for grills etc which cannot easily be kept warm); then serve fresh fruit, ending with the savoury.

Another possibility is to reverse the usual procedure of cold hors d'oeuvre followed by a hot main course. An excellent example of hot starter, cold main course is to be found in the Italian feast menu (see pages 171–178) with a hot, and quite filling, pasta course of tagliatelle followed by a light, cold vitello tonnato (veal in tuna fish sauce) and salad.

Steak tartare is a good example of a cold meat dish of dinner-party proportions. You could precede this with something hot like soup, or a hot vegetable dish like ratatouille.

Another break with tradition is to lavish money on the hors d'oeuvre course and be frugal over the main course. This is a good way to try the many excellent (but expensive) types of smoked fish and caviare.

This elegant luncheon menu is planned to start with rather expensive, but glorious, smoked trout in mustard cream sauce, followed by a more modest main course of stuffed peppers with scalloped potatoes. The protein of the meal is supplied by the fish, so the main course is basically vegetable dishes. This gets away from the accepted idea that the hors d'oeuvre is just to stimulate the appetite, and the real food value comes from the following dishes.

Instead of 'pudding' as such, this menu serves cream cakes, which might be nice taken with a pot of tea, rather than eaten on their own with coffee afterwards. If you don't have the time to make the cream slices, buy pastries from your local bakery in the morning.

THE GUESTS

There are lots of occasions when women want to be with other women, without necessarily needing a man around in order to turn the lunch into an 'event'. Take the arrival of your mother-in-law, for example. She is someone you doubtless have a sneaking desire to impress. Smoked trout would be just the thing for her, but only if it were followed by something fairly economical, such as the stuffed peppers. Can't have her thinking that you are an extravagant young woman for her son! There are also old school friends and former flat mates to whom you want to show off when they come over for lunch to talk about old times. Perhaps you may want to ask your own mother or godmother or favourite aunt to lunch—people who, in the past, were always giving you treat meals and whom you would now like to repay a little.

Lunch is a meal also when you can happily mix the generations. The 'best friend' you grew up with may know your mother almost as well as she knows you. Or perhaps you might like to turn your mother-in-law's visit into more of a party by inviting one of your neighbours to join you.

This menu has been planned around yourself and two guests, because threesomes are so seldom catered for in cookery books. Ingredients are always calculated, it seems, to feed even numbers, and sometimes amounts do not divide conveniently for three. So here you

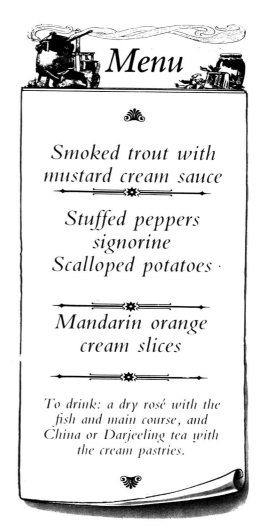

Menu

❦

Smoked trout with mustard cream sauce

*Stuffed peppers signorine
Scalloped potatoes* ·

Mandarin orange cream slices

To drink: a dry rosé with the fish and main course, and China or Darjeeling tea with the cream pastries.

have 3 small smoked trout, 3 stuffed peppers and 3 cream slices, with the appropriate amounts of sauces and fillings to go with them. On another occasion when you want to adapt this menu to feed a dinner party of 6, simply make twice as much.

GETTING ORGANIZED

This is not the kind of meal you plan days in advance; in fact, if your guests are local, you may even be issuing your invitations the day before. On the other hand the menu is rather too special to be ruined by bad organization.

To begin with, women—and especially older women—appreciate detail. They love flowers on the table, feel pampered at the sight of matching, pretty china, and they actually notice when you fold the napkins in attractive shapes, such as waterlilies. The appearance of the table is, therefore, important and for that reason the countdown timetable suggests you get it all set some hours before the lunch is due to start.

Countdown timetable

THE DAY BEFORE
Do the shopping.
Mandarin orange cream slices: make pastry and bake—steps 1–5. Cool and store overnight in an airtight tin.

ON THE DAY
In the morning
Set the table.
Mandarin orange cream slices: split

and combine with fruit, cream, jam and nuts—steps 6–15.
Smoked trout with mustard cream sauce: make sauce and chill in refrigerator—step 1.

1 hour before the meal
Stuffed peppers signorine: prepare the onions and peppers and blanch the peppers—steps 2–4.

50 minutes before the meal
Scalloped potatoes: heat oven. Parboil potatoes and prepare topping— steps 1–4.
Stuffed peppers signorine: make the filling and stuff the peppers—steps 5–9.
Scalloped potatoes: prepare the dish ready for the oven—steps 5–7.

30 minutes before the meal
Stuffed peppers signorine: pour on tomato juice and bake—step 10.
Scalloped potatoes: bake—step 8.
Smoked trout with mustard cream sauce: arrange fish on serving plate and garnish—steps 2–3.
Serve sherry to guests.

10 minutes before the meal
Smoked trout with mustard cream sauce: cut bread and butter—step 4.
Scalloped potatoes: uncover dish to brown the top—step 9.
Put plates to warm for the peppers.

Another job you can do well in advance is finish the cream slices. It is a good idea to do the baking part the previous day and also, of course, all the shopping.

The hors d'oeuvre course is cold and so will not require cooking; but the sauce can be mixed a couple of hours beforehand and left in the refrigerator to chill.

If you think that your guests are too figure-conscious to eat both potato and pastries at the same meal, (the potato portions are deliberately small) keep the lovely cream slices and omit the potatoes. Serve a green salad instead; there are several excellent salad ideas given in other menus in this book, such as Italian green salad. As the dish with the cheese is being omitted, a little cheese could be grated over each stuffed pepper for decoration (allow 15 g [½ oz] per person) before the dish is put in the oven.

About an hour before the meal is when you start work in earnest.

Begin by preparing the stuffed peppers and the scalloped potatoes to the point where they are ready for the oven—then you can start them baking. Arrange the trout on a plate.

During the last 10 minutes, apart from cutting and buttering the bread, there will be nothing at all for you to do but relax and talk to your guests.

SHOPPING CHECKLIST
The star of this meal is undeniably the smoked trout, so order that before you organize any other food: for if trout is unavailable in your area, then you may very well want to rethink your entire menu. Don't forget you want smoked trout, not fresh, and you are more likely to find it in a delicatessen than in a fishmonger's. If collecting it the day before, wrap it and store in the refrigerator.

The delicatessen may also be the place to buy Emmenthal cheese; but if you cannot find it, do not worry— Cheddar with the addition of a little parmesan would be perfectly acceptable as a substitute.

In the greengrocery department, take your time finding three small stumpy bell peppers, just the right shape for stuffing for your main course of stuffed peppers signorine. You will also want lettuce for garnishing the trout, 350 g [¾ lb] of old potatoes for the scalloped potatoes and 175 g [6 oz] each of onions and of mushrooms, plus garlic for the pepper stuffing. Finally, you will need parsley and a lemon for the trout.

In the general grocery department, buy a 150 ml [¼ pt] can of tomato juice and one of mandarin segments and, as necessary, Dijon mustard, tomato purée, cornflakes, sugar, bacon, butter, vanilla extract and mixed nuts. Also, buy frozen pastry or check your store cupboard for baking ingredients. If you have no apricot jam but do have a jelly marmalade (ie one without peel), use that instead for glazing your cream pastries.

As for the cream, if your supermarket stocks a 175 ml [6 fl oz] carton, that will be large enough for the cream slices and allow sufficient over for the trout sauce. You can always sour your own fresh cream with lemon juice. Otherwise buy 150 ml [5 fl oz] of fresh cream for the mandarins and the smallest size you can find of soured cream. Do not forget a brown loaf to accompany the trout.

If you think the idea of a speciality tea a good one, but find buying a whole packet just for this one lunch rather extravagant, look for gift packs of tea-bags instead. They are a neat way of obtaining several different luxury teas in one go. For this menu, a China tea or a Darjeeling would be excellent.

THE DRINKS
For a change, why not choose a rosé wine to accompany this meal? When offered the choice of anything on the wine-list in a restaurant, women very often opt for a rosé, and with trout and stuffed peppers on this menu, a rosé would certainly be very suitable. Do buy a dry one, and preferably a non-sparkling rosé, too—the celebrated Portuguese Mateus, for instance, would be too sweet for this particular menu.

If you are pampering your guests and serving an aperitif as well as table wine, then a medium sherry finds favour with most women.

Smoked trout with mustard cream sauce

This is an hors d'oeuvre from the luxury class which deserves to be eaten just as it is—merely garnished with lettuce and lemon wedges and accompanied with brown bread and butter. The mustard cream sauce makes a superb alternative to the more usual horseradish cream sauce. If you wish, the fish can be bought filleted and the heads and tails removed in the kitchen beforehand.

Filleting the smoked trout will be essential on an occasion when the fish is larger and a portion is only half a fillet. It is, however, more usual—if less convenient for the diners—to serve the fish unfilleted. Serve the sauce in a separate bowl.

SERVES 3
3 small smoked trout
1 lettuce heart
half a lemon
3 slices brown buttered bread
parsley for garnish (optional)

For the sauce:
**30 ml [2 tablespoons] Dijon
mustard**

**90 ml [6 tablespoons] soured
cream**

1 Make the sauce. Put the mustard and the soured cream into a jug and stir until thoroughly blended. Chill lightly in the refrigerator.

2 Wash and dry the lettuce leaves. Put these on a serving plate and arrange the trout on top decoratively.

3 Cut the lemon into wedges and arrange on the trout as a garnish. Use parsley, too, if wished.

4 Serve bread and butter separately.

Stuffed peppers signorine

An inexpensive and tasty recipe from the Mediterranean, this is an example of a vegetable dish interesting enough to serve as a main dish, but which could be served as an accompaniment at a grander meal. It can be accompanied with rice, bread or a salad, or the potatoes given here. Canned tomato juice is given here for simplicity's sake, but on an occasion when you have more time, make a tomato sauce using either fresh or tinned tomatoes. This dish is also attractive cold. Serve whole for a main course, halved as a starter for 6 people.

The dish in which the peppers are cooked is taken to the table. Choose one with a small diameter and high sides, such as a 15 cm [6"] soufflé dish or a small casserole with a lid.

SERVES 3
3 medium-sized peppers
salt
1 garlic clove
175 g [6 oz] onions
50 g [2 oz] bacon rashers
30 ml [2 tablespoons] oil
175 g [6 oz] mushrooms
30 ml [2 tablespoons] freshly chopped parsley
freshly ground black pepper
15 ml [1 tablespoon] lemon juice
15 ml [1 tablespoon] tomato purée
150 ml [¼ pt] canned tomato juice

1 Heat oven to 180°C [350°F] gas mark 4.

2 Prepare the peppers: cut off the stalk end, take out the seeds and fibres and rinse out. Chop the edible parts of the lid and reserve.

3 Half fill a saucepan with salted water, bring to the boil and blanch peppers for 5 minutes. Drain and refresh in cold water.

4 Peel and finely chop the garlic and onions.

5 De-rind the bacon and chop it into matchsticks. Put the oil into a heavy-based frying-pan and add the bacon. Sweat it for 1 minute.

6 Add the onions, garlic and chopped reserved peppers to the pan and fry over a low heat to soften.

7 Meanwhile, wipe and chop the mushrooms. Add them to the pan and cook stirring from time to time for 2 minutes.

8 Add the parsley, pepper, lemon juice and tomato purée. Season generously and stir to mix.

9 Spoon the mixture into the peppers and stand these in the casserole.

10 Pour round the tomato juice and season it. Cover the dish with a lid or foil and bake for 30 minutes.

Scalloped potatoes

This original way of serving potatoes makes them into a side dish fit for guests. This is a pleasant warming dish on a winter's day. On economy nights, it could be served as a main dish for two, with perhaps a hot soup to start.

If you cannot get Emmenthal use grated Cheddar with 15 ml [1 tablespoon] of parmesan. The easiest way to crush cornflakes is to put them in a large polythene bag and roll them with a rolling pin.

SERVES 3
350 g [¾ lb] small to
    medium-sized potatoes
65 g [2½ oz] Emmenthal
    cheese
40 g [1½ oz] cornflakes
salt and pepper
40 g [1½ oz] butter

1 Heat oven to 180°C [350°F] gas mark 4.

2 Peel and rinse the potatoes. Cut medium-sized potatoes in half. Parboil them in salted water for 10 minutes.

3 Meanwhile grate the cheese and crush the cornflakes finely.

4 Put the grated cheese and cornflakes in a bowl, season generously and mix together.

5 Drain the potatoes and pat dry on kitchen paper. Slice thinly.

6 Grease a small shallow ovenproof dish with butter and arrange a layer of potato slices. Top with a layer of cheese mixture and dot over half the remaining butter.

7 Make a second layer of potato slices, finishing with a layer of cheese. Dot over the remaining butter.

8 Cover the dish with lid or foil and bake at the top of the oven for 20 minutes.

9 Remove the lid or foil and continue cooking, uncovered, for a further 10 minutes to brown the top.

Mandarin orange cream slices

◪◪ *These are delicious pastries made of rough puff or flaky pastry, as described in the glossary. If you are making your own pastry, instead of using frozen, make double the amount to achieve the same rise and pair them rather than splitting them. The fruity filling and topping makes them suitable not only for afternoon tea but also for eating in place of a dessert course.*

SERVES 3
225 g [½ lb] home-made rough puff or flaky pastry or 125 g [¼ lb] frozen puff pastry, made weight
granulated sugar
225 g [8 oz] canned mandarin orange segments
150 ml [5 fl oz] carton thick cream
few drops vanilla extract
15 ml [1 tablespoon] apricot jam
15 ml [1 tablespoon] chopped mixed nuts

1 Heat oven to 220°C [425°F] gas mark 7. Position shelf to just above centre of oven.

2 Sprinkle rolling surface liberally with granulated sugar. Roll out the pastry and then trim it with a sharp knife to oblong 15 × 10 cm [6 × 4"].

3 Rinse a baking sheet with water. Cut frozen pastry into 3 strips (home-made pastry into 6) each measuring 5 × 10 cm [2 × 4"].

4 Place the pastry strips on the baking sheet and prick them well with a fork. Transfer the baking sheet to the refrigerator for 30 minutes to relax the pastry.

5 Bake for 15 minutes or until well risen and golden brown. Transfer the strips to a wire rack and cool.

6 Drain syrup from the can of mandarin segments and keep it for another dish. Reserve 18 segments for decoration and roughly chop the remainder.

7 Place the cream and a few drops of vanilla extract in a bowl.

8 Whisk the cream until it stands in soft peaks. Fold in the chopped mandarin oranges, using a metal spoon.

9 If home-made pastry is used, place slices in pairs. If frozen pastry is used slice pastry strip into 2, through the flakes, lengthways.

10 Using half the whipped mandarin cream, generously sandwich each pastry strip back together.

11 Spread the remaining cream evenly over tops of each pastry slice with a round-bladed or small palette knife.

12 Place sieved jam in a small saucepan, add 5 ml [1 teaspoon] of water and stir over a low heat until jam has melted. Remove from heat.

13 Pat reserved mandarin segments dry on kitchen paper and then arrange 6 in a line on top of each pastry slice.

14 Carefully brush mandarin segments with apricot glaze to coat.

15 Sprinkle slices with mixed nuts.

Slimmers' lunch party for four

Invite your female friends to this light, refreshing summer lunch. The variety of textures has appeal for dieters and non-dieters alike and the three courses add up to a mere 459 calories per person—giving leeway for a glass or two of wine as well for those who wish.

TO HELP YOU SLIM

No one enjoys slimming but today there is no need to deprive yourself unduly. There are many products on the market which, when included as part of a calorie-controlled diet, can increase the rate of weight loss quite noticeably. If you select your ingredients with care, cook them sensibly and add up the calories as you go, you will find that you can eat quite well and still lose weight. It is not necessary to starve.

There are also many non-fattening substitutes for fattening foods available to help you slim. Low-fat spreads are a substitute for butter, liquid and granular sweeteners can replace sugar for those who cannot banish the 'sweet tooth', while low-calorie salad dressings, sauces and soft drinks mean few drastic changes in everyday life. Skimmed milk in tea or coffee has only half the calories of whole milk and you can buy it either ready mixed or reconstitute it from powder.

The idea of slimming on a diet of unrelieved 'rabbit food' is a thing of the past. These days most slimmers know that lean red meat, chicken, eggs, cheese, white fish, fruit and vegetables are all available to them. These foods are rich in protein, vitamins and essential mineral salts, but low in calories. Cooked properly, they will remain so.

Counting the calories

To keep the calorie count low, trim the fat from meat and remove the skin from chicken. Grill food so that the fat drips away rather than frying in fat or oil which are then absorbed by the food, increasing its caloric value. Serve yourself generous portions of raw or plainly cooked green vegetables. But avoid pulses such as peas and beans, which are more fattening. Eat plenty of fruit with the exception of bananas. Grapes are also best avoided as they have a high sugar content.

One of the first things people eliminate from their diet when they start slimming is potatoes, but this is not essential. You may eat a small amount of potato if you wish, provided it is not fried or cooked with fat in any way. A baked potato is admissable for slimmers if served with low-fat spread or yoghurt instead of the usual butter. You can also eat a controlled amount of low-calorie bread.

Foods which are high in carbohydrate provide energy, but the body quickly converts them into fat if their full energy-value is not used. Chiefly to be avoided among these are sugar and sweets, closely followed by cakes, biscuits and snacks such as crisps. If you must eat between meals, have crunchy vegetables and cubes of cheese ready prepared in the refrigerator. These will stem your hunger without disrupting your diet too much.

A drink of tea or coffee, with sweetener if required, or even a glass of water helps fill the gap, while hot yeast and meat-extract drinks are helpful because their savoury taste discourages any tendency to nibble sweet things.

Cooking hints

When cooking, substitute low-calorie ingredients for high-calorie ones. For example, low-fat yoghurt can be used instead of cream when making cream soups and can be served in place of cream with fruit. Replace sugar with liquid sweetener when stewing or poaching fruit. For casseroles, always use the cold-start method where there is no need to fry the meat in fat first. Skim off any fat which comes to the top of casseroles and soups.

TEN TIPS FOR TROUBLE-FREE SLIMMING

1 Don't tell your friends you are on a diet. If they don't know, they won't be able to tempt you with fattening goodies. Dieting brings out the devil in even the best of friends—as many failed slimmers know to their cost.

2 Don't be discouraged if your weight does not drop by a consistent amount each week. You will reach several plateaux in the course of your diet, and after a rapid initial loss your weight may appear to remain static. This is only temporary, so don't give up.

3 Invest in a good calorie counting book and be scrupulously honest about weighing everything and recording everything you eat. Many slimmers claim they can't lose with calorie counting, but this is generally because they have been cheating. Anyone can lose weight on an intake of 1500 calories a day.

4 Use smaller plates to make portions look bigger.

5 Choose wisely when you go out for a meal so there's no need to do penance. Smoked fish, grapefruit, melon or antipasto are suitable starters. Good main courses are grills or plain casseroles with plenty of vegetables or salad. A small portion of baked or boiled potatoes is allowed, but never roasted or fried ones.

6 Puddings are many a slimmer's downfall. To avoid this choose cheese and celery or, if you must have something sweet, a water-ice or fresh fruit.

7 If you drink, stick to dry white wine and ration yourself to occasional spirits. Avoid beer—it is very fattening.

8 Always weigh yourself on the same scales every week and make yourself a progress graph. Remember the steeper you make the curve of the graph, the better it will look.

9 Join a slimming group if there is one near you—it always helps to find there are others in the same boat.

10 Never diet to excess. Check the correct weight for your age on a weight/height table and do not attempt to go below it. If you are attempting to lose a large amount of weight, you should not attempt this without the supervision of your doctor.

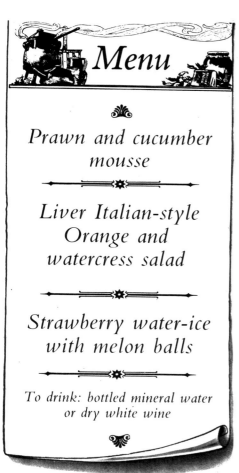

*Prawn and cucumber
mousse*

*Liver Italian-style
Orange and
watercress salad*

*Strawberry water-ice
with melon balls*

*To drink: bottled mineral water
or dry white wine*

Countdown timetable

THE DAY BEFORE
Buy all the food with the exception of the liver.
Prawn and cucumber mousse: make the mousse—steps 1–8.
Strawberry water-ice with melon balls: make the water-ice—steps 1–10.

ON THE MORNING
Buy the liver. Chill the mineral water or wine.

One hour before lunch
Prawn and cucumber mousse: turn out the mousse and decorate— steps 9–10. Put in cool place.
Liver Italian-style: prepare ingredients— steps 1–3.
Orange and watercress salad: prepare oranges and watercress— steps 1–3.

Half an hour before lunch
Remove wine from refrigerator or it will be too cold.
Strawberry water-ice with melon balls: make the melon balls—step 11.

10 minutes before lunch
Orange and watercress salad: combine ingredients in a serving bowl— step 4.
Strawberry water-ice with melon balls: remove the ice from freezing compartment and place on the least cold shelf in refrigerator—step 12.

After the first course
Liver Italian-style: cook the dish steps 4–7.

After the main course
Strawberry water-ice with melon balls: scoop ice on top of melon, decorate with one or two strawberries and serve—step 13.

ENTERTAINING ON A DIET
Going on a diet can wreak havoc with your social life, but entertaining needn't go by the board. Slimming need not be a lonely business or a culinary bore as this slimmers' lunch menu for four amply demonstrates. Though your weight-conscious friends may be quite content with iced mineral water over lunch, for dinner you could serve Perrier water as an aperitif, as the French often do, and serve a dry wine with the meal. This won't send the calorie count rocketing and will effectively transform the meal into something festive enough to serve even to non-slimming friends.

Getting organized
This is an easy meal to prepare as the water-ice can be made well in advance and the mousse can be made the day before. Remove the mousse from the mould and decorate with prawns just before serving.

You will need a 400 ml [¾ pt] container for the mousse. This will look best in a ring mould or could be served in a soufflé dish. If you own neither of these, it may be made in an 18 cm [7″] cake tin.

All the preparation for the liver Italian-style can be done in advance. It cooks in a matter of minutes so the frying can be done after you and your guests have eaten the first course. This has the advantage of allowing time for your guests to digest the first course and it is a good practice, particularly when slimming, to allow five minutes between each course for this purpose.

The frozen water-ice will need to soften slightly before it is eaten and should be removed from the freezer or ice-making compartment to the least cold shelf in the refrigerator (usually the bottom) 10 minutes before the meal begins. This will allow about half an hour before the water-ice is actually eaten.

SHOPPING CHECKLIST
All the shopping for this meal can be done a day in advance although, for the sake of freshness, the liver is better bought on the day if possible. Calf's liver is the tenderest but the most expensive and is not always available. As an alternative buy lamb's liver. Buy the liver in one piece and slice it yourself for maximum freshness.

Check that you have some green food colouring for the mousse and foil or cling film for covering cold dishes in the refrigerator. Cling film generally works out cheaper.

Look for a low-fat yoghurt which is appreciably lower in calories than ordinary yoghurt. If you cannot get fresh strawberries for the water-ice, buy frozen ones not canned, as these latter are highly sweetened.

DRINKS
For minimum calorie intake serve bottled spring water, such as the French Perrier water which has a natural 'sparkle' and which can be bought at many supermarkets. Serve in a jug with the strained juice of half a lemon, lemon slices and plenty of ice. Garnish with sprigs of mint if you wish.

If you must offer wine, a dry white wine has the least calories— about 19 calories per 25 ml [1 fl oz]; claret is also low in calories. Remember that an average wine glass two-thirds full contains around 125 ml [4 fl oz] which accounts for 76 calories. Once you start a second glass you will be adding nearly one-third to your calorie count.

Prawn and cucumber mousse

Calories per portion—86

⊠⊠⊠ *Roughly chopped pieces of cucumber give bite to this unusual mousse, providing a more satisfying taste and texture. Do not let the gelatine stand once melted, as it will begin to set. Use an attractive savoury mould—a fish-shaped one would be ideal—or a ring mould, and serve, garnished with prawns.*

SERVES 4
50 g [2 oz] cottage cheese
150 ml [¼ pt] natural low-fat yoghurt
1 large cucumber
100 g [¼ lb] peeled prawns
150 ml [¼ pt] chicken stock
15 g [½ oz] gelatine powder
10 ml [2 teaspoons] lemon juice
salt
freshly ground black pepper
2–3 drops green food colouring

1 Sieve the cottage cheese and mix with the yoghurt.

2 Peel and roughly chop the cucumber. Chop half the peeled prawns.

3 Place 30 ml [2 tablespoons] cold chicken stock in a small heavy-based pan. Sprinkle the gelatine over it and leave to soak for 5 minutes.

4 Place the pan with the gelatine over a very low heat until the liquid has cleared. This will take about 3 minutes.

5 Pour gelatine into the remaining cold chicken stock and mix well.

6 Stir chopped cucumber and prawns into the cheese and yoghurt mixture. Add lemon juice and season to taste.

7 Add the stock containing the gelatine to the mixture and just enough food colouring to turn the mousse pale green. Mix lightly but thoroughly.

8 Rinse out a 400 ml [¾ pt] mould with cold water and pour in the mixture. Cover and leave to set in the refrigerator for 2 hours.

9 Dip the mould into hot water for one minute and invert a plate over the top. Turn out the mousse on to the plate.

10 Decorate with the remaining prawns.

Liver Italian-style

Calories per portion—221

Liver is highly nutritious but low in calories. It remains so even when fried as it absorbs very little fat. The cooking time for the liver is brief so this can be done while diners are waiting. The addition of mushrooms makes this a fairly hearty dish, which will satisfy the largest appetite without piling on the pounds.

SERVES 4
450 g [1 lb] lamb's or calf's liver
225 g [½ lb] button mushrooms
6 fresh sage leaves
2 garlic cloves
40 g [1½ oz] unsalted butter
15 ml [1 tablespoon] lemon juice

1 Remove any ducts and fat from the liver and cut it into 6 mm [¼″] slices. If not cooking immediately, cover and refrigerate.

2 Wipe and thinly slice the mushrooms.

3 Chop the sage. Skin and finely chop or crush the garlic and mix with the sage. Add mushrooms and set aside.

4 Heat the butter in a heavy-based frying-pan over a low heat until the foam has subsided, then add the liver.

5 Cook the liver for 4 minutes on each side using a fish slice or tongs for turning the slices to avoid piercing the flesh.

6 Remove liver from the pan, cover and keep warm. Add the other ingredients, including lemon juice, to the juices in the pan.

7 Cook for 2 minutes, stirring occasionally. Spoon over liver and serve.

Orange and watercress salad

Calories per portion—20

There is no need for a dressing on this salad as the juice from the oranges and the naturally strong flavour of the watercress give it plenty of bite. This is good news for slimmers for whom salad dressings are a calorie-laden pitfall.

SERVES 4
2 oranges
1 large bunch watercress

1 Using a sharp vegetable knife peel the oranges, cutting as close to the flesh as possible.

2 Holding the oranges over a plate so that no juice is lost, cut between the membrane and the flesh to divide the oranges into segments. Put the segments in a bowl and chill in the refrigerator until ready to put the salad together.

3 Wash the watercress and cut off stringy stalk ends, discarding any dead or yellowing leaves. Shake or dry in a salad spinner. Wrap in a polythene bag and reserve in the refrigerator if not using at once.

4 Place the watercress in a salad bowl and mix in the orange segments. Pour over any remaining orange juice and serve.

Strawberry water-ice with melon balls

Calories per serving—132

▨▨▨ *Strawberry water-ice looks as luscious as it tastes and has the joy of being low in calories as well. Melon is a great friend to slimmers; some varieties contain only four calories per ounce. Here it provides an attractive colour contrast to the ice.*

Make sure your melon is ripe. Choose a cantaloupe or two small Ogen melons. A honeydew melon will do but it is more fattening.

This water-ice will serve 6 so if you do not eat all of it the calorie count will be reduced.

SERVES 4-6
450 g [1 lb] strawberries
100 g [¼ lb] caster sugar
45 ml [3 tablespoons] lemon juice
45 ml [3 tablespoons] orange juice
1 cantaloupe or 2 Ogen melons
1 egg

1 Set the refrigerator to its lowest setting and remove food not to be frozen.

2 Measure 250 ml [½ pt] water into a pan. Add the sugar and stir once. Bring to the boil over medium heat, lower heat and simmer for 5 minutes.

3 Pour into a jug, leave to cool and then chill.

4 Wash and hull the strawberries, reserving 100 g [¼ lb] for decoration. Use a liquidizer or push the remaining 350 g [¾ lb] through a sieve to purée.

5 Mix the orange and lemon juice with the strawberry purée.

6 Mix the strawberry purée with the sugar syrup. If using a refrigerator pour into an ice-cube tray or loaf tin. If using a freezer you can leave the mixture in a plastic bowl. Cover and seal with a double thickness of foil or cling film and freeze for about 45 minutes until slushy.

7 Just before removing the ice from

the freezing compartment, separate the egg white and reserve the yolk for future use. Whisk the white until it stands in thick peaks.

8 Turn the slush into a bowl if necessary and beat the harder outside into the softer inside. Then beat in the egg white a spoonful at a time.

9 Re-cover and freeze until the mixture again forms a slush (about 45 minutes).

10 Turn out the ice and beat as

before. Return to freezing compartment and freeze until firm.

11 Halve the melon and remove the seeds. Use a melon-baller to scoop out balls of melon flesh. Place in individual serving dishes.

12 Ten minutes before the meal, remove water-ice from the freezing compartment and place on the least cold shelf of the refrigerator.

13 Scoop water-ice on top of the melon balls and decorate with one or two strawberries.

A Sunday lunch for six

Sundays, most families agree, would not be Sundays without the traditional roast. Bacon joints are always reasonably priced and are delicious roasted. Bacon is meaty enough to please the traditionalists and a rather more enterprising choice than the usual Sunday fare of roast beef, lamb or pork. To go with the roasted bacon, there are broad beans and potatoes cooked in delicious and unusual ways. To start the meal there is an appetizing sardine salad and as a grand finale, strawberry baked Alaska, a 'conjuring trick' dessert that never fails to delight.

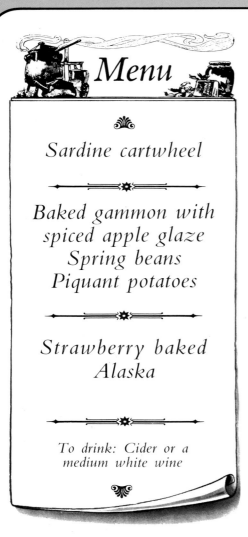

Menu

Sardine cartwheel

Baked gammon with spiced apple glaze
Spring beans
Piquant potatoes

Strawberry baked Alaska

To drink: Cider or a medium white wine

Countdown timetable

THE DAY BEFORE

Do shopping.
Strawberry baked Alaska: make or buy sponge flan case and ice-cream.
Baked gammon with spiced apple glaze: soak if necessary—step 1.

ON THE DAY

6 hours before

Baked gammon with spiced apple glaze: soak if not already done—step 1.

2¾ hours before

Baked gammon with spiced apple glaze: if not previously soaked, blanch and drain—step 1.

2½ hours before

Baked gammon with spiced apple glaze: place in water and start simmering—step 2. Heat the oven—step 3.

1 hour 40 minutes before

Baked gammon with spiced apple glaze: skin and decorate with cloves. Place in the oven—steps 4–7.

1 hour before

Sardine cartwheel: prepare—steps 1–6. Cover and leave in a cool place until required.

40 minutes before

Baked gammon with spiced apple glaze: prepare the glaze—step 8. Remove gammon from the oven and glaze then roast—steps 9-10.
Strawberry baked Alaska: place flan case on an ovenproof plate and add strawberries—steps 1–2. Leave in a cool place.
Spring beans: shell—step 1.
Piquant potatoes: prepare and start cooking—step 1. Prepare celery—step 2.

I f your family are traditionalists about Sunday lunch, you may have found serving the same roast and vegetables week after week a rather restrictive business. A roasted bacon joint gets away from this but still provides Sunday meat for those who would feel lost without it.

Here, quite a large joint of gammon was used. Gammon is one of the more expensive cuts of bacon but its flavour is excellent, it cuts well and if you buy a boned joint of the weight given in the recipe, there will be enough to eat hot at lunchtime and cold in the evening or the next day.

In order that the joint does not become the most important thing in the meal (always a risk when a large piece of meat is served), the first course, vegetables and dessert have been chosen carefully. The first course makes clever use of canned sardines and removes the edge from appetites before the more expensive meat arrives on the table. To accompany the meat, there are herb-scented broad beans and an unusual dish of creamed potatoes, mixed with raisins and chopped celery. To end the meal, there is strawberry baked Alaska, a delicious pudding that really must be eaten all at once because it won't keep. Warn the diners of this in advance then they'll have room for a generous helping.

GETTING ORGANIZED

None of these dishes is particularly difficult to make, but the strawberry baked Alaska does require close attention to detail for success.

A baked Alaska is made with ice-cream which is piled into a sponge flan case with fruit, topped with meringue and then browned for a few minutes in a very hot oven. The result is a dish hot on the outside with an icy filling. The great risk, of course, is that the ice-cream will melt, but if you follow instructions carefully, all should be well.

The day before, make the sponge base and the ice-cream for the Alaska (or buy the ice-cream). Follow your favourite recipe for whisked sponge cake or if you like buy a ready-made sponge flan case.

The flan can be filled with the fruit in advance but it is essential that the ice-cream and meringue are assembled at the very last moment.

Usually, recipes tell you to remove ice-cream from the refrigerator or freezer 30 minutes before serving to take away hardness. With baked Alaska this would be disastrous because the ice-cream would begin to melt in the oven. It is important to leave the ice-cream in the freezer until the very last minute.

Meringue cannot be prepared in advance because it will collapse, so between courses you will have to whisk the meringue (use an electric whisk to save time), quickly remove the ice-cream from the freezer, pile into the fruit-filled flan and top with meringue. When spreading the meringue topping, be sure that it covers the sponge flan case completely—even the sides—otherwise it will not do its job of being an insulating jacket between the heat and the ice-cream. Always have the oven pre-heated to the correct temperature when making baked Alaska so there is no waiting around. This might seem like a lot of work between courses but it will take only 5 minutes. This gives guests time to digest the

12 minutes before
Spring beans: start cooking—step 1.

6 minutes before
Piquant potatoes: remove from heat, drain, mash and make additions—steps 3–5. Dot with extra butter, cover and place either in a warming drawer or over a pan of water.

5 minutes before
Strawberry baked Alaska: heat oven to 220°C [425°F] gas mark 7—step 3. Spring beans: drain and toss in butter with herbs—steps 1–2. Keep hot as given for potatoes.
Baked gammon with spiced apple glaze: remove from the oven and leave in a warm place—step 11. Remove drinks from refrigerator.

Between main and dessert courses
Strawberry baked Alaska: make meringue. Fill flan case with ice-cream, cover with meringue and cook—steps 4–8.

main course before being faced with the splendid pudding.

SHOPPING CHECKLIST
As this is a Sunday meal, all your shopping will have to be done the day before. The gammon is quite a large joint, so it might be a good idea to order it in advance. For the gammon you will need cloves and apple juice. Both can usually be obtained from supermarkets. Or you can ask your milkman for apple juice or ask for it at a liquor store and buy the wine or cider there, too.

Don't forget the ingredients for the ice-cream and the sponge flan as these are not actually mentioned in the recipes. If there are no fresh strawberries available, substitute frozen, or use fresh raspberries, peaches, nectarines or apricots.

DRINKS
Cider makes a pleasant and refreshing accompaniment to all three courses but if wished, a medium white wine could be served instead. Older children could have the cider but if there are younger ones present provide soft drinks.

Sardine cartwheel

The idea of combining oranges and sardines sounds unpromising, but the result is a delicious hors d'oeuvre—and one which is decorative enough to provide a handsome centrepiece for a lunch or buffet party.

SERVES 6
100 g [$\frac{1}{4}$ lb] canned sardines in oil
4 oranges
1 small Spanish onion
bunch of watercress
75 g [3 oz] canned pimento

1 Peel the oranges, removing all pith, and cut into thin slices. Arrange the slices overlapping around the edge of a circular dish.

2 Peel the onion. Cut it into slices and push into rings. Arrange a few of the rings over the orange slices and place the remainder in the centre of the dish.

3 Chop most of the watercress, reserving a few sprigs for garnish. Put chopped watercress on top of the onions in the centre of the dish.

4 Drain the sardines and arrange, radiating from the centre of the dish (tail ends pointing to the centre and bodies fanning out).

5 Drain the pimento and cut into thin strips. Arrange a strip along the length of each sardine.

6 Garnish the centre of the dish with reserved watercress sprigs.

Baked gammon with spiced apple glaze

◫◫◫ *Gammon, first boiled to cook it and then skinned and finished off in the oven with a fruity, slightly spicy glaze, makes a delicious and unusual alternative to the usual Sunday joint. The gammon is marked in the traditional criss-cross pattern and studded with cloves before a liquid glaze is applied. Bottled apple juice is quick and easy to use.*

Pre-soaking of very mild-cured bacon is unnecessary. Simply place the joint in a pan, cover with cold water, bring to the boil and drain. If using a smoked joint, it must be soaked. Soak in cold water for at least 4 hours or overnight if wished and omit the blanching.

Removing the gammon from the oven 10–15 minutes before serving allows the meat to set and makes it easier to carve.

SERVES 6
**1.8 kg [4 lb] boneless gammon
   joint
20 whole cloves
30 ml [2 tablespoons] cooking
   oil
100 g [¼ lb] Demerara sugar
60 ml [4 tablespoons] apple
   juice
pinch of mixed spice**

1 According to the cure or the cut purchased, either soak the gammon in cold water for at least 4 hours and drain, or blanch by placing in a pan of water and bringing to the boil and then draining the meat.

2 Place the gammon in a large, heavy-based saucepan with enough water to cover. Slowly bring to the boil, cover and simmer for 40 minutes.

3 Remove the gammon from the pan as soon as it is cool enough to handle. Set the oven to 200°C [400°F] gas mark 6.

4 Using a sharp knife, cut away the rind from the gammon, making sure you do not cut too deeply into the fat.

5 Cut the fat into diamond patterns, cutting diagonally in one direction and then another to form a criss-cross pattern. Make shallow cuts, being sure to cut the fat only, not the flesh.

6 Brush the fat with oil, using a pastry brush. Stud each diamond with a clove.

7 Place in a roasting tin. Place in the centre of the oven and roast for 1 hour. Baste from time to time with the pan juices.

8 Meanwhile, prepare the glaze. Mix together the sugar, apple juice and mixed spice in a heavy-based pan. Stir over low heat until the sugar has dissolved and the mixture is just about to boil.

9 Remove the gammon from the oven and brush the glaze over the fat using a pastry brush. Reduce oven temperature to 190°C [375°F] gas mark 5.

10 Return the gammon to the oven and roast for a further 35 minutes, basting from time to time with pan juices.

11 Remove from the oven 10–15 minutes before serving and keep in a warm place.

Spring beans

◫ *Broad beans are at their very best when young, before the dark line characteristic of age has developed along the side of the beans. Summer savory is a natural complement to broad beans but if you cannot obtain it, use chopped parsley instead. Allowing for the weight of the pods buy 1.8 kg [4 lb] of beans.*

SERVES 6
**900 g [2 lb] broad beans,
   shelled weight
sprig of parsley
salt
50 g [2 oz] butter
sprig of savory**

1. Shell the beans and cook with the parsley in lightly salted water for 8 minutes. Drain.

2. Cut the butter into dice and put into the saucepan. Add the beans. Finely chop savory and add. Toss over low heat until the beans are coated in melted butter. Serve immediately.

Piquant potatoes

This mixture of creamed potatoes, celery and raisins may seem un-usual but was a popular favourite among the Victorians, who were very discerning about food. A pinch of mace accentuates flavours and the touch of sweetness from the raisins goes particularly well with the gammon. To keep the potatoes warm until needed, dot with a little butter, cover loosely with foil and keep in a warming drawer or over a pan of hot water.

SERVES 6
700 g [1¼ lb] potatoes
salt
4 celery sticks
1 large egg
25 g [1 oz] butter
pinch of mace
45 ml [3 tablespoons] seedless raisins

1. Peel the potatoes, cut into chunks and boil in salted water for 15 minutes or until tender.

2. Meanwhile, scrub celery sticks and chop finely.

3. Drain the potatoes and then return them without additions to the pan over a low heat for 3–4 seconds to dry out. Remove from the heat and mash with a potato masher.

4. Break the egg into a bowl and beat with a fork. Stir quickly into the potatoes. Chop the butter into dice and stir into the potatoes.

5. Season with mace. Stir in raisins and celery. Return to heat for 10 seconds to warm through before serving.

Strawberry baked Alaska

⊠⊠ *A magical combination of cold ice-cream and hot meringue, strawberry baked Alaska is an appealing dessert—especially when the ice-cream and the sponge flan base are home-made. But, if you are short of time, buy a ready-made sponge flan case and the ice-cream, choosing one with plenty of luscious pieces of fruit in it.*

The secrets of success with this dessert lie in using really well frozen ice-cream and in careful and accurate covering with the meringue. If even a tiny amount of ice-cream is exposed when the Alaska goes into the oven, the whole thing will melt and be spoiled. Baked Alaska must be cooked for exactly the right length of time and served immediately or the ice-cream will melt.

SERVES 6
25 cm [10"] sponge flan case
350 g [¾ lb] fresh strawberries
15 ml [1 tablespoon] sherry
(optional)
4 egg whites
pinch of salt
225 g [½ lb] caster sugar
550 ml [1 pt] strawberry
ice-cream

1 Place the flan case on an oven-proof serving plate. Sprinkle with sherry if used.

2 Wash, hull and slice the strawberries. Place on the flan case.

3 Heat the oven to 220°C [425°F] gas mark 7.

4 Place the egg whites in a large bowl. Add a pinch of salt and stir once.

5 Using a balloon whisk, whisk the egg whites until they will stand in soft peaks.

6 Gradually whisk in one-quarter of the sugar. Fold in the remainder gradually, using a metal spoon.

7 Slice the ice-cream and arrange in a dome shape over the strawberries. Spread with meringue, covering all the ice-cream and the sides of the flan case. Be sure that no flan case or ice-cream is exposed.

8 Place in the centre of the oven for 4 minutes until the meringue is lightly browned. Serve immediately.

Traditional Christmas lunch for ten

Roast turkey with all the trimmings is a must for almost every family on Christmas Day—so here it is complete with chipolatas and bacon rolls, bread sauce and cranberry jelly and accompanied by Brussels sprouts, roast potatoes and parsnips. Mincemeat tart with brandy butter or cream is served for pudding. The menu is as familiar as Santa Claus and carol-singing, and each individual dish is easy to cook. The difficulty comes in the organization: how to get all those bits ready at the same time—on a morning already brimming over with present-giving, guest-greeting and probably church-going too. Turn the pages for an unharassed countdown timetable and all the recipes, and make it a Happy Christmas for you, the cook, as well!

Christmas is a time for family gatherings—for a Christmas lunch with granny and grandpa and, of course, children, perhaps nephews or nieces, with their parents, as well as your own family. A big family gathering, however, presents a considerable challenge to the cooking skill and organizing abilities of the cook, who may have been one of the visitors on other years.

Family parties mean several children and so Christmas dinner will be lunch, perhaps at 1.30 pm. Everyone will be expecting traditional Christmas fare, with only the subtlest of alterations.

One of these changes for the better could be a new stuffing with your roast turkey. Two tried and trusted stuffings—parsley and thyme and chestnut—are undeniable favourites, but this Christmas menu introduces you to something new: fruity stuffing of orange, apple, raisins and walnuts.

Christmas pudding has deliberately been omitted because few guests can eat much of it after a huge hot main course; it is often more successful to leave that famous dish for Boxing Day. Mince pies make a less solid pudding and are still traditional. This menu includes one big handsome jalousie, made with flaky pastry and filled with a glorious mincemeat you make yourself: Victoriana mincemeat. The adults can eat their portion of tart with brandy butter and the children theirs with cream.

Brussels sprouts are naturally on the menu, but glamourized for the occasion by being served with fresh chestnuts. Roast potatoes are there, too, to remind you of past Christmases and also roast parsnips, because they make such a perfect complement to the rest of the food—providing, of course, you have room for them in your oven.

It is not really a difficult menu and, if organized properly, leaves you all the time you need to enjoy your family's own cherished routine for Christmas Day. You should be able to relax with your family when they are unwrapping their presents and actually be organized enough to go to church, if you wish, instead of being tied to the kitchen.

GETTING ORGANIZED

Christmas Day is probably the last morning of the year when you would choose to be bogged down in the kitchen, missing all the fun and festivities; so this timetable arranges for you to do as much cooking as you can in advance, leaving you as free as possible on the big day.

Since Christmas Eve is often almost as hectic as Christmas Day itself, what with last-minute gifts to be wrapped, balloons to be blown up, stockings to be filled—not to mention the neighbours inviting you in for a quick drink which lasts all evening— as much preparation as possible has been moved back even further to the preceding days.

Three days before Christmas, you must start thawing your turkey: it will take 52 hours, and it is vital for health reasons that a turkey is completely thawed before it goes in the oven. Also on this day, clean your home from top to bottom—the last thorough clean it will probably receive for a week, when the holiday is officially over.

The next day, attend to all the Christmas cooking that will not be harmed by being stored: the mince-meat, breadcrumbs for the sauce, and the flaky pastry.

Sometime on Christmas Eve, make the mincemeat tart Victoriana, so that when you wake up on Christmas morning, at least you can comfort yourself that the pudding is all done and needs only reheating. If you are super-efficient, it can be assembled and cooked on Christmas morning itself. Relax it in the refrigerator while you are attending to the vegetables, and put it into the oven when you sit down for the main course. Many cooks, however, regard the main course as enough cooking for one day!

Christmas Eve is scheduled for roasting and peeling chestnuts—a lovely winter's job when you don't have to rush it—and for extracting the giblets from the turkey and making stock. Before you go to bed, do as much as you can towards getting the sideboard ready—for instance, finding the nutcrackers. Last of all, start the stuffing and get the turkey ready, so that when you put out your light, you can tell yourself you are really on your way.

ON CHRISTMAS MORNING

Set your alarm clock for 7.15 and, before you so much as brush your hair, stagger downstairs and heat the oven for the turkey. Quickly finish the stuffing, so that ten minutes later, you can put it in the turkey and start the roasting. After that, apart from popping back to baste, your time is your own. You can have a leisurely bath, and dress yourself to suit the occasion, or even go back to bed for half an hour. From then on, you must remember to turn the turkey every hour, but otherwise you are free to be

Menu

*Roast Christmas
turkey
with fruity stuffing
Chipolata sausages
Bacon rolls
Giblet gravy
Home-made bread
sauce and
cranberry jelly
Roast potatoes
Roast parsnips Noël
Brussels sprouts
with chestnuts*

---

*Mincemeat tart
Victoriana
Brandy butter and
cream*

Christmas sideboard

---

*To drink: claret or Côtes du
Rhône for adults, fizzy drinks
for children.*

with the family and slip away to church, provided you turn and baste the turkey thoroughly last thing before you leave and first thing after you return. The only other job for the morning is setting the table.

A late lunch is always permissible on Christmas Day—everyone knows it is worth waiting for! Some of the family can even go drinking with neighbours, provided they are back just before lunch, because your last 20 minutes are very hectic and you are going to need help. Get someone to carve for you, while you are dishing up. Even so, the timetable has allowed you 10 minutes to toast yourself a wonderful Christmas.

Very few people have a second oven or warming place big enough to keep a turkey in after it has been removed from the oven. The top of the cooker with foil wrapped around it is probably the best that can be managed, while you make the gravy.

SHOPPING CHECKLIST

The most important item on your shopping list is, of course, your turkey. Order it at least a week in advance and, if it is to be a frozen one, pick it up 3 or 4 days beforehand in order to give it time to thaw out. If when your turkey arrives, it is not the precise weight you wanted—it is a little under or over that weight— do not panic. All it will mean is that you will merely have to adjust the length of cooking time very slightly on your timetable. Do not forget when you are in the butcher's to buy the chipolatas and the streaky bacon which is a must with turkey (each rasher makes 2 rolls, remember, and they are always popular).

Then there are the special Christmas things like dates, nuts and dried fruit. There is not usually any shortage of them, but around December 25th there is likely to be a sudden rush for them. To be sure, shop a good week or two ahead. You need 450 g [1 lb] of chestnuts to accompany the sprouts, 50 g [2 oz] of chopped walnuts for the stuffing and 15 g [½ oz] of almonds for the mincemeat, in addition to the nuts you want for your sideboard. When buying dried fruit to make your mincemeat, remember you need an extra 50 g [2 oz] of raisins to go in the stuffing. On the other hand, if you are using ready-made mincemeat, buy a 450 g [1 lb] jar.

Equally, if you're buying commercial cranberry jelly, be sure to get enough—not less than 350 g [12 oz]. The family may well ask for it with cold turkey on Boxing Day or after and would be very disappointed if you had to say it had all been eaten up with Christmas lunch.

The greengrocery order for this menu alone is large without including all the other vegetables and salad stuffs you will doubtless be purchasing for the holiday period. Along with the oranges and pears you will

almost certainly be buying for your sideboard, make sure you have an extra orange for the stuffing (also a spare cooking apple) and allow 100 g [¼ lb] grapes for the Victoriana mincemeat. This mincemeat also takes half a lemon. Buy two or three lemons while you're about it; they will come in useful for garnishing. You want sprouts—at their firmest and best in midwinter—parsnips, potatoes of course, onions for bread sauce and giblet stock, and also watercress.

In the dairy department, bear in mind you need thin cream (no need to go the expense of thick) and cheeses. Remember the little extras, like cocktail sticks for the bacon rolls and sprigs of holly while not essential, give the mincemeat tart a festive air.

Finally, a little brandy is essential: for the Victoriana mincemeat as well as the brandy butter. If you do not have cooking brandy in your store-cupboard, buy a miniature bottle.

THE DRINKS

Christmas lunch is a family affair and not really an occasion for expensive wines. Although white wine is traditionally drunk with all poultry, turkey has a strong enough flavour to take a bold red like a claret or a Côtes du Rhône.

In a mixed party of children and adults, two bottles will probably be right. As for the children, give them whatever's their current favourite drink—even if you don't fancy their fizzy preferences!

SPECIAL EQUIPMENT

This familiar menu requires familiar equipment. The real problem is that for a big meal you need so many things at once, and you cannot rely on borrowing from kind neighbours.

First, you must have a giant roasting pan for the turkey and no less than two more for the roast Noël. Use cake tins for the vegetables if you have no pans, or buy commercial foil containers, which are inexpensive. Then you need a big platter for the turkey, at least three large vegetable dishes, a gravy boat, two sauce-boats or little jugs (one for your bread sauce and the other for cream), a dish on which to decant the cranberry jelly and a small pot for the brandy butter. If your gravy boat is not large enough, you will have to refill it from the pan. This means you will get hotter gravy

too! It is also worth sharpening up your carving knife for such a big meal.

If you do not have a second big platter for the tart, try covering the baking tray with foil before cooking and send it to the table just as it is, with a little holly (real or artificial) on the corners so it will look festive.

Even finding china, cutlery and glasses for 10 may present a problem. Giving children tumblers and small-sized knives and forks (or even plastic ones) and smaller dinner plates is the usual answer, and this also marks out children's places at table. Kitchen stools between the chairs will help to squeeze 10 places in round your dining table. Keep table decorations to a minimum. With so many place settings and an array of vegetable dishes and sauce-boats, there will be very little room for them.

Work out what you are going to need ahead, so that you know in good time if you need to ask any of your guests to bring a vegetable dish or so with them on loan.

Christmas turkey

Despite turkey's growing availability and the abundance of new recipes around for cooking it in different ways, for Christmas lunch a simple roast is still voted tops— stuffed, of course, with the family's favourite stuffing. A turkey can be cooked enclosed in foil or in a roasting bag to help contain all the juices, but that method takes longer and, with a large bird like this one, would necessitate getting up very early in the morning to get it roasted in time for lunch. So for the sake of cooks without automatic ovens, in this recipe the bird is cooked uncovered, except for legs and breast which may need the protection of a little loose foil towards the end to prevent over browning.

The giblet stock, made by simmering the chopped giblets in water, is best prepared in advance; but if you do prefer to make it while the turkey is roasting, remember that it needs to simmer for 2 hours. This version of giblet gravy contains no cranberry jelly; the jelly is served separately.

Streaky bacon is almost obligatory with turkey. Rolls are decorative and much easier to serve. With a very large turkey there is insufficient room in the pan for the extras so necessary to a Christmas spread. The bacon rolls can be fitted under the rack beneath the

Countdown timetable

THREE DAYS BEFORE
Start thawing turkey.

TWO DAYS BEFORE
Victoriana mincemeat: make and store in a covered bowl in the refrigerator—steps 1–8.
Mincemeat tart Victoriana: make the flaky pastry (see glossary) and then store in a polythene bag in the refrigerator.
Bread sauce: make breadcrumbs by coarsely grating white bread. Store in a polythene bag and chill.

CHRISTMAS EVE
In the morning
Mincemeat tart Victoriana: remove flaky pastry from the refrigerator 1 hour before needed to bring to room temperature. Make tart and bake—steps 1–12.
Brussels sprouts with chestnuts: roast and peel the chestnuts—steps 1–3.
Make giblet stock: simmer giblets in water with sliced onion, carrot and celery for 30 minutes. Strain.

In the evening
Arrange nuts, fruit etc in dishes for sideboard.

Fruity stuffing: make the bread squares and prepare the orange; store in the refrigerator—steps 1–4.
Roast Christmas turkey: rinse and season the bird—step 2.

CHRISTMAS MORNING
6¼ hours before the meal
Roast Christmas turkey: heat the oven—step 1.
Fruity stuffing: finish—steps 5–8.

6 hours before the meal
Roast Christmas turkey: butter, stuff and truss it and put in oven. Baste frequently—steps 3–6.
Get dressed for Christmas Day.

5 hours before the meal
Family breakfast.
Roast Christmas turkey: turn and baste—step 7.

4 hours before the meal
Present-giving time.
Roast Christmas turkey: turn and baste—step 7.
Leave for church.

3 hours before the meal
Roast Christmas turkey: turn and baste—step 7.
Set the dining table.

1½ hours before the meal
Roast Christmas turkey: turn and baste—step 7.
Roast Noël: parboil the potatoes and parsnips and transfer to roasting pans in the oven—steps 2–7.

1 hour before the meal
Bread sauce: infuse milk with flavourings and leave to stand in a warm place for 20 minutes. Strain and return to the pan.
Uncork red wine.
Pour out Christmas aperitifs—and take 10 minutes off to enjoy a well-earned celebration drink.

50 minutes before the meal
Roast Christmas turkey: make and add the bacon rolls. Remove foil, if used. Heat giblet stock—steps 8–11.

40 minutes before the meal
Brandy butter: make and transfer to a bowl—steps 1–4

30 minutes before the meal
Roast Christmas turkey: remove bird and bacon rolls from oven and keep in a warm place—step 12.
Roast Noël: turn vegetables. Increase oven heat to 180°C [350°F] gas mark 4 and put them on the upper shelf. Add chipolatas to parsnip pan—steps 8–9.
Brussels sprouts with chestnuts: heat a pan of salted water—step 4.

---

turkey, but the potatoes and sausages must be roasted in a different pan (or pans) on the shelf below the turkey.

The meal is planned to serve 10. The turkey is deliberately big enough to serve twice that number—so that you will have plenty left over for a cold buffet or see for eating over the remaining holiday. Leftover roast turkey makes a delicious stuffing for pancakes, or use it to make a pâté.

SERVES 10 HOT
PLUS 9–10 COLD
6.8 kg [15 lb] turkey
salt
freshly ground black
**   pepper**
425 g [15 oz] fruity
**   stuffing**
175 g [6 oz] butter
550 ml [1 pt] giblet stock
15 bacon rashers
15 ml [1 tablespoon] plain
**   flour**
watercress

1 Set the oven to 160°C [325°F] gas mark 3.

2 Rinse out the turkey, pat dry thoroughly inside and out, and season inside with salt and black pepper.

3 Stuff the breast with the stuffing, secure the flap of skin with a skewer if wished, and then truss the bird securely.

4 Fork the butter in a bowl until soft then spread the legs and breast generously with it. Sprinkle with salt.

5 Place the bird on a rack in a large roasting tin and place in the oven.

6 Roast for 5½ hours, basting every 10 minutes for the first hour and frequently thereafter.

7 Turn the turkey round after an

hour to make sure the skin browns evenly. After another hour turn it again, and so on for each further hour. If the breast is browning too quickly, cover with a piece of foil.

8 Make the bacon rolls by cutting each rasher in half and rolling the bacon up. Secure each with a cocktail stick.

9 Twenty minutes before the end of cooking time, cook the bacon rolls in the pan below the turkey rack.

10 Remove the foil, if used, 5 minutes from the end of cooking time to complete browning of breast.

11 Remove the surface fat from the giblet stock. Put the stock into a small saucepan and bring to the boil over medium heat.

12 Remove the turkey from the oven,

20 minutes before the meal

Brussels sprouts with chestnuts: boil the chestnuts and prepare the sprouts—steps 5–6.

Warm plates, vegetable dishes etc.

15 minutes before the meal

Bread sauce: combine milk and bread crumbs; leave to stand for 15 minutes in a warm place. Stir in a little cream if you like.

Roast Christmas turkey: make giblet gravy—steps 13–15.

10 minutes before the meal

Brussels sprouts with chestnuts: add sprouts to the pan—step 7.

Roast Noël: transfer chipolatas to serving platter—step 10.

Roast Christmas turkey: arrange bird and bacon rolls on platter with sausages. Garnish with watercress and carry to the table for carving—steps 16–17.

2 minutes before the meal

Bread sauce: reheat and transfer to a sauce-boat—step 7.

Roast Noël: transfer vegetables to vegetable dishes—step 11.

Brussels sprouts with chestnuts: strain and transfer to a vegetable dish—step 8.

Mincemeat tart Victoriana: put in oven for about 20 minutes.

Guests to be seated for Christmas lunch.

place on a warm plate and allow to rest in a warm place for about 20 minutes before carving.

13 Pour the fat from the roasting tin, leaving the sediment behind. Stir in the flour off the heat then return to the heat for a moment, stirring.

14 Pour the hot giblet stock into the roasting tin off the heat. Stir and scrape the sediment from the bottom.

15 Return to the heat and bring slowly to the boil. When ready, transfer to a sauce-boat.

16 Place the turkey on the serving platter. Remove the sticks from the bacon and surround the turkey with bacon rolls and accompanying chipolata sausages.

17 Garnish with watercress and carry platter to the table for carving.

Fruity stuffing

This is an original stuffing for poultry, which is crunchy and refreshing—and one that makes a welcome change on an occasion like Christmas when there is a lot of rich food about. Stuff the breast end of the bird to keep it moist.

SERVES 10 GENEROUSLY
3 slices white bread
1 orange
1 dessert apple
25 g [1 oz] butter
50 g [2 oz] raisins
50 g [2 oz] chopped walnuts
5 ml [1 teaspoon] salt
pinch nutmeg
60 ml [4 tablespoons] well-flavoured stock or red wine
1 medium-sized egg

1 Heat the oven to 180°C [350°F] gas mark 4.

2 Remove the crusts from the bread and cut into cubes.

3 Toast in the oven for about 15 minutes until brown.

4 Prepare the fruit: peel the orange removing all pith and segment it.

5 Melt the butter in a pan and toss the toasted bread in it. Remove pan from the heat and mix in the orange, raisins, walnuts, salt and nutmeg. Peel, core and chop apple. Add this to the pan and mix.

6 Bind the ingredients together with the stock or wine.

7 Beat the egg and mix in.

8 Leave this stuffing to stand for at least 10 minutes before putting into the turkey.

Roast Noël

⊠⊠ *Along with the turkey, people expect other standards with their Christmas lunch: bacon, sausages, roast potatoes and a colourful, comparative newcomer—roast parsnips. Ideally, these should all be cooked round the turkey in the bird's own juices. However, few cooks have a large enough pan—let alone an oven—to get them all in at once. So it is usually necessary to have a separate roasting pan for the majority of the potatoes and yet another for the parsnips and chipolatas.*

The vegetable roasting time is longer than usual to compensate for the temperature being lower—necessary for the turkey.

SERVES 10
15 medium-sized potatoes
15 small parsnips
450 g [1 lb] dripping
20 chipolata sausages

1 Heat the oven to 160°C [325°F] gas mark 3.

2 Put water and salt into two pans and bring to the boil.

3 Meanwhile prepare the vegetables: peel, rinse and halve the potatoes; peel, rinse and halve lengthways the parsnips.

4 Put the potatoes in one pan of water and the parsnips in the other and parboil for 5 minutes.

5 Meanwhile take two roasting pans and divide the dripping between them. Place the pans side by side in the oven and heat until fat is sizzling but not smoking.

6 Drain the potatoes in a colander. Place several layers of kitchen paper on top of a clean, spread kitchen towel. Turn the potatoes on to the paper and blot dry. Dry the parsnips in the same manner.

7 Put the blotted potatoes in one hot pan and the parsnips in the other. Spoon over the fat so that the vegetables are well coated. Roast for 1 hour, basting occasionally.

8 After half an hour's roasting time, turn the vegetables over with a pair of tongs or a fish slice. Add the chipolatas to the parsnip pan.

9 When you take the turkey out of the oven, move the vegetable pans up a shelf and turn up the oven to 180°C [350°F] gas mark 4 in order to brown them.

10 Ten minutes before the end of cooking time, remove chipolata sausages and arrange with the bacon rolls on a serving platter.

11 When cooked, use a perforated spoon or tongs to transfer the potatoes and parsnips to two warm vegetable dishes.

Brussels sprouts with chestnuts

⊠⊠ *Boiled sprouts with roast turkey has become a classic combination. This recipe mixes the Brussels with hot chestnuts for a special treat. Because chestnuts take time to peel, it is best to do this in advance to cut down on time in the kitchen on Christmas day itself.*

SERVES 10
450 g [1 lb] chestnuts
1.4 kg [3 lb] Brussels sprouts
salt

1 Position the shelf at the top and heat the oven to 220°C [425°F] gas mark 7.

2 Make a small cut through the tufty end of each chestnut and roast on a baking sheet until the skins crack—about 10 minutes.

3 Peel the two layers of skin from the chestnuts while still warm.

4 Choose a large pan and half fill it with water. Salt and bring to the boil.

5 Add the peeled chestnuts and boil for 20 minutes.

6 Meanwhile trim away the base and any yellowing leaves from the Brussels sprouts. Cut a neat cross with a sharp knife at the bottom of each stalk. Rinse.

7 After 12 minutes of cooking time, add the sprouts to the chestnut pan.

8 When both sprouts and chestnuts are tender, strain. Transfer to a warm vegetable dish.

Victoriana mincemeat

⊠⊠⊠ *This is a mincemeat from the nineteenth century which contains some fresh fruit, making it rather lighter than the mincemeats which have come to us from medieval England. It is also one of the few mincemeats that does not contain suet. Most mincemeats must mature for at least a fortnight before use, but this one can be made a couple of hours before eating. It is therefore the answer when you are unprepared, or have been unable to buy a jar of made mincemeat, on which you were relying.*

Over Christmas and other periods of entertaining, you can make a batch of mincemeat Victoriana and store it in the refrigerator, using it in various dishes as required. Thanks to the brandy, it will keep a week. The quantity given here will make one large tart and 6 small individual pies or 18 small pies.

MAKES ABOUT 700 G [1½ LB]
1 apple
half a lemon
100 g [¼ lb] raisins
100 g [¼ lb] currants
50 g [2 oz] sultanas
15 g [½ oz] candied peel
75 g [3 oz] grapes
15 g [½ oz] almonds
25 g [1 oz] glacé cherries
100 g [¼ lb] sugar
15 ml [1 tablespoon] brandy

1 Peel, core and quarter the apple.

2 Pare thinly the zest from the lemon.

3 Put the apple, lemon zest, dried fruit and candied peel through a mincer. Put the resulting mixture in a bowl.

4 Skin and de-seed the grapes, chop roughly and add to the bowl.

5 Blanch and roughly chop the almonds and add to the bowl.

6 Chop the cherries and add to the bowl.

7 Squeeze the juice from the lemon and add to the bowl.

8 Stir in the sugar and brandy and mix all ingredients thoroughly together. Cover bowl and store in the refrigerator for a minumum of 2 hours or until needed.

Mincemeat tart Victoriana

This is a straightforward recipe, using puff or flaky pastry with a filling of traditional mincemeat—your own Victoriana mincemeat (given opposite) or a 450 g [1 lb] jar of a commercial variety. For a large lunch party it is easiest to serve a jumbo-sized jalousie, big enough to allow for 'seconds'. The rich dark mincemeat shows temptingly through the Christmas-tree-shaped slashes in the top of the pastry. Here it is made on a baking sheet, but a baking tray would also be suitable. If both the mincemeat and pastry are prepared in advance, the tart takes only 10 minutes of your time to assemble on the baking day.

To serve, cut it in half lengthways and then carve slices off each side— delicious with cream or brandy butter. Any leftovers not gobbled up can be served cold over the next day or two.

The tart can be reheated for 15 minutes at 160°C [325°F] gas mark 3.

SERVES 10 GENEROUSLY
**450 g [1 lb] puff or flaky
  pastry
450 g [1 lb] mincemeat
1 egg**

1 Position the shelf just above the centre and heat the oven to 200°C [400°F] gas mark 6.

2 Roll out the pastry to a long thin rectangle 40 × 25 cm [16 × 10"]. Cut the pastry in half crossways to make two rectangles 20 × 25 cm [8 × 10"].

3 Carefully roll one piece of pastry over the rolling pin and transfer it to a rinsed baking sheet. Unroll the pastry on the baking sheet and ease back into shape.

4 Spread the mincemeat on top to within 12 mm [½"] of the edges.

5 Beat the egg and brush edges.

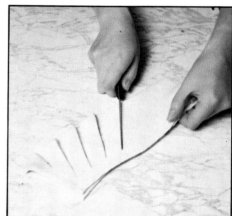

6 Fold the remaining rectangle of pastry in half lengthways. Using a sharp knife, cut diagonal slits right through the double layer of pastry on the folded edge to within 12 mm [½"] of the raw edge. Hold the pastry firmly in the other hand.

7 Carefully lift slit pastry on to one half of the filling and unfold. Ease it into shape to cover filling. The filling should just be visible through the decorative slits in the pastry.

8 Firmly press the pastry edges together to seal. Knock up and flute the edges.

9 Glaze the pastry top with beaten egg taking care not to brush between the slits.

10 Put the tart into the refrigerator for 30 minutes to relax.

11 Bake for 20 minutes, until the pastry is risen and golden brown.

12 Leave the jalousie to cool on the baking sheet for 5 minutes. Then transfer to a warm serving dish and serve hot. Alternatively allow to cool, cover with cling film and chill overnight.

Brandy butter

The seasonal spirited accompaniment to mincemeat tart and mince pies is brandy butter. This one looks like clotted cream when first made but becomes harder if kept. Serve it in a glass or china dish or in a small pot.

SERVES 6–7
75 g [3 oz] unsalted butter
75 g [3 oz] icing sugar
30 ml [2 tablespoons] brandy

1 Cream the butter until white.

2 Gradually beat in the sugar.

3 When thoroughly mixed, add the brandy a few drops at a time, beating continuously. Take care that the mixture does not curdle.

4 When it looks white and foamy, pile into a dish. If necessary store covered in the refrigerator until needed.

CHRISTMAS SIDEBOARD

One of the treats of Christmas is all the little extras available to pick at over the holiday: the dish of nuts, the bunch of grapes, the bowl of fresh fruit, a box of dates, a wedge of ripe Stilton. These seasonal titbits seem expensive if purchased all at one time, but they are helpful for quick suppers through the entire holiday and are not all consumed on the day itself. They look festive and attractive beside the table, and it is a generous gesture to produce them at the end of lunch. They fit in with that period when the children have got down from the table and rushed off to play with their new toys, while the adults linger for the last of the wine, coffee and perhaps even port or liqueurs.

The cheese, if not Stilton, should certainly be a blue cheese: for after this mammoth lunch, guests will be looking for a savoury taste rather than something filling. In your fruit dish, be sure to include a few lovely, easy-to-peel tangerines among your oranges, and also some large ripe pears, which are at their finest at this time of the year. Grapes are expensive but you may want a little bunch, because they are beautiful to look at and give an air of luxury and Bacchanalian feasting.

Brunch for twelve

Brunch is the thing to eat when everyone rises too late for breakfast and too early for lunch—it combines the two meals into one relaxed, sophisticated occasion with the minimum of last minute cooking for the hostess. The art comes in choosing a whole range of simple dishes, rather than in the complicated cooking of one or two. This menu offers some old Victorian favourites like scrambled eggs, jugged kippers and slices from a cold gammon joint, as well as introducing a couple of tempting new ones. Serve your food with endless pots of fresh coffee and, in addition, some of the traditional alcoholic drinks, such as black velvet, Bloody Mary and buck's fizz.

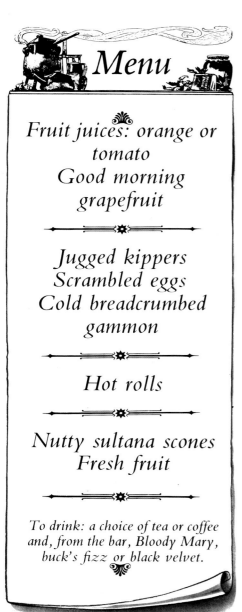

Menu

Fruit juices: orange or tomato
Good morning grapefruit

Jugged kippers
Scrambled eggs
Cold breadcrumbed gammon

Hot rolls

Nutty sultana scones
Fresh fruit

To drink: a choice of tea or coffee and, from the bar, Bloody Mary, buck's fizz or black velvet.

This civilized meal of brunch is often thought to be an American invention, but really it has its roots in the extended and splendid breakfasts served in English country houses in the 1800s. These breakfasts were a kind of running buffet, lasting from quite early in the morning, when the sportsmen might rise for refreshment, until late morning when the last of the house guests would come down.

A contemporary account by Ethel, Lady Raglan, shows the kind of food that might be served at one of these meals. 'There would be a choice of fried fish, eggs and crisp bacon, a variety of egg dishes and sizzling sausages. During the shooting parties, hot game and grilled pheasant always appeared on the menu but were served, of course, without any vegetables. On a side table was to be found a choice of cold viands: delicious home-smoked hams, pressed meats, a large raised pie consisting of cold game and a galantine with aspic jelly. The guests drank tea, coffee or ale, and there were the inevitable accompaniments of hot rolls and scones and stillroom preserves of apple and quince. The meal usually ended with a fruit course of grapes or hothouse peaches and nectarines. . .'

It all sounds very tempting—and what is more, in certain circumstances, it's also a very practical idea. Just think of those big 'mornings after', Boxing day or following a wedding or a big party, for instance. You may find that you are left with half the family quartered on you or billeted out on your neighbours—plus the odd guest who never quite made it home the previous night!

How and, more important, on what can you feed them all? You cannot very well let your neighbours cook breakfast for your overspill, too, and yet no one wants to get up early for a fixed-time breakfast and the hostess does not want to land herself with a big lunch party, and more elaborate cooking.

A running brunch is the answer. It cuts out that scramble of trying to cook two meals at the same time. It also makes a post-church breakfast.

Serve only early-morning tea—10 a.m. is quite early-morning enough after a late night—and tell guests brunch will be from 11 o'clock. Then they join you when they are ready, and it's a meal that permits them to eat as much or as little as they fancy—from just coffee and rolls to the brunch with courses the Victorians enjoyed.

This menu is representative of the sort of spread of courses you will want—a refreshing appetizer, two or three main hot dishes and one cold and some sort of bread to accompany them. Preferably your main dishes should be able to be eaten together if desired. For example, here scrambled eggs is an obvious choice to go with ham; but it is, surprisingly, also a delicious complement for kippers. The menu finishes with a taste of sugar: fruit-and-nut scones.

You need not stick to these particular dishes if you think they will not suit your family or friends. You could equally well use some of the examples given from the country-house breakfast. How about kidneys, bacon and sausages in place of scrambled eggs? Let each guest cook his own or put a member of the family in charge, but don't get involved in a lot of on-the-spot cooking. Kedgeree would make an interesting alternative to the kippers (make it the day before and reheat it in a double-boiler). If you're not a scone-lover in any form, then finish with a compote of stewed fruit.

Brunch parties are fun and an informal way of entertaining mixed age groups. Americans don't need the excuse of a big morning after to have one, so why not brunch out next Sunday? It provides an excellent way to please, at the same time, those who think Sunday morning should be devoted to drinking and those who like a slow start. You can all enjoy the morning without anyone having to worry about getting back in time to cook a Sunday lunch.

GETTING ORGANIZED

This brunch includes very little which needs to be cooked from start to finish on the actual morning. The gammon can be dealt with completely the day before—two days before or more if the previous day is your big day. Allow an extra day (or overnight) to give the gammon the maximum time if you are soaking it. Once cooked, wrap it, put it in the refrigerator and forget about it. If your plans go awry and you do not manage to put it to soak early, it can always be blanched before cooking to remove saltiness.

The night before, advance preparations further: see to the fruit for the good morning grapefruit and mix the dry ingredients for the nutty sultana scones. Then, because you don't have to worry about a sit-down breakfast, you can lay the buffet table and arrange the fresh fruit.

On the morning itself you can actually have a lie-in until almost 10 o'clock, until it is time for you to be making early morning tea and buying the Sunday papers for your guests. The cooking does not need you until half an hour before the meal is promised. Half an hour is enough to finish the grapefruit and the scones, make coffee and tea, heat the jugged kippers and the rolls, and scramble the eggs.

Brunch is a running meal, catering for guests as they arrive, but the additional cooking will be minimal.

Countdown timetable

1 OR 2 DAYS BEFORE
Do the shopping.
Breadcrumbed gammon: soak then cook and refrigerate—steps 1–11.
Put the 'champagne' in the refrigerator to chill.

THE NIGHT BEFORE
Good morning grapefruit: prepare and mix the fruit and refrigerate—steps 1–7.
Nutty sultana scones: mix together the dry ingredients—steps 2–4—and store in a polythene bag in the refrigerator.
Put the orange and tomato juice in the refrigerator to chill.
Fill ice-cube trays and put in freezer compartment.
Lay the buffet table.
Arrange fresh fruit in a bowl.

ON THE MORNING
Transfer gammon joint from refrigerator to serving platter on table.
Set up the bar, opening necessary cans of fruit juices for drinks.

30 minutes before the meal
Good morning grapefruit: mix the yoghurt into the fruit segments and pile into shells—steps 8–9.
Nutty sultana scones: heat the oven—step 1.

25 minutes before the meal
Nutty sultana scones: beat the eggs, make the dough and bake the first batch—steps 5–11.

15 minutes before the meal
Make coffee, and tea if serving it.
Jugged kippers: boil kettle of water—step 1.

10 minutes before the meal
Scrambled eggs: mix together the eggs, butter or thick cream and seasoning ready to cook.

5 minutes before the meal
Jugged kippers: put a pair in each jug to warm—steps 2-3.
Rolls: wrap in foil and put half in the oven to warm.

2 minutes before the meal
Scrambled eggs: cook first portions.

During buffet
Make fresh pots of coffee and tea.
Mix drinks as required.
Cook further batches of scrambled eggs and scones.
Heat second batch of rolls.
Continue to heat kippers as required.

DRINKS
The drinks have been chosen to cater for all tastes. Those who prefer can stick to tea or coffee. But for those who feel that Sunday morning is for drinking, or who fancy alcohol after a heavy night as 'the hair of the dog . . .', three possible cocktails are suggested.

For a strong pick-me-up, there is Bloody Mary, which can be made mild with plenty of ice and tomato juice or strong and spicy with lots of vodka, Worcestershire sauce and Tabasco. For those who are still in the party mood there's buck's fizz, which uses cheaper forms of a champagne-type wine and ekes it out with orange juice; and finally for beer drinkers, there is black velvet: half and half 'champagne' and Guinness.

If you have vodka in the house anyway, you may be in a position to offer all three cocktails; otherwise, to reduce expense, you will probably have to settle for either Bloody Mary, which is vodka-based, or the other two, which need 'champagne'.

As you will be buying at least one variety of fruit juice for your cocktails, these can also be served at the beginning of the meal and to any youngsters who may be present.

SHOPPING CHECKLIST
The first thing to decide is what you are going to serve in the way of drinks, and buy accordingly. For Bloody Mary, to serve 12, you will need a bottle of vodka, plus 3 large cans of tomato juice for everybody. According to taste you also need lemons, Worcestershire sauce, garlic salt, Tabasco—check you have them in stock. For buck's fizz and black velvet, buy 3 bottles of 'champagne' (any dry sparkling wine but preferably made by the champagne method) and 2–3 cans of orange juice, plus about 4 litres [8 pints] of Guinness or stout. That should give you enough to offer the odd confirmed beer drinker neat Guinness if he wants it. You could, of course, also serve the 'champagne' on its own as an alternative but if you are going to do this, buy 4 bottles.

If you need to shop for coffee, it is worth investing in a breakfast blend for this meal—Colombian and Kenyan are the two most popular. You could also buy a special breakfast tea such as Assam or Darjeeling. A famous breakfast tea is the Lady Londonderry's blend: strong, aromatic and a perfect wake-you-up.

As for food, all the shopping can be done a day or two before. It is worth ordering the gammon joint well in advance of this, however, just to make sure you can get it. Ask the butcher how long to soak the gammon, when you buy it.

Buy 12 kippers; not everyone will say 'yes' to them and this will allow a pair each for the guests who do have the appetite for them. When choosing your kippers, beware of the orange-coloured ones; there has been dye at work. The genuine article, which is slowly smoked in true Scottish tradition, is more of a dusty yellowy-orange.

Look for large, firm oranges with bright skins, and try to get the pink Texas grapefruit if you can. While you are in the greengrocer's, select fruit for your fresh fruit platter; buy anything that is in season and cheap that week. Finally, the yoghurt: it must be plain and unsweetened for this particular grapefruit dish.

Remember also to buy rolls or bread and check that you have a sufficient quantity of butter.

SPECIAL EQUIPMENT
The only special equipment for this menu is the unusual use of a familiar piece of equipment—a jug in which to heat the kippers. A big pottery one, nearly 30 cm [1'] tall is most suitable. If you do not have such a jug, you could achieve the same result with a frying-pan of boiling water with a lid but the surface area is larger and the heat loss is therefore much faster. If possible do it the proper way, in a jug—much more stylish and far less smelly!

If you own or could borrow two or three jugs you can jug several batches of kippers at one time.

The brunch bar

Here are recipes for three traditional potent drinks, suitable for a brunch. All can be served in squat tumblers.

Bloody Mary

This drink is named after the Tudor Queen, Mary I, because she spilled so much blood! If you have a cocktail shaker, this drink can be made for two or three people at one time—shake it well, then serve. Alternatively make individual glasses, stirring each one well before serving. (Provide a long spoon for this.)

Americans start this drink by putting in 2–3 cubes of ice, but some purists think that the melting ice dilutes the tomato juice too much. Add 1 part vodka to 3 parts tomato juice. Add a dash of Worcestershire sauce and a squeeze of lemon juice and stir well.

For a stronger pick-me-up, a pinch of dried mixed herbs, another of garlic salt and a dash of Tabasco added will really wake you up. The advantage of plenty of ice is that the first sips are strong: when the ice melts the drink becomes weaker.

Buck's fizz

This drink was a favourite 'morning after' drink of the Regency bucks. Pour 1 part well-chilled orange juice into a glass and top up with 2 parts non-vintage 'champagne', well-chilled. Serve immediately before the bubbles can evaporate, and you have a bubbly champagne cocktail to start the day in lively fashion.

Black velvet

Versions as to the origin of this drink vary; one is that it was originated by a barman on the death of Queen Victoria, because he felt champagne, too, should go into mourning. Another story makes it a favourite drink of Bismarck, and for a long time called 'a Bismarck'.

Fill a tumbler two-thirds full of stout or Guinness and top up with non-vintage 'champagne'—a luscious concoction that certainly beats the Sunday morning pint of ale! Those who disagree can always drink their stout or Guinness on its own.

Good morning grapefruit

⊠⊠⊠ *Plain grapefruit can be a little sharp for some tastes. Mixed with orange segments and cucumber and stirred into plain yoghurt, however, it makes an interesting dish which is refreshing but not too tart. Pink Texas grapefruit are better as they are marginally sweeter than the yellow kind, but either may be used. In this recipe the cucumber skin has been left on for a prettier effect, but it can be removed when this hors d'oeuvre is served at breakfast, if you wish. Also, if you have time, removing the cucumber seeds makes a less watery mixture.*

SERVES 12
6 large grapefruit
6 large oranges
about 20 cm [8"] cucumber
275 ml [½ pt] plain yoghurt
sprigs of mint to decorate

1 Cut the grapefruit in half through the middle from stalk end. Using a grapefruit knife, cut out the flesh in one piece. Retain the shells.

2 Divide the grapefruit flesh into segments, discarding the pith but reserving the juice.

3 Peel the oranges, removing the pith. Divide into segments, carefully removing membranes, but retaining the juice.

4 Mix the grapefruit and orange segments in a bowl, with all the juices.

5 Remove all pith and membranes from the grapefruit skins so they are clean inside. Be careful not to pierce the shells.

6 Cut the cucumber into dice, preferably removing seeds. Add to the fruit segments in the bowl.

7 Cover bowl with cling film and refrigerate for at least 2 hours.

8 When fruit is chilled, add the yoghurt to the bowl and lightly toss all ingredients together.

9 Pile the mixture back into the grapefruit shells and decorate each with a sprig of mint.

Jugged kippers

⊠ *Kippers are the classic breakfast and in this recipe are heated in style at the table. Because smoked fish is already cured, it needs only warming through to make it ready for eating. This method of cooking kippers is unbelievably simple, and it has the great advantage of being odour-free. Have two or three jugs of water on the go simultaneously to save time.*

SERVES 12
12 kippers

1 Boil a kettle of water and warm a tall jug.

2 Place a pair of kippers in the jug, tail upwards, and fill jug with boiling water. Leave for 10 minutes to heat.

3 Pull the kippers out of the water by

their tails and serve. Repeat process for remaining kippers with fresh boiling water.

Breadcumbed gammon

◫◫◫ *Buy a large joint of gammon— either boneless or on the bone—for a really fine flavour. The shank end of the joint is particularly recommended because it is easy to carve and is such an attractive shape— it will make an impressive-looking centrepiece on your brunch table. A half gammon will more than feed your party, and leftovers can always be used up in sandwiches, salads and snacks. The traditional breadcrumb finish to this gammon gives a pleasant contrast in texture.*

SERVES 12
2.7–3.1 kg [6–7 lb] mild cured half gammon joint
2 onions
15 ml [1 tablespoon] cloves
1 bay leaf
6 peppercorns
125 g [¼ lb] white bread, crusts removed

1 Weigh the joint and calculate the cooking time: 20 minutes per 450 g [1 lb].

2 Immerse the joint in cold water and soak for at least 3 hours to remove excess saltiness. Change water at intervals and sip water to test for saltiness. Alternatively place in a pan of cold water and bring to the boil. Drain.

3 Choose a heavy-based pan that is only slightly larger in diameter than the joint. Place the joint in it and cover with fresh cold water.

4 Place the pan over a low heat and bring slowly to boiling point.

5 Remove any scum that rises to the surface with a perforated spoon.

6 Peel the onions and stud them with the cloves. Add these with the bay leaf and peppercorns to the pan. Reduce heat to low and cover the pan. Time the cooking from this point, and simmer gently for the calculated period.

7 When the cooking time is up, lift the joint out of the pan, and place it in a colander under cold running water to reduce temperature quickly. Discard the onions and flavourings.

8 Place the joint in a clean pan, pour on enough cold water to cover and set aside to cool.

9 Meanwhile, make breadcrumbs. Place them on a baking tray under the grill for 5 minutes to toast.

10 When the joint is quite cold, drain and dry it with kitchen paper. Then peel off the outer skin and, using a knife, press the browned breadcrumbs into the fat.

11 Wrap the breadcrumbed joint in foil and refrigerate until required. Serve on a platter and carve into large thin slices just before eating to prevent gammon drying out.

Nutty sultana scones

◩ *This recipe is for an enriched scone for a special occasion. It uses an egg in addition to the other ingredients and a higher proportion of fat to flour than is used for making traditional scones. The difference between them is comparable to that between a rich cake and a plain one.*

All scones should be eaten as soon as possible, so bake only as many in one batch as guests are ready to eat.

MAKES ABOUT 30
450 g [1 lb] plain flour
20 ml [4 teaspoons] baking powder
5 ml [1 teaspoon] salt
175 g [6 oz] butter
50 g [2 oz] caster sugar
225 g [½ lb] sultanas
50 g [2 oz] flaked almonds
2 medium-sized eggs
about 60 ml [4 tablespoons] milk to mix
beaten egg to glaze

1 Position shelf in the middle of the oven and heat oven to 220°C [425°F] gas mark 7.

2 Sift the flour with the baking powder and salt into a bowl.

3 Cut the butter into the flour, and then rub in until the mixture resembles even-sized bread-crumbs.

4 Stir in the sugar, sultanas and half the almonds.

5 Beat the eggs, adding 30 ml [2 tablespoons] milk.

6 Make a well in the centre of the dry ingredients and lightly and quickly work in the beaten egg mixture until a soft dough is formed. Add extra milk if necessary.

7 Gather the dough together with your fingers and turn out on to a lightly floured board.

8 Knead the dough until it is elastic and smooth and free from cracks.

9 Roll out dough to about 1.2 cm [½"] thick and, using a 5 cm [2"] round cutter, cut dough into rounds.

10 Place scones on a baking tray 2.5 cm [1"] apart. Glaze with beaten egg. Top with remaining almonds.

11 Bake for 15 minutes. Serve warm.

Informal Menus

A summer sporting picnic for four

Catering at sports grounds always seems to be abysmally bad and outrageously expensive, usually consisting of sad, packeted pies and bags of crisps. Next time you attend a summer sporting event, be it the thrills of a test match at Lords or just the village team doing their best out on the green, why not take your own picnic? This menu features a meal which is easy to pack and to eat. Best of all, there's no need for knives and forks or precarious balancing of paper plates on laps to distract your attention from the pitch.

Menu

❧

Pavilion eggs
Finger salads

❈

Peach
upside-down cake

❈

To drink: cider cup

❧

Somehow, food eaten out of doors always tastes better than food eaten indoors. Picnics have been a popular pastime ever since the Edwardians, who ate 'al fresco' in grand style and would never have dreamed of attending a sporting event without taking substantial nourishment with them.

Today, appetites are smaller and picnics are a much simpler affair. With modern packaging such as foil, cling wrap or cling film, snap-top plastic boxes and that boon to outdoor diners, the vacuum flask, a whole family picnic can be packed easily into one bag.

Picnics offer a way to spend a day out of doors, whether walking in the woods or attending a sports event, without meal problems. Picnics are

also much cheaper than buying food at catering establishments. Here is a meal that's cheap and simple to prepare, easy to pack and delicious to eat out of doors.

SHOPPING CHECKLIST

All the food in this menu is easy to obtain, so there is no need for special shopping. As almost everything is perishable, the best time to buy is the morning of the day before. This gives you enough time for advance preparation and ensures the food won't deteriorate.

Finger foods are really best for picnics unless for a semi-formal occasion. For salads, select the best quality fresh vegetables that can be eaten without forks or mess.

Fresh mint leaves are needed for a first-class cider cup. If you don't have a mint plant in the garden, you will probably find some sprigs for sale at a good greengrocers. Fresh mint is easy to grow and well worth the effort. It will even flourish in a pot if you don't have a garden. Planting and growing instructions can be found on the back of seed packets.

GETTING ORGANIZED

If a picnic is to be an enjoyable experience and not a disaster of squashed, limp food and frayed tempers, organization is essential. There is nothing more annoying than reaching your picnic spot and finding half the feast has been left behind. For this reason, most of the food featured in this menu is packed well in advance so all you have to do is

Countdown timetable

THE EVENING BEFORE

Peach upside-down cake: make the cake, then turn out to cool. Do not remove the foil covering from top—steps 1-18.

Pavilion eggs: make—steps 1-17. Cool, wrap well in foil or cling film and store in the refrigerator—step 18.

Cider cup: make the cider cup and put in the refrigerator to chill—steps 1-4 or put the bottles in the refrigerator.

Finger salad: wash all vegetables and store in plastic bags in the refrigerator, or do this next morning.

IN THE MORNING

1½ hours before leaving

If you are not planning on an early start, you may make the cider cup from previously chilled bottles and wash the finger salad in the morning.

½ hour before leaving

Peach upside-down cake: return this to its tin and put in a plastic bag. Pack your picnic making sure you have cups for the cider, paper napkins, cologne wipes and, of course, the knife.

remove the packages from the refrigerator and stow them in your picnic bag—no chance that way of leaving home with only half the salad!

Raw fruit can present problems on picnics; while apples are perfect, oranges are difficult and messy to peel without a knife and peaches drip when skinned. The fruit here is neatly incorporated in a cake.

People always seem to get hungrier out-of-doors, and especially when walking, so this menu includes two items with carbohydrates. The cake is also big enough to allow a second slice later in the day.

Put the cider bottles into the refrigerator 24 hours before you plan to make the cider cup.

Packing

For the cider cup, you will need two one-litre or 1¾-pint vacuum flasks. If the cider cup is placed in the flask when made and put uncovered in the refrigerator, it will keep cool.

If you are purchasing a vacuum flask, a wide-necked one is very useful because it can be used for soup or ice-cream, or stew in mid-winter. A small insulated flask is also useful. It can be used for ice cubes for drinks in summer, and is handy to hold fresh milk for cups of tea.

The neatest way to transport salt for the finger salads is to make individual portions twisted up in a small square of foil.

A rigid container such as an airtight plastic box will stop your softer salad items, such as tomatoes, getting squashed. The pavilion eggs should also go in a rigid box. Celery and radishes can be transported in a plastic bag. The bag will also be

useful to bring home any rubbish, such as food that was accidentally dropped on the ground and cologne wipes that were used to clean fingers.

Remember to take a knife for the cake: it is the only piece of cutlery you will need.

The simplest way to transport the cake is to return it, when completely cold, to the tin in which it was cooked. If you are using a loose-bottomed tin, put the cake back on to the base and reverse the top over, but don't turn it upside down again. Remove the foil at the last moment before cutting the cake, as it will help to keep the topping in place while travelling. The base of the cake tin provides useful support on which to cut the cake.

To carry your picnic you will need a sturdy picnic bag. Choose one that is fairly capacious but not awkward to carry. When buying, look for comfortable handles and a spongeable lining in case of spills. An insulated zip bag is ideal and does not take up much room when empty. Insulated buckets keep food cool and fresh but are awkward to carry and mean that you must always picnic near the car.

Follow the country code

When you get to your picnic ground, be it a sports field or out in the country, please follow the country code. If you are in a field, make sure the farmer does not object and that you are not destroying crops. Keep dogs and children under control, shut all gates behind you and above all, don't leave litter. A plastic bag carelessly discarded by a picnicker can easily kill a cow should she try to swallow it. Perfect picnickers leave no trace of their presence.

Pavilion eggs

Pavilion eggs are a meal in a bun that's both filling and easy to eat. Choose plump, soft rolls for pavilion eggs. Hard dinner rolls should not be used; they would be like concrete after being cooked in the oven.

Pavilion eggs taste equally good hot or cold. They will keep for up to one day if well wrapped, in the refrigerator.

SERVES 4
1 lettuce heart
4 spring onions
75 g [3 oz] butter
3 rashers of streaky bacon
4 soft rolls
4 medium-sized eggs
60 ml [4 tablespoons] thick cream
salt and black pepper

1 Shred the lettuce heart finely using a sharp knife.

2 Trim the green part and root of the

spring onions. Chop the onions finely.

3 Heat the oven to 190°C [375°F], gas mark 5.

4 Melt 25 g [1 oz] of the butter in a heavy-based pan over medium heat.

5 When the butter has melted but is not sizzling, add the lettuce and onions. Season with black pepper.

6 As soon as the lettuce and onions begin to simmer, reduce the heat and cover the pan. Cook for 5 minutes, shaking the pan from time to time.

7 Meanwhile, set the grill to very hot. Cut the rind off the bacon.

8 Place the bacon on the grill rack about 5 cm [2"] from the heat. Grill until crisp, turning once. This will take about 4 minutes.

9 Cut a slice from the top of each of the rolls and set aside.

10 Using a knife, scrape out the crumb (interior) of the main part of each roll so that a shell is left. Keep the crumbs for use in making breadcrumbs.

11 Using the remaining butter, butter the insides and cut side of the lid of each roll.

12 Distribute the lettuce and onion evenly between the rolls.

13 Remove the bacon from the grill. Allow to cool slightly then crumble. Divide bacon equally between each roll.

14 Break an egg into each roll so it sits on top of the lettuce and bacon mixture.

15 Place 15 ml [1 tablespoon] of thick cream on top of each egg. Season

with salt and freshly ground black pepper.

16 Replace the lids on the rolls.

17 Place on a baking tray and cook in the centre of the oven for 12 minutes.

18 Either serve immediately or, if to be eaten cold, allow to cool then wrap individually in foil or cling film and store in the refrigerator.

Finger salad

Choose your salad items to pick up in the fingers from what is freshest and cheapest on the day of purchase. Remember that you will have neither plates nor forks to eat the salad with, so make sure the things you choose can easily be picked up in the fingers. Whole baby tomatoes, radishes, young carrots, celery, fennel and spring onions can all be picked up and bitten into. If young broad beans are on the market, very small and fresh in the pod, take a bagful and eat them just as they are.

SERVES 4
4 baby tomatoes
1 bunch radishes
225 g [$\frac{1}{2}$ lb] new carrots
1 head celery
1 small fennel bulb (optional)
bunch spring onions
700 g [1$\frac{1}{2}$ lb] broad beans in pod (optional)
juice 1 lemon (optional)

1 Wash the tomatoes.

2 Wash the radishes and carrots and trim the roots but not the radish tops.

3 Strip the coarse outer sticks of the celery and select four of the inner tender sticks. Rinse.

4 Trim the bulb base of the fennel and cut it into quarters. Dip the cut sides into the lemon juice so that they will not discolour.

5 Trim roots from the spring onions and wash.

6 Place the vegetables into plastic bags and put in the refrigerator to crisp.

Peach upside-down cake

◻◻◻ *This cake, made by the all-in-one method, has a lovely fruity topping which helps to keep it moist. The number of eggs is reduced because the orange juice provides extra liquid. The method of lining the tin is a little different from usual because the sugar crust is very runny when hot, and you do not want it dripping through the lining.*

If the cake is to be taken on a picnic, wait till it is to be cut before removing foil over the topping.

MAKES 6-8 SLICES
1 medium-sized orange
100 g [4 oz] self-raising flour
5 ml [1 teaspoon] baking powder
100 g [4 oz] caster sugar
50 g [2 oz] soft margarine
2 medium-sized eggs

For the topping:
820 g [1 lb 13 oz] can sliced peaches
45 ml [3 tablespoons] margarine
100 g [4 oz] brown sugar
3 maraschino or glacé cherries

1 Position the shelf in the centre and heat the oven to 160°C [325°F] gas mark 3.

2 Grease a 17.5 cm [7"] cake tin and line it with foil rather than grease-proof paper. Cut strips and line the sides of the tin.

3 Cut the circle to line the base 6 mm [¼"] larger than the tin. Place the base lining in the tin and work all round the edge with the tips of your fingers, so that the foil just turns up the side and fits the shape neatly.

4 Grease the lining thoroughly.

5 Drain the peaches into a sieve placed over a bowl.

6 Put the margarine for the topping into a small pan and melt over medium heat. Add the brown sugar and stir with a wooden spoon until the sugar becomes runny.

7 Pour the sugar paste into the lined cake tin and spread it out over the bottom of the tin with the back of a spoon. The covering will be rather uneven.

8 Lift the peach slices with a spoon, one by one, on to kitchen paper. Turn them over and blot all sides.

9 Arrange the peach slices on the sugar, starting at the edge of the tin. Lay each slice with the high side towards the rim. Make concentric circles of peach slices, until the tin bottom is covered.

10 Drain the maraschino cherries, if using, and blot on kitchen paper. Arrange maraschino or glacé cherries in the middle of the peaches. Set the tin aside while you make the cake mixture.

11 Grate the zest from the orange with a citrus zester and squeeze the juice.

12 Sift the flour and baking powder into a large warmed mixing bowl.

13 Add the sugar, margarine, orange zest, and 50 ml [2 fl oz] orange juice and eggs to the bowl. Beat for 2-3 minutes with a wooden spoon.

14 Scrape the mixture into the prepared cake tin with a spatula.

15 Smooth the top with the spatula and then bake for 70 minutes.

16 Test that the cake is cooked with a fine warmed skewer. It should come out clean.

17 Let the cake rest 3 minutes before turning out on to a cake rack as the topping will drip while it is warm.

18 Remove the lining from the side of the cake but leave the foil over it for travelling.

Cider cup

This drink is only mildly alcoholic and a good choice in hot weather when one always wants to drink more than usual. The cider loses its sparkle while cooling in the refrigerator but is pleasantly refreshing. For a picnic you will need two one-litre [one and three-quarter-pint] containers. If you pour it over ice cubes, it is even more refreshing and goes further.

Cider cup makes an excellent party drink for teenagers. For a party, multiply the quantities and decorate the serving jug with more mint and orange slices. If wished, 550 ml [1 pt] of soda water can be added to the quantities given in the recipe. Do this at the last moment before serving to make the drink slightly fizzy. Cool the siphon in the refrigerator for the same length of time as the cider cup.

MAKES 2 L [3½ PT]
1.7 L [3 pt] medium-dry cider
225 ml [8 fl oz] orange juice
50 ml [2 fl oz] dry sherry
a few drops of angostura bitters
half a cucumber
mint sprig

1 Peel the skin from the cucumber and crush the mint leaves with your fingers so that they are oozing juice. Put these into a small jug.

2 Choose a container large enough to hold all the liquid. A large mixing bowl is suitable.

3 Add all the liquids and stir lightly to mix. Fill up the jug containing the rind and mint. Divide the rest between the two vacuum flasks.

4 Put the flasks, without their tops, and the jug into the refrigerator to cool for at least two hours.

5 When ready to travel, pour half of the contents of the jug into each vacuum flask, removing the skin and mint. Close the flasks and put straight into an insulated bag.

An insulated container will keep cider cup cool and refreshing for your picnic.

Dead-broke dinner for six

Everybody enjoys buying special luxuries or more expensive ingredients out of the common run when friends are expected for a meal. But sometimes this is not possible and you have the problem of how to entertain your guests in style at minimum cost. Cheap ingredients badly cooked are, to say the least, uninspiring and anyway smack of penny-pinching. Here is how to turn economical everyday foods into dishes worthy of a party.

SPENDING TIME AND TROUBLE

Giving a good dinner party on a shoe-string is a considerable challenge but there is an enormous satisfaction to be gained from transforming ordinary food into festive fare. Spending extra time and trouble instead of money is the secret for success. Cheap, everyday ingredients treated with loving care can taste every bit as delicious as luxury foods – and, if the spread looks handsome as well, no-one will ever guess how little money you've spent.

Attention to detail is also important when it comes to preparing the table. Crisply laundered napkins, soft light and sparkling glasses cost nothing at all but a little extra time, and they create a wonderfully welcoming atmosphere.

This colourful table centre is dismantled and the parsley and lemon used in the kitchen next day.

51

Menu

French onion soup

*Lamb scrumpets
with carrot puree*

Apple dumplings

*To drink: Lager or a strong cider
such as Strongbow*

Flowers are often too expensive to buy, yet for guests a supper table does need something extra as a decoration. Make a pretty and economical centrepiece using 6–8 lemons and a bunch of fresh parsley. (All of them can then be used in the kitchen next day.) Choose a pretty dish about 15 cm [6"] in diameter. Pile the lemons on to it and push curly green heads of parsley into the gaps.

SHOPPING CHECKLIST
All the ingredients for this party are everyday ones. However, French bread is more exciting in the soup than ordinary toast. Old carrots are more suitable for the purée (as well as cheaper) than new ones.

SPECIAL EQUIPMENT
No special equipment is needed for these recipes. However, if you do not own a pastry board, you can press the meat with the bottom of a roasting tin. Fill the tin with weights from your scales, or use other heavy objects such as full container jars.

THE DAY BEFORE

Lamb scrumpets: cook, bone and press – steps 1–8.
French onion soup: make a well-flavoured brown stock with beef bones or stock cubes.

ON THE DAY

Lamb scrumpets: make and coat the triangles and refrigerate – steps 9–14.
Apple dumplings: make the pastry and prepare – steps 1–17.
Lay the table.

1 hour before the meal
French onion soup: make the soup and prepare the cheese mixture – steps 1–4.

45 minutes before the meal
Apple dumplings: heat the oven – step 18.
Carrot purée: prepare and cook the vegetables and prepare the additions – steps 1–3.

Lamb scrumpets: heat the grill – step 15.

25 minutes before the meal
Apple dumplings: put the dumplings in the oven to cook – step 19.
Carrot purée: make the purée – steps 4–7.
Put the serving dishes and plates in the warmer.
French onion soup: toast the bread under the grill – steps 5–6.

15 minutes before the meal
French onion soup: transfer the soup to a tureen or bowls, float the bread on top, cover with a layer of cheese and bake – steps 7–9.
Lamb scrumpets: grill the meat and put on a temporary dish in the warmer – steps 16–17.

5 minutes before the meal
Carrot purée: heat through and put in serving dish – steps 8–9.
Lamb scrumpets: pile round the purée and put in warmer while you serve and eat the first course.

French onion soup makes an economical and satisfying start to the meal.

French onion soup

This classic soup is unusual because it introduces cheese at the beginning of the meal. Serve the soup in a large oven proof tureen or six individual oven proof bowls, each topped with an island of sizzling toasted cheese. Each person submerges his own cheese island under the soup as he eats it, pressing the bread against the bottom of the bowl with the edge of a soup spoon to cut it into bite-sized pieces. If you do not have time to make beef stock, you could use canned consommé. For an extra rich soup add 15 ml [1 tablespoon] of brandy per serving. Stir in the brandy just before the end of cooking.

SERVES 6
350 g [¾ lb] onions
75 g [3 oz] margarine
1 L [2 pt] well-flavoured beef
  stock
bay leaf
salt and pepper
6 thick slices of French bread
100 g [¼ lb] Emmenthal cheese
30 ml [2 tablespoons] Parmesan
  cheese

1 Skin and finely chop the onions.

2 Melt the margarine in a heavy-based pan. Add the onions and cook over a low heat, stirring occasionally, until browned.

3 Add the stock and bay leaf. Season with salt and pepper. Cover pan and simmer gently for 30 minutes.

4 Grate the Emmenthal cheese, put it in a bowl, add the Parmesan cheese and mix the two together.

5 Heat the grill and heat the oven to 200°C [400°F] gas mark 6.

6 Toast the bread lightly on each side.

7 Remove the bay leaf and pour the soup into an oven proof soup tureen or six individual bowls.

8 Cover each slice of bread with cheese and float the bread on top of the soup.

9 Carefully put the soup tureen or bowls into the oven and cook for 10–15 minutes, or until the cheese is melted and sizzling.

Lamb scrumpets with carrot purée

⬛⬛⬛ *This recipe transforms one of the cheapest cuts of meat into a dish fit for a party. There are three stages of preparation, so it needs to be started on the day before it is eaten. The second stage of preparation can also be done well before the meal. The third and final stage is quickly done just before serving.*

Buy two small breasts of lamb to make the weight of 1.15 kg [2½ lb].

SERVES 6
1.15 kg [2½ lb] lean breasts of lamb
1 medium-sized onion
1 medium-sized carrot
1 stick celery
5 ml [1 teaspoon] salt
1 bay leaf
6 peppercorns
10 ml [2 teaspoons] French mustard
50 g [2 oz] seasoned flour
1 large egg
50 g [2 oz] dried white breadcrumbs
10 ml [2 teaspoons] oil
lemon wedges for serving

1 Peel and chop the onion and carrot. Wash and chop the celery.

2 Put the whole breasts of lamb into a large saucepan. Add the onion, carrot, celery, salt, bay leaf, peppercorns and water just enough to cover.

3 Bring to the boil, cover and simmer very gently until the meat is very tender – about 1½ hours.

4 Lift out the meat, discard the vegetables and reserve the liquid for soups.

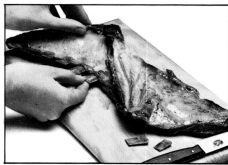

5 When cool enough to handle, remove the skin and top layer of fat from the meat. With your fingers pull out the ribs.

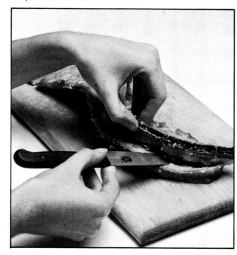

6 Remove the breastbone from the opposite side of the meat, cutting it free with a small knife.

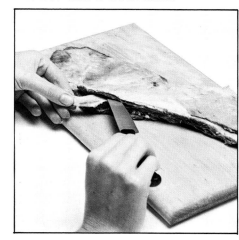

7 Free the cartilage by cutting through horizontally from the edge and then pulling it out. Try not to break up the outer layers of meat. Discard the bones.

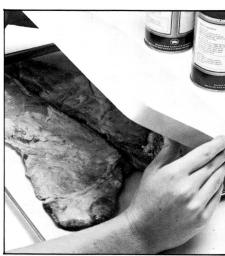

8 Lay the boned breasts flat side by side on a baking tray. Cover the meat with a pastry board and put heavy weights on top. Leave the meat for several hours, or overnight, until firm, cold and flat.

9 Lift off the board and weights. Remove any congealed fat adhering to the outside of the lamb.

10 Using a sharp knife, cut the meat into triangles. Small spare scraps can be reserved for soup.

11 Spread one side of the meat (or both sides if liked) with mustard, then coat on all sides with seasoned flour (flour seasoned with a little salt and pepper).

12 Break the egg into a saucer, add 20 ml [4 teaspoons] of water and beat together with a fork. Arrange the breadcrumbs nearby on a piece of greaseproof paper.

13 Dip each triangle first into the egg to coat both sides and then into the breadcrumbs to cover. Press the crumbs in place with a palette knife.

14 Put them on a plate with grease-proof paper between the layers. Cover and chill in the refrigerator.

15 Heat the grill until medium hot. Brush the base of the grill pan with a thin coat of oil.

16 Put the lamb triangles in a single layer in the base of the grill pan. Reduce the heat and grill under a gentle heat for 3–4 minutes. Turn with tongs and grill the other side. The scrumpets will heat through and become crisp and golden on the outside.

17 Transfer the cooked scrumpets to a heatproof dish until ready to serve.

Crunchy lamb scrumpets contrast favourably with smooth carrot purée.

CARROT PUREE

The use of a vegetable mill, rather than a liquidizer, gives a better texture to this purée. The addition of potato helps to make it smoother, while the orange peel adds interest.

SERVES 6
550 g [1¼ lb] carrots
550 g [1¼ lb] potatoes
30 ml [2 tablespoons] butter
 or margarine
2.5 ml [½ teaspoon] caster sugar
grated zest of one orange
30 ml [2 tablespoons] chopped
 parsley
salt and pepper

1 Scrub carrots and peel potatoes and then, if necessary, cut to make them the same size.

2 Bring water to boil in a saucepan, add the vegetables and simmer for 15 minutes or until they are tender.

3 Meanwhile, grate the orange zest on a citrus zester or the fine holes of a cheese grater. Chop the parsley.

4 Drain the vegetables carefully.

5 Put the empty saucepan back on to the cooker, over a low heat and dry the vegetables by tossing gently for 1 minute.

6 Purée the vegetables in a liquidizer, or pass them through the fine grinder of a vegetable mill straight into the saucepan.

7 To the purée in the saucepan add the butter, sugar and orange zest. Season generously with salt and pepper and stir to mix well.

8 Re-heat the purée over low heat, stirring all the time.

9 Pile the purée into the centre of a warm serving dish. Arrange the lamb scrumpets around it and garnish with parsley and lemon wedges.

Apple dumplings

⧗⧗ ▲▲ *This is a substantial pudding, very handsome in appearance and particularly good if served with thin cream. The inclusion of a little black treacle when making suet crust will give a golden glow to the final pastry and this greatly improves its appearance.*

The apples may be prepared well in advance of the meal and be kept in the refrigerator.

SERVES 6

350 g [¾ lb] self-raising flour
2.5 ml [½ teaspoon] salt
175 g [6 oz] suet
30 ml [2 tablespoons] black treacle
175 ml [6 fl oz] water
6 small apples each weighing 120-150 g [4–5 oz]
60 g [2½ oz] mincemeat

1 Make the suet crust following the method described in the glossary and add 30 ml [2 tablespoons] of black treacle with the water. This pastry may need a little more kneading than usual to distribute the treacle thoroughly.

2 Peel and core the apples.

3 Roll out the pastry on a floured board into an oblong about 45 x 30 cm [18 x 12"] and 1·5 mm [1/16"] thick.

4 Cut it into 6 equal pieces, each measuring about 15 cm [6"] square.

5 Place a cored apple in the middle of each piece of pastry. Fill the hole in the centre of each apple with 10 ml [2 teaspoons] of mincemeat.

6 Now work the pastry around the

Measuring black treacle.
Taken straight from the cupboard, all syrups stick to the spoon and are therefore difficult to measure. Stand the

first apple. Gather the opposite corners together at the top to make a pastry envelope. With floured fingers press the pastry close to the apple.

7 The pastry will be thicker where the seams meet, but it is still very malleable. Push the thickness upwards by pressing it gently with the tips of your fingers. You should end up with an equal thickness of pastry all over the apple, and fitting it like a tight coat.

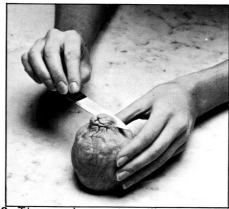

8 The surplus pastry will now all be at the top of the apple. Cut it off

tin in a saucepan with hot water half way up the sides. Bring to the boil and remove from the heat. The runny liquid is easy to measure.

neatly with a knife, leaving a small hole at the top for steam to escape during cooking. Reserve the scraps of pastry.

9 Cover the other apples with pastry.

10 Work all the scraps of pastry together to make a ball of dough and roll out again.

11 To make the pastry decorations, cut long thin strips 12 mm [½"] across with a knife.

12 Cut diagonally across the strips at 12 mm [½"] intervals to make a series of diamond shapes. With the point of the knife, mark each diamond to indicate the stem and veins of a leaf.

13 Divide the pastry leaves equally among your apples. There should be 3 or 4 each.

14 Pinch the leaves with your finger and thumb on the 2 long sides until they look rounded and leaf-like. Brush the underside of the leaves with a little water and stick them firmly on to the top of each apple dumpling, taking great care not to cover the small steam-hole.

15 Cut a 17.5 cm [7″] square of foil for each apple and grease it with oil or margarine.

16 Wrap up each apple dumpling by

Hearty apple dumplings are made with suet pastry and filled with treacle and mincemeat. Serve them with thin cream or with custard.

standing it in the middle of the foil square, folding the foil upwards so that it forms a tight coat around most of the apple. At the top turn back the foil, leaving the decorations exposed so that they will take colour in the oven.

17 Put the dumplings on a baking sheet and reserve in the refrigerator.

18 Heat the oven to 200°C [400°F] gas mark 6.

19 Cook in the centre of the oven for 35 minutes.

A family supper to come home to
serves 6

Here is a menu that solves every mother's dilemma of whether to join the rest of the family on a Saturday afternoon's outing or to stay at home and prepare a meal for their inevitably hungry return. In this menu all the food is prepared well in advance, so you can applaud your offspring's sporting prowess, jeer and cheer with the best of them on the terraces, attend the school concert or go out with your children and still produce a satisfying meal for six within half an hour of getting home. There's even enough time to check that aspiring young sportsmen and women have washed muddy hands and knees before sitting down to hearty thick green pea soup, subtly spicy chicken with crunchy coleslaw and a rich but simple sweet—all dishes that will win favour with young diners and prove interesting enough to please the adults.

Menu

❧

*Green pea and
bacon soup*

━━━✿━━━

*Sportsman's chicken
Coleslaw*

━━━✿━━━

Banana Fluff

━━━✿━━━

*To drink: cider, lemonade
shandy or ginger beer*

GETTING ORGANIZED

When a family outing is being planned and there are children to organize, it is wise to start things as far in advance as possible. When the family says that kick off is at two, then one o'clock is no time to be thinking about what to make for supper. If you know there is a match coming up on Saturday, it's good sense to make the stock and start soaking the peas for the soup well in advance on Thursday. This means you can cook the soup on Friday, leaving Saturday morning free to make the coleslaw and dessert and to marinate the chicken, and still have plenty of time to get yourself and any small children ready.

It is also a good idea to set the table before you go. This means that when you all return home, you only have to reheat the soup and cook the chicken, make the coleslaw dressing and toss the coleslaw in it. The soup will take only a few minutes to heat through and the chicken is timed so that grilling should be completed just as the last spoonful of soup is downed.

SHOPPING CHECKLIST

At least two days in advance, buy a

Countdown timetable

TWO DAYS BEFORE

Green pea and bacon soup: make the stock and soak the peas—step 1.

THE DAY BEFORE

Green pea and bacon soup: make— steps 2-8.
Sportsman's chicken: start thawing if using frozen chicken.

ham bone to make the stock for the soup (its flavour goes well with dried peas or other pulses). If you can't get a ham bone, buy a small boiling bacon joint such as knuckle. This means you can use some of the meat in place of the bacon rashers listed in the recipe, and save most of it for another meal.

The dried peas should also be bought in advance as they need prolonged soaking before use.

For the chicken you will notice that the recipe says use either tarragon or German mustard. Both these mustards have a mild but spicy flavour. If neither of these is available, French mustard may be used instead.

The chicken breasts can be either fresh or frozen. Bone the breasts because they are easier to eat— especially important when there are children involved.

Finally, make sure you put the chocolate flake for the dessert in a safe place, otherwise someone might come across it and be tempted to eat it on the way to the match.

SPECIAL EQUIPMENT

No special equipment is needed for any of these recipes, but do make sure you have a good supply of kitchen foil. As most of these dishes

ON THE MORNING

Sportsman's chicken: cover the chicken breasts with mustard and honey marinade and refrigerate— steps 1-5.
Coleslaw: prepare and refrigerate— steps 1-4.
Banana fluff: make—steps 1-4. Cover and refrigerate.
Set the table.

ON THE EVENING

15 minutes before the meal
Coleslaw: make dressing and dress — steps 5-7.
Sportsman's chicken: heat the grill and start cooking—steps 6-7.

10 minutes before the meal
Place plates and soup bowls in the plate warmer.
Banana fluff: add chocolate flake— step 5.
Green pea and bacon soup: reheat, add milk and serve—step 9.

are made in advance and kept in the refrigerator until needed, they must be covered to prevent any transfer of flavours and smells.

For the soup, all that is needed is a heavy-based pan to allow gentle cooking. If you don't own one of these use a thin-based pan with an asbestos mat placed underneath it to make the heat more gentle. Asbestos mats with metal mesh on each side are the best to use for modern gas and electric cookers.

To marinate the chicken, you will need a glass or glazed earthenware bowl which will not absorb the flavour of the marinade.

If you have no tall sundae glasses, banana fluff will look just as appetizing piled into ordinary wine glasses.

DRINKS

Most children like a fizzy drink to go with their meal—obviously this must not be too alcoholic. A not-too-dry cider or a shandy made with a lot of lemonade are sufficiently grown-up looking drinks to please the children without doing them any harm. Ginger beer is also a popular choice. Reduce the lemonade in the shandy for the adults. An attractive touch is to float orange slices in the drinks— just like the footballers get at half-time.

Green pea and bacon soup

▲▲▲ *Serve this hearty soup with crisp French bread.*

Dried green peas are very hard when they are bought so they must be soaked overnight before they can be used. Green peas are available either whole or split. Both can be used to make this soup.

You can use 75 g [3 oz] diced cooked ham instead of bacon rashers. Add it at step 9.

If you make the soup in advance, up to step 8 in the recipe, it will keep, covered, in the refrigerator for 3 days. It will not keep quite so long after the milk has been added so if you have any soup left over, eat it within 2 days.

SERVES 6
200 g [7 oz] dried green peas
1.7 L [3 pt] ham or bacon stock
1 large onion
1 small carrot
a small piece of turnip
4 bacon rashers
50 g [2 oz] butter
bouquet garni
150 ml [$\frac{1}{4}$ pt] milk

1 Soak the dried peas in water for at least 8 hours or overnight. The water must be cold and must cover the peas.

2 Peel and chop the onion into small pieces.

3 Scrub and chop the carrot. Peel and chop the turnip.

4 Remove and discard bacon rind. Cut bacon into small pieces using kitchen scissors.

5 Melt the butter in a large heavy-based saucepan over low heat. Do not allow it to brown.

6 Add the bacon and chopped vegetables. Cook until the bacon and onion are just transparent.

7 Drain any surplus water off the peas and add to the pan with the stock and bouquet garni. Bring to the boil and cover.

8 Simmer over low heat for 2-2$\frac{1}{2}$ hours until the vegetables are reduced to a pulp.

9 Just before serving, remove the bouquet garni, check seasoning, add cooked ham if used, stir in the milk and reheat if necessary.

Sportsman's chicken

⧖⧖ *It is best, but not essential, to bone the chicken breasts. This is easily done by loosening the bone with a sharp knife.*

Mild mustard is used in the dish so that the chicken is well flavoured but not too spicy for children. The mustard could be omitted for those who are against it in any form, but add a good grinding of black pepper if you omit mustard. The chicken and marinade must be prepared at least 2 hours before cooking to allow the flavour to be absorbed into the meat.

SERVES 6
6 chicken breasts
125 g [¼ lb] butter
30 ml [2 tablespoons] tarragon or German mustard
90 ml [6 tablespoons] clear honey

1 Place the butter (which should be at room temperature) in a bowl and soften with a wooden spoon.

2 Add the mustard and honey and beat until well blended and smooth.

3 Place the chicken breasts in a shallow dish and prick the flesh with the point of a knife or a large darning needle.

4 Using a round-bladed knife, spread the honey and mustard butter over the chicken pieces, making sure all sides are well covered.

5 Cover and leave in the refrigerator for at least 2 hours.

6 Heat the grill to medium heat.

7 Grill the chicken breasts 15 cm [6"] from the heat for 20-25 minutes, basting with the buttery drips and turning occasionally.

Coleslaw

Either English salad cream or mayonnaise (use bought or home-made) can be used as a dressing for coleslaw.

Dress the coleslaw about 30 minutes before you plan to eat it. This gives the flavours a chance to amalgamate with the salad and softens the hard crunchy vegetables without them turning soggy and unappetizing.

SERVES 6
**1 small or half a medium-sized
   Dutch cabbage
2 celery sticks
a small onion
50 g [2 oz] walnuts
50 g [2 oz] sultanas
75 ml [5 tablespoons] English
   salad cream or mayonnaise
10 ml [2 teaspoons] white
   vinegar or lemon juice
freshly ground black pepper**

1 Remove any ragged outer leaves from the cabbage. Cut into quarters and discard the tough stalk.

2 Shred the cabbage into a large salad bowl.

3 Trim and scrub the celery sticks and chop into small pieces. Skin and chop the onion. Add to the cabbage.

4 Roughly chop the nuts then add to the bowl with the sultanas.

5 Put the salad cream or mayonnaise in a small mixing bowl. Add the vinegar and black pepper and stir to mix well.

6 Pour the dressing over the salad and toss lightly.

7 Cover and set aside in a cool place for about 30 minutes before serving the salad.

Banana fluff

This simple sweet can be made well in advance as it will keep in the refrigerator for several hours. Overripe bananas with black spotted skins are best as they mash well, and they are usually cheaper to buy. After mashing it is essential to add lemon juice or the banana pulp will turn a most unappetizing colour—this is particularly important when you are catering for children because they are usually sensitive to the colour of food.

Banana fluff will keep well in the refrigerator for 24 hours if covered with foil or cling film. Do not exceed this time—the bananas develop an unpleasant fermented flavour. Sprinkle the chocolate over banana fluff just before serving—if added earlier it might go soggy.

SERVES 6
6 large bananas
150 ml [¼ pt] whipped cream
1 large chocolate flake bar

1 Peel the bananas and mash to a pulp with a fork. Add the lemon juice to prevent discolouration.

2 Pile the mashed banana into tall glasses.

3 Pile the whipped cream on top of the banana mixture.

4 Chill for at least one hour but not more than 24 hours.

5 Just before serving, break up the flake bar and sprinkle some on top of each glass of banana fluff.

Two-in-one dinner for four adults and two children

Here's a menu that solves the problem of how to feed the kids excitingly when you are expecting guests. You don't want to cook twice and yet the grown-ups' food is too sophisticated as it stands for young tastes, yet the younger element will feel left out if they aren't offered any of the goodies. So this is one neat routine for adapting a meal to suit both sittings.

The night you are entertaining guests to dinner is not the time to be cooking something special for the children's supper as well. Yet who can blame the kids, when they see their dull little plate of fish fingers approach, for feeling disappointed and left out?

Now, obviously if you have older teenagers, they can join you for a late dinner, or the very young can be put to bed. The 8–14 year-olds, however, will be up and will want to join in, if only for the food.

So, here is what you do: you feed them an amended version of your dinner at their suppertime, set out as prettily as possible on a tray or side-table. Then invite them to be there with you to greet your guests and share a drink (they can always have lemonade), then shortly before you adjourn to the dinner table, they go to their bedrooms.

Menu

DINNER MENU FOR ADULTS

Cheesy fish mousse

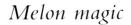

*Mediterranean lamb
with peppers
and olives*
Italian green salad
*Hot French bread and
butter*

Melon magic

To drink: *medium-dry white
wine
such as hock or Moselle*
Coffee

SUPPER MENU FOR CHILDREN

Mediterranean lamb
Plain green salad
*French bread and
butter*

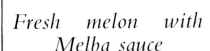

*Fresh melon with
Melba sauce*

To drink: *a glass of milk*

THE FOOD

For simplicity's sake, the main course is cold: succulent medium-rare slices of roast lamb in a fresh tomato sauce. The youngsters' sauce is the basic tomato and onion with a dash of lemon juice; but after their portions have been extracted from the pan, red and green peppers, garlic, chopped basil and handsome black olives are added to please the grown-ups. That way, the adults get something out of the ordinary without the children complaining that the sauce is 'too hot' or that they hate olives.

The accompanying green salad can be treated in a similar way. Cos or Webb's lettuce is used for both salads. If your children like French dressing, you can make a little specially for them—the adult version can then be spicy. Most children prefer bottled salad cream or mayonnaise anyway! To go with their lettuce, the children have radishes and mustard-and-cress. For adults you toss in courgettes, a few raw young peas, green pepper and basil again to echo the flavour of the lamb sauce, plus the shredded heart of a bulb of Florentine fennel to give a touch of piquancy. With the lamb, everybody eats French bread and butter. The bread can be warmed in the oven for the adults.

The dessert is a large melon which is divided into balls for the adults, battered, fried and served with Melba sauce. The remains of the melon are used for the junior dessert, once again with Melba sauce.

And that, apart from coffee for adults and milk for the kids, brings the meal to a spectacular close.

However, that makes only two courses—which seems a little sparse when you are entertaining. It is fine for the kids; very few people regularly have an hors d'oeuvre course when eating with the family. For the adults, at the second sitting, there is a tasty mousse made using cottage cheese and smoked haddock. Serve the mousse with hot crusty French bread or with toast fingers.

GETTING ORGANIZED

Once you have established the theme of your dinner—this two-tier idea of catering—then organization becomes simple. Apart from the salad and melon, everything can be done the day before, making this an ideal meal for Saturday when the children are at home all day and serious cooking is difficult.

In the morning of the day before take on the big job of the Mediterranean lamb and get that tucked away in the refrigerator. Also make the mousse and the sauce for the lamb. Store everything covered in the refrigerator.

Early next day (depending, probably, on the time you awake and how well Dad occupies the kids), see to the vinaigrette for the salad and prepare and chill the lettuce.

About an hour before you plan to serve the children, divide up the melon, leave to soak in fruit juice and make the Melba sauce. You can also wash the salad vegetables and set both the tables.

Giving the children their meal is simplicity itself. Simply carve their portion of the joint of lamb, prepare their salad and arrange it all on a plate with the tomato sauce. Cut some French bread for them and let them spread their own butter. The melon with its sauce can go on the junior table at the same time as the rest of their food.

Then, while they eat that, you can be mixing your own Italian green salad; wash up the children's supper things and any lurking kitchen utensils and, after extracting a promise from the kids that they won't play anything that involves making a mess, take a leisurely hour off to get yourself ready for the evening.

There are just four things to do before your guests' arrival: fetch out the mousse and garnish it, toss the salad in the vinaigrette, make a batter and carve and arrange the Mediterranean lamb. The last one could be a job for Dad. After spending the first quarter of an hour with your guests, you will have to disappear to the kitchen to warm the bread and the plates, and to part-fry the melon dessert. Also it would be as well to pack the kids off at this stage, otherwise they may start wangling it so that they are still around at coffee time! Finally, carry in the warm French loaf and the cheesy fish mousse and eat.

Between the main course and the sweet, re-heat the oil and quickly immerse the half-cooked melon balls in it so that the batter crisps. Transfer the melon balls to a serving dish and pour a little of the sauce over to add a dash of colour. Serve the remaining sauce separately.

THE DRINKS

On the subject of after-dinner coffee, you might like to serve a richer blend than usual, or a liqueur coffee. For the latter you'll need some whipped cream.

For the main adult drink, you will need 1 litre of white wine, choose dry or medium-dry wine, according to preference. Frascati and Soave are dry, Riesling, hock and Moselle are medium dry. If white wine is not a favourite, try a rosé.

Don't forget you also need a small bottle of cooking wine (dry this time) for the melon batter or, if you don't want to buy cooking wine specially, you could use some of the table wine instead.

As for aperitifs, serve anything you happen to have in the house. Dry sherry will be particularly suitable as the first course is fish.

SHOPPING CHECKLIST

There are one or two special items to be bought for this menu, including some dairy produce; then, after that, it's just a matter of store-cupboard items and a mammoth greengrocery list. If you have a street market within reach, this is one occasion when a visit will be really worthwhile.

Special items first, starting with the main course, a cold roast which uses the best end of neck of lamb—this is a fairly meaty cut and has an excellent flavour. As you will see from the recipe introduction, the joint needs to be boned and rolled—and there is some advantage in doing it yourself. In any event, you have to serve 6 off it, so buy the largest joint in the shop—at least 900 g [2 lb] with the bone included.

If you have a local delicatessen, pay him a visit and buy coriander seeds for lamb (not always available in an ordinary supermarket) and plump black olives for the Mediterranean lamb.

For the fish mousse, you need only 225 g [½ lb] of fish, so you can afford to buy the very best smoked haddock around.

Stop off at the baker's for a long French loaf—and keep it in a cool, dry place until it is required.

Thinking of lovely crusty French bread to accompany both the mousse and the lamb, you had better buy an extra packet of butter from the dairy department—it's amazing how quickly it goes. Also from the dairy you need 225 g [½ lb] carton of cottage cheese or buy it at the cheese department of your supermarket or store.

Finally, just check that you have an egg for the batter—or rather just the egg white.

From the greengrocer you will need a large cantaloup or honeydew melon—700 g [1½ lb] in weight, 2 lemons, a punnet of raspberries (strawberries could be substituted), a Cos or Webb's lettuce, a box of mustard-and-cress and/or a small number of radishes, a medium-sized red pepper (for the adult's lamb sauce) and a jumbo-sized green pepper (for the sauce plus the Italian green salad), 900 g [2 lb] ripe tomatoes, 2-3 courgettes, 1 garlic bulb, 450 g [1 lb] onions, fennel if you're using it, and just 100 g [¼ lb] of fresh peas in the pod for the salad or 45 ml [3 tablespoons] frozen peas as a substitute.

Check too that you have sugar, wine vinegar, flour, icing sugar, olive oil, cooking oil, basil, a bay leaf and lots of fresh parsley.

Countdown timetable

THE DAY BEFORE

Do the shopping.

Cheesy fish mousse: make and turn into dishes. Cover and store in the refrigerator—steps 1-4.

Mediterranean lamb: cook the lamb. Make both sauces—steps 1-13. Cover meat and sauces and store in the refrigerator until required.

ON THE DAY
In the morning

Italian green salad: chill the lettuce and make the vinaigrette.

50 minutes before children's supper

Italian green salad: prepare children's plain salad—step 1.

Set the supper table/tray and the dinner table.

Melon magic: divide melon into balls and slices. Prepare Melba sauce—steps 1-5.

Mediterranean lamb: carve off children's portions and spoon over chilled tomato sauce—steps 14-15. Serve children's supper.

During children's meal

Italian green salad: mix adult's ingredients—steps 2-3.

Wash up children's supper dishes. Get yourself ready.

45 minutes before adults meal

Cheesy fish mousse: transfer from refrigerator to table, unmoulding if necessary, and garnish—step 5.

Italian green salad: toss in vinaigrette—step 4.

Mediterranean lamb: carve adults' portions and arrange with sauce in centre of serving plate; garnish—step 16.

Melon magic: make a batter and leave to rest—steps 6-7.

30 minutes before the meal

Greet guests with aperitifs.

15 minutes before the meal

See children off to bed.
Warm dessert plates and bread.

Melon magic: whisk egg white and heat the oil; fry melon balls a few at a time and keep hot under a low grill—steps 8-11.

Between main course and dessert

Melon magic: refresh the melon balls in hot oil so that they are pleasantly crisp when served—step 12. Serve—step 13.

Cheesy fish mousse

▧▧▧ *This sophisticated mousse of smoked haddock and cottage cheese is simple to make and a good recipe for the weight conscious to bear in mind. The fish is heated in water— the cooking principle adopted for the jugged kippers.*

Here the mousse is intended as a first course, but served with whole-meal rolls and a tomato or French bean salad, it would make a lovely summer lunch.

Press the mousse into ramekin dishes and serve turned out on small plates or make in a plain dish and spoon out. Garnish the mousse with lemon and parsley.

SERVES 4
225 g [½ lb] smoked haddock fillet
1 bay leaf
225 g [½ lb] cottage cheese
juice of ½ lemon
45 ml [3 tablespoons] freshly chopped parsley
salt
lemon slices for garnish
parsley sprigs for garnish

1 Place the haddock fillets in a pan with the bay leaf. Pour on just enough boiling water to cover the fish. Cover the pan with a well-fitting lid and leave for 10 minutes.

2 Meanwhile sieve the cottage cheese into a bowl.

3 Remove the fish from the pan of water. Bone, skin and divide the fish into small flakes. Fold these fish flakes into the cheese.

4 Add lemon juice and parsley. Season. Turn into 4 ramekins or one large dish. Chill until required.

5 Garnish with lemon slices and parsley sprigs before serving.

Italian green salad

This crisp salad, with its pretty mixture of greens, makes a welcome and refreshing complement to a rich cold meat dish. For children, the more exotic ingredients can be omitted and plain mustard-and-cress and /or radishes served in their place. The recipe serves 4 adults and 2 children.

A home-made French dressing is best, but a boiled dressing is a good substitute if time is short. If desired, the raw young peas may be replaced by frozen ones. They should be thoroughly thawed but not cooked.

Fresh basil is needed, but it is not always to hand, so substitute any other fresh herb you have.

SERVES 6
1 Cos or Webb lettuce, trimmed, rinsed and chilled

Additional ingredients for children:
10-14 radishes
box of mustard-and-cress

Additional ingredients for adults:
2-3 courgettes
1 small green pepper
1 fennel heart, optional
15 ml [1 tablespoon] chopped fresh basil
45 ml [3 tablespoons] chopped fresh parsley
45 ml [3 tablespoons] peas
salt and black pepper
75 ml [3 tablespoons] vinaigrette

1 Prepare the children's salad first. Remove about a quarter of the lettuce to a separate plate. Top and tail and rinse the radishes; rinse and cut off edible part of the mustard-and-cress. Mix lettuce, radishes and mustard-and-cress together and share between two plates.

2 Now attend to the adults' salad. Thinly slice the courgettes without peeling; rinse, de-seed and cut the pepper into narrow strips; shred the fennel heart.

3 Place the above ingredients in a salad bowl and add the herbs and peas. Mix and season lightly.

4 Just before serving, toss in the prepared vinaigrette.

Mediterranean lamb

If in your book, cold roast lamb is synonymous with washday dinner, then here is a recipe so tasty and different it will dispel that unfortunate image for ever. The roast lamb in this case is a joint of best end of neck which has been boned and rolled. The butcher may do this for you or you can try to do it yourself. The thick chine bone is removed, then the rib bones are eased out. If boning the meat yourself, take the opportunity to sprinkle the seasoning on the meat before rolling it up so that you gain a subtle flavour on the inside of the joint and not just on the outside as with a pre-rolled joint.

The accompanying richly coloured and flavoured tomato sauce is not unlike a cold ratatouille but with a different combination of vegetables—olives and herbs in place of courgettes and aubergine. By removing children's portions of sauce before these sophisticated ingredients are added, you can turn this into a dish to suit younger members of the family as well. The quantities given serves 4 adults and 2 children.

Serve with hot, crusty French bread and lots of butter.

SERVES 6
1 best end of neck of lamb boned and rolled
salt
freshly ground black pepper

For the sauce:
450 g [1 lb] onions
1 garlic clove
90 ml [6 tablespoons] olive oil
900 g [2 lb] tomatoes
pinch of sugar
10 ml [2 teaspoons] lemon juice

Additional ingredients for adults:
1 medium-sized red pepper
1 medium-sized green pepper
1 garlic clove
10 ml [2 teaspoons] coriander seeds
15 ml [1 tablespoon] chopped fresh basil
75 g [3 oz] black olives

For the garnish:
sprig of parsley

1 Heat the oven to 180°C [350°F] gas mark 4.

2 Rub the surface fat of the joint with a mixture of salt and pepper. Do not rub the mixture into the flesh.

3 Stand the joint on a rack in a roasting pan and roast for 45 minutes to each 450 g [1 lb].

4 Meanwhile prepare the sauce. Peel and chop the onions and crush the garlic.

5 Heat the oil in a frying-pan and lightly sauté the onion and garlic—about 5 minutes.

6 Skin, de-seed and chop the tomatoes and add them to the pan, together with the sugar and lemon juice. Simmer, uncovered, until tomatoes begin to pulp down—about 10 minutes.

7 Spoon half the sauce into a separate pan for the children and simmer it for 30 minutes, stirring occasionally to prevent sticking.

8 Prepare the additional ingredients. Rinse and de-seed both peppers and cut into thin strips; crush the second clove of garlic. Add peppers, garlic and basil to the adult pan and simmer for 30 minutes, stirring occasionally.

9 When the cooking time is up, the liquid in both pans should have evaporated, leaving a rich, juicy stew. Season both pans with salt and pepper. Leave junior sauce in saucepan to cool.

10 Crush the coriander seeds and stir into adult sauce with the olives. Adjust seasoning if necessary. Transfer to bowl.

11 When cool, transfer to the refrigerator to chill.

12 When the meat is ready (when the flesh pierced with a thin skewer gives out slightly rosy juices) remove the joint from the oven and leave in a cold place to cool rapidly.

13 When the joint has cooled, wrap in foil or cling film and refrigerate.

14 Shortly before serving, unwrap the joint and carve into thin slices, removing string as necessary. If adults are not eating at this stage, leave carving their portions until later because cut meat tends to dry. Re-wrap joint until needed again.

15 For children, serve meat on individual dinner plates with their special sauce on top.

16 For adults, arrange their carved slices of meat in an overlapping circle round a serving dish, with the sauce spooned into the centre and garnished with a sprig of parsley.

Melon magic

This is an unusual way to serve melon but well worth trying. When catering solely for an adult party, choose a specially ripe melon and soak it in a glassful of your favourite liqueur.

For a mixed group gathering, the melon recipe divides halfway through—the children eat their melon with Melba sauce, and the adults have theirs fried in batter. If raspberries are not available for the Melba sauce, frozen berries may be used. Or substitute fresh or frozen strawberries if you prefer or other berries such as blackberries or a ginger syrup sauce. As melon is naturally sweet and full of flavour there is no need to macerate or toss in sugar before frying.

SERVES 6
1 large cantaloup or honeydew melon weighing about 700 g [1½ lb]

For the Melba sauce:
450 g [1 lb] raspberries
50 g [2 oz] icing sugar

Additional ingredients for adults:
50 g [2 oz] plain flour
salt
15 ml [1 tablespoon] olive oil
75 ml [5 tablespoons] dry white wine
1 large egg white

1 Cut the melon in half and remove seeds.

2 Using a parisienne cutter, cut the melon into as many balls as possible.

3 Chop remaining melon and place in a bowl for the children.

4 Push the raspberries through a nylon sieve. Sift the icing sugar and use to sweeten the raspberry purée to complete Melba sauce.

5 Spoon the children's melon pieces into 2 sundae glasses. Pour over a little Melba sauce and serve.

6 Make a batter for the adult's melon by sifting flour and a little salt into a bowl. Make a well in the centre of these dry ingredients and gradually stir in the olive oil.

7 When the oil is smoothly incorporated, gradually add the wine and stir in smoothly. Leave batter to rest for 30 minutes.

8 Heat the cooking oil in a deep fryer until it reaches 180°C [350°F].

9 Meanwhile whisk the egg white with a pinch of salt until stiff. Fold in the batter.

10 Dip each melon ball in turn into the batter to coat lightly and fry, about 8 at a time, until golden.

11 Remove fried balls from the oil with a draining spoon and blot on kitchen paper. Keep hot in a single layer on a baking tray in a low oven or under a low grill.

12 If not serving immediately, refresh the melon balls in hot oil just before you take them to the table. This will crisp the batter.

13 When all the melon balls have been fried, pile them in a warm dish. Spoon some sauce over top and serve rest separately.

Entertaining eight for the day from the freezer

When you are expecting a big crowd for two or three meals, a freezer can really come into its own. It allows you to cook at your leisure in advance, so that catering on the day is merely a matter of thawing out a ready-made dish or popping one into the oven to reheat. With next to no trouble, you can offer your guests superb savouries and sweets as well as home-made bread and cakes. What is more, should the visitors be unexpected droppers-in, you can still feed them—thanks to your surprise storehouse.

The point of a freezer is that you are able to cook when you are in the mood and time is your friend, and not when you are in a panic and working against the clock. This means that when it comes to entertaining—especially for more than one meal at a time—all the food can be put into the freezer, ready-cooked, anything from a month to a whole year before the day (according to what it is) and quietly reappear on the table ready to eat.

The whole process makes those towering 'family visits' child's play. If you are four in family yourselves and invite a couple of friends and their youngsters to spend a Sunday with you, before you know it, you have a crowd to feed. Even if you do not have children of your own, just your married sister's brood, your parents, and you and your partner add up to eight—a number which is quite a challenge to cook for at one session. With a freezer, though, the problem melts away.

With children in mind—and die-hards who expect Sunday lunch to be a proper dinner—the menu card suggests that meat and vegetables are served at lunchtime, with a pâté pie for supper. Danish pastries come up with afternoon tea. If, however, your guests have to make an early departure—before 7 pm—then omit the tea and pastries in mid-afternoon and instead serve high tea at around 5.30, with Danish pastries as a sweet to follow the pie.

These useful pastries can be suc-cessfully cooked in advance and open-frozen. However, instead of just thawing them when they are required, you will find they are greatly improved if you take the trouble to refresh them briefly in the oven first. They are still, of course, eaten cold.

In order to save money and work, the lunch has no hors d'oeuvre course. If you would like to serve something, how about fruit juice? Tomato and pineapple juice are the most popular choices for adults and kids respectively. Frozen concentrated fruit juices (more often orange and grapefruit juice) will keep for 9 months in your freezer; so it is well worth tucking a can or two in there for use on such an occasion as this one.

The main course on the menu is Italian beef rolls: thin slices of sirloin braised in a rich, Marsala-flavoured sauce and stuffed with exotic ingredients including salami and raisins. It is served with mange-tout peas, lovingly preserved from their brief spring season, and pommes Anna, which are potatoes baked in butter and well flavoured with garlic.

If, when you cook your pommes Anna, you freeze them in servings for four, you then have the choice of fetching out the dishes in pairs for parties like this one, or individually for feeding just the family on ordinary week nights.

The pudding is a real spectacle: a bombe with a centre containing raw blackberries and a surrounding ice-cream made from puréed blackcurrants. A natural for the freezer, it is

Menu

❦

LUNCH:

Italian beef rolls
Pommes Anna
Mange-tout peas

⸻ ✧ ⸻

Black bombe

⸻ ✧ ⸻

To drink: home-brewed beer

❧

❦

AFTERNOON TEA:

Tea and Danish pastries

❧

❦

SUPPER:
Chimney pâté en croûte
Italian green salad
Hot home-made bread rolls

⸻ ✧ ⸻

Fresh oranges

❧

handsome to look at as well as delicious to eat—tops with children and parents alike. This is served with fruit; fresh blackberries are suggested but you could use frozen fruit if fresh is unavailable.

The chimney pâté for the evening meal is enclosed in a pastry case, making it easy to eat on a lap, should supper in your home be an around-the-fire affair. Serve it accompanied by the Italian green salad which was first introduced for the Two-in-one menu. The recipe appears on page 69, with a plainer version for fussy children. Look it up again—it is a perfect contrast in both texture and flavour to the pâté. The salad will have to be fresh, of course. Lettuce goes hopelessly limp on thawing out. This salad is so quick to prepare that it would not be labour saving to do it ahead anyway.

The pie and salad will probably be sufficient sustenance in themselves for the majority of diners; but for the odd insatiable teenager or traveller facing a long journey home, you could offer your own home-made bread rolls, perhaps on a wicker platter or in a basket. With oodles of butter, they are almost irresistible. Bread rolls freeze like a dream and can be heated up to give that fresh, home-made bread appeal.

Pastry and pâté will keep for a month, so that the pie is worth stashing away for unexpected visitors and yet it is not so grand or expensive that it will not make excellent family fare if visitors do not come.

Cook all the recipes listed as and when you have the opportunity and freeze them. Then come the day when six friends drop in, this entire menu will be to hand: waiting to be lifted out of the freezer, thawed and served.

For a finale to your supper, put a bowl of fresh oranges on the table. They make a colourful and refreshing end to a perfect day.

GETTING ORGANIZED
Vegetables, ice-cream, braised meat dishes, pies and, of course, bread and cakes of all descriptions, can be cooked when you have the urge and the ingredients and stored in the freezer for times ahead. So it is very possible that at the stage when you freeze these specific recipes, you may not know precisely when you are going to use them. You may not even

have considered entertaining eight people on any particular day. The point is, as soon as you do issue an invitation, check your freezer to see that it contains the necessary meals to suit. Watch out for the dates on your labels: although some foods remain in prime condition for a good year, others, such as pâté, start to deteriorate within a month. Consult the timetable to see how far ahead

you can make the different recipes on this menu; they vary considerably.

Beer can be made several months beforehand, giving you a wide choice of dates to start; the minimum time for maturing is three weeks, so make sure you open up your kit and begin work in time.

After that, there is nothing that you absolutely must do until the day itself. However, if you do have 24

Countdown timetable

FREEZING THE FOOD

Up to 1 year before
Mange-tout: prepare and blanch peas and freeze—steps 1–2.

Up to 3 months before
Black bombe: make and freeze—steps 1–6.
Home-brewed bitter: make, bottle and store.

Up to 2 months before
Italian beef rolls: make and freeze—

steps 1–12. Freeze them in a foil-lined casserole.

Up to 1 month before
Pommes Anna: make and freeze—steps 1–7.
Danish pastries: make and freeze—pack in polythene bags.
Chimney pâté en croûte: make and freeze—steps 1–15.
Home-made bread rolls: make and freeze.

SERVING THE FOOD

The day before
Italian beef rolls: transfer from freezer to refrigerator to thaw. (Return meat to casserole used for freezing.)

First thing in the morning on the day
Chimney pâté en croûte: transfer from freezer to refrigerator to thaw.

1 hour before lunch
Heat the oven.
Home-brewed bitter: put bottles in refrigerator if beer is preferred chilled.
Black bombe: remove blackberries from freezer and spread out on a plate in the refrigerator to thaw.

45 minutes before lunch
Pommes Anna: transfer foil dishes from freezer to oven.
Set the table.

30 minutes before lunch
Italian beef rolls: reheat in oven.

10 minutes before lunch
Mange-tout: boil a pan of salted water, add frozen mange-tout peas and simmer until tender but still 'al dente'. Transfer to warm vegetable dish.

**Danish pastries: remove from freezer to thaw.

1 minute before lunch
Black bombe: remove from freezer and unmould. Place in refrigerator. Serve the beef rolls and vegetables. Open the beer.

Between courses
Black bombe: decorate with blackberries and serve.

During the afternoon
Danish pastries: refresh in the oven and leave to cool.

1 hour before supper
Chimney pâté en croûte: transfer from refrigerator to table to get the chill off it.

30 minutes before supper
Heat the oven.
Set the supper table.

15 minutes before supper
Home-made bread rolls: take out of the freezer and thaw and warm in the oven.
Italian green salad: prepare—steps 1–4.
Serve supper.

hours notice, it is worth taking the beef rolls out of the freezer to thaw slowly in the refrigerator instead of cooking them from a frozen block in the oven.

First thing in the morning, fetch out the pâté pie and leave that to thaw gently and then relax and enjoy yourself till an hour before lunch. At that point, chill the beer, if this is the way you like it, heat the oven and then a little later put the pommes Anna and the beef rolls to cook and set the table.

Finally, ten minutes before the meal, cook the mange-tout and fetch out the Danish pastries from the freezer ready for the afternoon. (They will have to be refreshed later on.)

Also, before you sit down, transfer the bombe from freezer to refrigerator to soften slightly. It can be decorated with blackberries just before serving.

Before supper it will be necessary to make the salad, heat the bread rolls (from frozen) and switch the pâté pie from refrigerator to table.

THE DRINKS
An informal lunch is the perfect occasion to bring out your home-made bitter and fill your guests' glasses. Your own beer makes both a very economical drink and also a notably fine one. Many home-brewers regard their more successful

A day's entertaining is made easy when you have a freezer. Every dish on the menu — bar the salad — can be cooked weeks ahead and frozen.

results as superior to the commercial varieties pumped up from bar cellars. At least it makes a talking point!

Bitter has been suggested on the menu card because it pleases more of the people more of the time, and it is also the very simplest to make with a kit. But if your friends' and family's tastes tend to run towards lager or stout, etc, then obviously choose a different kit instead. Making home-made beer is fun as well as being relatively cheap and easy.

Italian beef rolls

There is a wide and delicious range of stuffings that can be used to stuff meat. To make this dish memorable, the stuffing contains salami, hard-boiled egg and raisins in addition to the more usual ingredients, and the rolls are cooked in a mixture of rich stock, Marsala and red wine. If Marsala—the genuine Italian fortified wine—is unavailable, substitute sweet sherry.

Unless you have a very large frying-pan, it may be necessary to cook the beef rolls in two pans side by side.

In common with all braised and casseroled beef dishes, this one freezes well. To cut recooking time, it is thawed a day ahead. If, however, it is required at short notice, reheat from frozen at 190°C [375°F] gas mark 5 for 1¼ hours.

SERVES 8 ADULTS
16 thin slices sirloin of beef each weighing about 50 g [2 oz]
16 wafer-thin slices cooked ham
3 garlic cloves
16 thin slices salami
5 hard-boiled eggs
200 g [7 oz] raisins
1 large onion
120 ml [8 tablespoons] chopped fresh parsley
50 g [2 oz] white breadcrumbs
4 ml [¾ teaspoon] grated nutmeg
2.5 ml [½ teaspoon] oregano
salt
freshly ground black pepper
1 egg
45 ml [3 tablespoons] cooking oil
5 ml [1 teaspoon] flour
400 ml [14 fl oz] beef stock
400 ml [14 fl oz] red wine
30 ml [2 tablespoons] Marsala
5 bay leaves

1 Trim the meat as necessary. Put each slice between sheets of greaseproof paper and beat flat.

2 Cover each slice with ham cut to fit. Peel and crush the garlic and spread a little on each slice of ham.

3 Finely chop the skinned salami, hard-boiled eggs and raisins and put them in a bowl.

4 Peel the onion, chop roughly and mince. Add to the bowl.

5 Add the parsley, breadcrumbs, nutmeg, oregano and seasoning and mix all ingredients together.

6 Beat the egg lightly and use to bind the stuffing together.

7 Divide the stuffing into 16 and place a ball in the centre of each slice of ham.

8 Roll up the slices of meat, tucking in the edges. To tie securely, loop strong cotton thread at least three times around the rolls.

9 Heat the oil in a large, heavy-based pan and fry the rolls for 5 minutes, turning to brown all surfaces.

10 Remove the rolls from the pan and reserve. Off the heat, add the flour to the remaining oil. Cook for 1 minute, stirring.

11 Add the stock, the wine and the Marsala. Bring to the boil and boil rapidly for 2 minutes, scraping up the sediment.

12 Return the rolls to the pan, add the bay leaves, cover tightly and simmer gently for 45 minutes.

Pommes Anna and mange-tout add colour to Italian beef rolls.

To freeze

Leave to cool quickly and then remove bay leaves. Line a casserole with foil and spoon the beef rolls with their sauce into it. Freeze until firm. Remove the foil-covered block from the casserole, fold the foil over and over-wrap with polythene. Seal, label and return to freezer. Store for up to 2 months.

To serve

Unwrap the frozen meat and place it in the casserole in which it was originally frozen. Cover and leave in the refrigerator for 24 hours. Reheat in the oven for 30 minutes at 190°C [375°F] gas mark 5.

Pommes Anna

Potatoes are bulky to store whole in a freezer but fortunately freeze very well as a made-up dish, which is far more economical on space. This is a classic recipe for slices of potato baked in garlic butter and it can be stored in a freezer for a month. If you want to keep it for a longer period—up to 6 months—omit the garlic, because it is this ingredient which goes musty and gives pommes Anna such a short storage life.

Cook the potatoes in purpose-made, round foil dishes, so that they can go straight from oven to freezer and back to oven again, with no need to wash up in between.

SERVES 8
1.4 kg [3 lb] old potatoes
225 g [½ lb] butter
4 garlic cloves
salt
freshly ground black pepper

1 Heat the oven to 200°C [400°F] gas mark 6.

2 Peel and slice the potatoes thinly.

3 Butter two foil freezer dishes and cover the bases with overlapping slices of potato.

4 Peel and finely chop the garlic. Season the potato in the dishes generously and sprinkle on a little garlic.

5 Melt the butter and pour a little butter over each dish of potatoes.

6 Continue with similar layers of potato, garlic, seasoning and butter until all the potato has been used.

7 Cover the dishes with foil and bake for 45 minutes.

To freeze

When cool, over-wrap the dishes with foil or heavy-duty polythene, label and freeze. Store for up to 1 month.

To serve

Bake in the oven at 190°C [375°F] gas mark 5 for 45 minutes. (There is no need to thaw first.) When reheated, transfer the pommes Anna carefully to a warm serving dish.

Mange-tout peas

Peas in their pod are a delicious rarity—delicious because of the fascinating contrast between crunchy pod and the sweet peas inside, and rare because it is only for a couple of weeks right at the beginning of the pea season that the pods are tender enough to eat. For this reason it is sensible to freeze them, since they will not be available again fresh for another year.

SERVES 8
900 g [2 lb] peas in their pods
salt

To serve:
25 g [1 oz] butter

1 Wash the pods and trim the ends.

2 Blanch the peas in boiling salted water for 2–3 minutes. Cool and then pat dry.

To freeze

Place in a gusseted polythene bag (inside a rigid container if a regular shape is desired for packing) and fast freeze. Seal and label and return to the freezer. Store for up to 1 year.

To serve

Bring a large pan of salted water to the boil. Add the mange-tout peas and simmer for 5–7 minutes. Drain in a colander and transfer to a warmed dish. Put a knob of butter on top.

Black bombe

![icons]ΧΧΧ *This impressive and refreshing dessert can feed a big party, especially when eked out with a border of fresh fruit.*

Bombes and cassatas are frozen for at least a couple of hours as part of their preparation. Decorate the bombe with fresh blackberries if they are in season, or use thawed frozen ones.

The basic proportion for a fruit ice-cream is an equal quantity of fruit purée and cream, but this is varied for individual ice-creams.

SERVES 8
For 425 ml [¾ pt] blackcurrant ice-cream:
350 g [¾ lb] blackcurrants
175 g [6 oz] icing sugar
half a lemon
200 ml [7 fl oz] thick cream

For 150 ml [¼ pt] bombe mixture:
40 g [1½ oz] caster sugar
2 large egg yolks
30 ml [2 tablespoons] fresh blackberries
5 ml [1 teaspoon] orange juice
5 ml [1 teaspoon] lemon juice
5 ml [1 teaspoon] grated orange zest
30 ml [2 tablespoons] lightly whipped cream

For serving:
450 g [1 lb] fresh or thawed frozen blackberries

1 Combine the ingredients for the blackcurrant ice-cream and allow the mixture to freeze.

2 To line the bombe mould, beat the frozen ice-cream with a whisk or wooden spoon until sufficiently soft to be workable. Use it to line the inside of a thoroughly chilled 575 ml [1 pt] mould. Cover and freeze until quite hard.

3 Cook the bombe mixture (see glossary for method) and allow to cool in a bowl of water and ice cubes.

4 Put the (cleaned) blackberries for the bombe mixture into a small bowl. Pour over the fruit juices. Add to grated orange zest and toss gently.

5 Lightly whip the cream. Fold this and the macerated blackberries and juice into bombe mixture.

6 Turn the bombe mixture into the ice-cream-lined mould, level the top with a palette knife and cover. Refreeze as described below.

To freeze
Overwrap the mould and label. Then store in freezer for 2 hours to 3 months.

To serve
Remove wrappings and lid. Wrap the mould in a cloth and dip in hot water. Unmould on to a plate and then smooth the surface of the ice-cream. Pop this back into the freezer for a few minutes to firm up the outside if much of it melts during unmoulding. Place uncovered in the refrigerator for 15 minutes. Decorate with a border of blackberries (thawed in refrigerator for an hour if frozen).

DANISH PASTRIES
Use the method as described in the glossary. There is a large choice of fillings but note not all fillings are suitable for freezing. Pineapple and banana or custard fillings, for instance, cannot be frozen successfully.

If freezing, a glacé icing finish must be omitted at the original baking stage and brushed on after the pastries have been refreshed in the oven—see below.

To freeze
Open-freeze the Danish pastries on trays in order to protect decorations and intricate shapes. Then wrap in a single layer of polythene and stack carefully in a rigid foil container. Seal, label and store in the freezer for up to 1 month.

To serve
About 3 hours before required, transfer the pastries to room temperature. Remove the rigid foil container but keep them wrapped in polythene; leave to thaw for 1½–2 hours. Heat the oven to 180°C [350°F] gas mark 4. Take off the polythene covering and refresh in the oven for 5 minutes. While still hot, brush with glacé icing if required. Cool and eat while fresh.

HOME-MADE BREAD ROLLS
Use any traditional bread dough recipe, then, using the palm of one hand, roll 50 g [2 oz] dough into a ball shape. Bake and leave to cool.

To freeze
Wrap the freshly made rolls in heavy-duty polythene bags, seal and label. Store for up to 1 month in the freezer.

To serve
Heat oven to 200°C [400°F] gas mark 6. Unwrap the rolls and place, frozen, in the oven for 15 minutes to thaw and warm. Serve hot with butter.

Chimney pâté
en croûte

◩◩◩ *This is a raised pie made with hot water crust—an essentially English pastry which is both strong and pliable. This delicious pie can be cooked in a tall mould, but here an ordinary loaf tin is used. It freezes very successfully, and is served cold. Just one thing to note: make sure your redcurrant preserve is a good one.*

SERVES 8
**450 g [1 lb] hot water pastry
(made weight)
350 g [¾ lb] chicken livers
45 ml [3 tablespoons] port
2 bay leaves
1 slice white bread
45 ml [3 tablespoons] milk
15 ml]1 tablespoon[butter
25 g [1 oz] cooked ham
50 g [2 oz] sausage meat
50 g [2 oz] lean pork
salt
freshly ground black pepper
450 g [1 lb] turkey breast
150 ml [¼ pt] redcurrant
preserve
beaten egg yolk for glazing
60 ml [4 tablespoons]
redcurrant jelly
60 ml [4 tablespoons] jellied
meat stock**

1 Clean and slice the livers. Put in a large bowl with the port and bay leaves. Leave to marinate for 2 hours.

2 Cut the crusts off the bread. Soak in the milk for about 5 minutes. Squeeze dry.

3 Lift the livers out of the marinade, reserving the liquid. Blot them dry and sauté them in a little butter for 2 minutes, to seal outside.

4 Put the soaked bread in the mincer. Add the ham, sausage meat and pork and mince the mixture into a bowl. Add seasoning.

5 Add sufficient marinade to make a wet mixture.

6 Heat the oven to 200°C [400°F] gas mark 6.

7 Cut off one-third of the pastry and wrap in cling film and a damp cloth ready to make the lid. Roll out the remainder and use to line a 20 cm [8"] long loaf tin.

8 Pack the pâté mixture inside. Add liver in layers.

9 Skin the turkey breasts, cut into thick slices and place on top.

10 Cover with a layer of redcurrant preserve.

11 Use the remaining pastry to make the lid. Use the trimmings to decorate the pie, but make sure these are flat, as the pie will be inverted when turning out. With a knife, cut a hole big enough to take the tip of a funnel.

12 Brush the raised pie with beaten egg yolk to glaze and bake for 30 minutes.

13 Lower heat to 180°C [350°F] gas mark 4 and cook for a further 2 hours.

14 Ten minutes before the end of cooking time remove the pie from the oven. Protect the top with a teacloth and very carefully invert on to a wire rack. Stand upright pie on a baking sheet and brush its sides with beaten egg. Return to the oven for 10 minutes in order to brown the sides.

15 Remove the cooked pie from the oven. In a small pan, melt the redcurrant jelly together with the stock. Using a funnel, pour the redcurrant stock through the hole in the lid. Leave to set for at least 3 hours.

To freeze
Wrap carefully in aluminium foil and, if possible, place in a rigid foil container. Label, seal and freeze. Store for up to 1 month.

To serve
Remove wrappings and place on a serving plate. Cover lightly with cling film and leave in the refrigerator for 12 hours to thaw. One hour before required, transfer to room temperature.

A cook-ahead dinner for eight

Here is a truly economical meal to serve to a crowd on a cold night. It consists of a classic cassoulet from **Southern France** followed by **Norwegian cream**. It's a menu to put a warm, satisfied glow in your guests—and in you as well, because all the work for it is done in advance so that you, too, can have the night off.

Menu

❧

Country cassoulet

✲

Norwegian cream

✲

To drink: beer or a light red wine

❧

During the winter, when nights are cold and folk are hungry, there are dozens of occasions when you want to come home and find dinner waiting. You do not mind a big crowd; you do not even mind taking a lot of time and trouble over cooking for them—but not at that precise moment, when you stagger in at the end of a long day.

Perhaps it's the weekend of the car rally when your family foursome get together with another quartet and spend the entire day clambering in and out of a chilly car looking for non-existent marshal checkpoints! Or it's the big football match and you seem to wind up with half the team and their wives coming back for supper. Or, maybe, you are a working wife who likes to have midweek guests, but just does not physically have the time to cater for them after arriving home in the evenings. In all likelihood you do not get back from work till around seven and, with guests usually invited for eight, that leaves only an hour for everything—including getting yourself ready. On a night when you're feeding eight, that just is not practical.

So for whatever reason, you need a cook-ahead menu, with virtually all the work carried out the evening before, and only the minimum of reheating and decorating to be done on the night.

The meal chosen here is deliberately not fancy, expensive dinner party fare, but rather food more suited to an informal get-together, when you want something hot, filling and tasty. Yet at the same time you still want to make a bit of an impression, to serve something just a little out of the ordinary. So for the main course a classic—cassoulet, a dish, sadly, that is seen all too rarely outside its native France.

A cassoulet is basically a special rich stew which combines pulses with several types of meat. A nourishing peasant dish, the cassoulet is the subject of infinite argument. In Toulouse, they say a cassoulet isn't a cassoulet unless it contains Toulouse sausage and preserved goose. Certainly there they would use goose because it is the area famous for foie gras (fat goose liver pâté) and they obviously have a lot of the rest of the goose left over!

In Castelnaudary, a traditional cassoulet contains beans, pork and sausage—and nothing else. In Arabia—which makes some claim to the origination of a cassoulet—the meat is mutton on religious grounds, and not pork.

This seems to lead one to the conclusion that any mixture of meats and beans will do—and that's true, within reason. Chucking in any left-over chicken or beef, or sundry extra vegetables or the odd fancy herb is definitely cheating and would only destroy the authentic flavour. Even to think of using canned beans in commercial sauce would be little less than sacrilege.

Flavourings, of course, are very important. In the menu cassoulet, country cassoulet, you will find garlic, onions, herbs and tomato—all most important to give flavour to the beans. There are three different types of meat, each performing a different function. There is lean lamb for texture, spicy salami for flavour and fatty belly of pork to enrich the bean sauce.

Although the weight of meat exceeds the weight of dried beans, once cooked, the beans will swell up and exceed the meat. Cassoulet is a peasant dish, remember, designed to feed a lot of people economically.

That is not to say it cannot be upgraded for an elegant party. The Toulouse cassoulet is definitely very exclusive, and so are the many recipes for cassoulet which feature game. Variations using pigeons or boned duck are given at the end of the country cassoulet recipe. Other favourites are also included—economical family-filling recipes for feeding a ravenous horde, one with salt pork, another with breast of lamb, and one with a bacon knuckle. All these cassoulets have three types of meat: one lean, one spicy and one fatty.

Any of them could be served as a buffet supper if you want to be casual and not go to the trouble of a laid table. Cassoulet is a one-dish dinner which can easily be negotiated standing up, wielding only a fork—it isn't runny and it doesn't need cutting up. This dinner definitely saves on the washing-up—a fork for the main course and only a spoon to follow for the pudding—a big advantage when there are eight of you.

You will notice that there is no hors d'oeuvre course to go in front, nor any accompanying vegetable to be eaten with it, although you could serve a green salad.

The well-known and great French chef, M. Colombie, advised that cassoulet should be eaten on a day when no great exertion was called for afterwards! It really is very satisfying, and nobody is going to have room for any additions. A first course would be a waste of good time and money. (The French would hoot with derisive laughter if you did serve one!)

For the same reason the dessert which follows must be really light and the proportions small. Norwegian cream, a variation on a baked egg custard, is therefore just the thing. It slips down deliciously and is the sort of pudding that raucous kids and sophisticated adults enjoy equally. What is more, like the cassoulet, it is cooked ahead of time.

GETTING ORGANIZED

The price you pay for a ready-and-waiting dinner is putting the work in the night before. Cassoulet isn't difficult, indeed it would be difficult to go wrong with it. Nor does it demand a lot of time in the kitchen from the cook, but it is a long drawn-out business, requiring slow cooking and starting in plenty of time. So start shopping two days before the cassoulet is to be eaten.

The most crucial job to do ahead is to put the beans to soak. They need 4-8 hours and remember—no salt. If you are out all day and so are planning on cooking at night, put the beans to soak in the morning before you go to work. Otherwise they can be soaked overnight and cooked in the morning.

Countdown timetable

2 DAYS BEFORE
Do the shopping.

THE DAY BEFORE

In the morning
Country cassoulet: soak the beans—step 1.

In the evening
Norwegian cream: heat the oven and infuse the vanilla pod in milk—steps 1-2.
Country cassoulet: simmer the beans in flavoured stock—steps 2-5.
Norwegian cream: spread jam in the soufflé dish(es), make egg custard and pour on top and bake—steps 3-7.
Country cassoulet: bone the lamb if necessary and reserve meat not needed for this meal. Cut up other meat and make breadcrumbs—step 6. When the beans are ready, drain and season them; layer the casserole—steps 7-16.
Norwegian cream: remove baked custard from the oven and leave to cool—step 8.

Reduce oven temperature to 150°C [300°] gas mark 2.
Country cassoulet: cook for 3 hours—step 17.
Norwegian cream: cover when cold and transfer to refrigerator—step 9.
Country cassoulet: transfer from oven to cool place before going to bed.

ON THE NIGHT

1¼ hours before the meal
Country cassoulet: set the oven to 150°C [300°F] gas mark 2. While waiting, make new crust and add extra liquid—step 18.
Set the table or prepare buffet.
Country cassoulet: top with fresh batch of herbed breadcrumbs and reheat in oven—step 19.
Norwegian cream: make Chantilly cream and spoon on to custard. Grate chocolate over for decoration—steps 10-14.
Get yourself ready.
Serve beer or aperitifs to guests and relax with them until cassoulet is cooked.

set the automatic timer for 3¾ hours before dinner-time. When you come home just add the extra crust.

As an added bonus, if for some reason one or two of your diners have not arrived at the point when you feel like eating, you can happily start without them. Their portions won't spoil in the least if left in the oven. Cassoulet is quite a marriage-saver for a husband-host who suddenly gets delayed at work!

SHOPPING CHECKLIST
This menu is a shopper's dream. Even though you are buying food for eight, it is so reasonable in price it will not throw your housekeeping budget for the month; and all the foods on your list are available at any supermarket. Certainly you may get better or more convenient buys from a local butcher, greengrocer and corner delicatessen, but there is nothing so out of the ordinary that you have to go to such places. The working wife can dash into the nearest supermarket during her lunch hour and get the lot.
Meat department: here you need to buy 350 g [¾ lb] belly of pork and a small joint of shoulder of lamb. If you buy meat from a butcher, he will bone this for you. However, do not cut the meat into pieces until you are ready to cook it.
Grocery: in this department buy haricot beans. You will probably have to buy 900 g [2 lb], but the portion not used for this dish will store well. Buy a can of tomatoes, tomato paste and a jar of apricot jam (or the conserve, which has larger pieces of fruit in it, if you feel generous). Then there's the salami—buy it in the piece and chop it up yourself. The vanilla pod may cause some difficulty. If you cannot find one, make do with vanilla extract. But next time you go into town, do make a point of buying a couple of vanilla pods. Although they are expensive initially, they can be wiped and used again, and their flavour is infinitely superior to that of vanilla essence, etc.
Dairy department: you need extra eggs and a bottle of milk and 150 ml [5 fl oz] carton of thick cream.
Greengrocery: all you need here is 225 g [½ lb] onions and a bulb of garlic—look for a good fresh one with nice fat cloves.

Before your shopping trip, check your herb rack for supplies of

The night before the party is when you do all your cooking. It will take you 4½ hours from beginning to end, though the last three hours can be comfortably spent in front of the television, waiting for the main dish to finish cooking.

Your first job on your cooking night, almost before you take your coat off, is to put the vanilla to infuse in hot milk for the Norwegian cream. It is important to move smartly with the pudding because it needs to come out of the oven before the cassoulet goes in. Next job is to put the beans to cook. Make stock from cubes at twice the usual dilution if you have no saltless home-made stock. Prepare the onions and garlic and put the beans to simmer in a large saucepan or your casserole. You have 20 minutes here to grab a snack. Later on you will have time to eat something more substantial, if you wish.

Make the custard and put the pudding into the oven and then turn your attention to the meat. You have 40 minutes before the custard comes out of the oven, ample time to prepare the cassoulet. Cut up the lamb and

reserve the extra lamb not needed for this meal. Cut up all the pork and salami into bite-sized pieces. Also prepare the breadcrumbs.

When the beans are ready, drain and rinse them, reserving the liquor as well as the beans. Then make the cassoulet in layers right up to step 16. When the custard completes cooking, turn the oven down to 150°C [300°F] gas mark 2, put in the cassoulet and your work is done. You can now spend a restful evening just waiting to take the casserole out. When you go to bed, late it is true, you will know that the following night will be an effortless one. All you have to do is to add the new layer of breadcrumbs and cook the cassoulet. This leaves you plenty of time to decorate your pudding and lay the table. So for once you can sit with your friends, instead of being busy behind the scenes.

Of course, if you have an automatic oven, you can forget about cooking the cassoulet in advance. Prepare it following the countdown up to step 16 and then leave it, uncooked, in the refrigerator overnight. Next day put it in the oven and oregano, thyme, bay leaves and bouquet garni. You also need a two-day old white loaf for breadcrumbs and three squares from a block of plain chocolate—hide it from the eyes of children and greedy menfolk!

SPECIAL EQUIPMENT

An absolute must when making a cassoulet is a very large casserole (or 'cassoulet' as it would be called in France). It needs to be at least 4.5 L [8 pt] size; in imperial terms that means it must hold a gallon of liquid. If you do not have anything that large, put an order on your birthday list and this time, sadly, settle for the small-sized cassoulet variation for your family given at the end of this recipe.

The other things you need for this menu are individual soufflé or ramekin dishes in which to cook and serve the Norwegian cream. Individual pudding dishes make a pleasant change after a one-pot main course. As the recipe states, technically the cream works equally well in one large soufflé dish (or any small ovenproof casserole for that matter). If you do not own ramekins, a set of little soufflé dishes are a present you might give yourself. The cost of the food for this menu is so modest that you might spend the money 'saved' on something useful for the future.

Country cassoulet

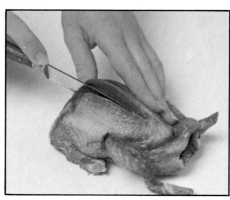 *The secret of a successful cassoulet is in the long cooking which blends the meat and the beans into one excellent whole. It needs to be very well flavoured to avoid the final result being rather dull—hence the inclusion of onions, garlic, herbs and tomatoes. Note that the garlic and onions are added to the stock used to pre-cook the beans. It is important that they are introduced at this early stage because this is when the haricot beans are swelling and absorbing flavour. When afterwards they enter the cassoulet with the meat, they will only take on a little extra from the tomatoes and sausage.*

The stock has to be unsalted because salt toughens bean skins and makes them resist the tenderizing effect of simmering. Therefore, if you are using commercial stock cubes, which are often very salty, use only half the recommended amount for the liquid. If desired, you could always crumble in an extra stock cube at step 9, when the seasoning of salt and pepper is added.

Use up the left-over stock not required for the cassoulet in soups, stock for other savoury dishes, or for cooking rice.

Since only 450 g[1 lb] of lean lamb is needed and you will have to buy a shoulder weighing around 1.4 kg [3 lb], you will have plenty of meat left over. Even after removing bones and fat you will have enough meat for a meal for 4, for instance any of your favourite mince recipes or shish kebabs. Since kebabs demand well-shaped pieces of meat and in a cassoulet the meat is not 'on show', it makes sense to reserve the cubes and to use up any scrappy pieces of lamb here.

SERVES 8-10
575 g [1¼ lb] haricot beans
225 g [½ lb] onions
6 large garlic cloves
about 2.8 L [5 pt] unsalted stock or 2 stock cubes
bay leaf
350 g [¾ lb] belly of pork
450 g [1 lb] shoulder of lamb, boned
225 g [½ lb] salami
salt and freshly ground black pepper
bouquet garni
400 g [14 oz] canned tomatoes
30 ml [2 tablespoons] tomato paste

175 g [6 oz] fresh breadcrumbs
10 ml [2 teaspoons] fresh oregano chopped, or 5 ml [1 teaspoon] dried
10 ml [2 teaspoons] thyme, chopped

1 Put the beans in a large bowl or pan which will comfortably hold 2.8 L [5 pt] water. Cover them with 3 times their volume in cold water. Cover with a clean cloth and leave them to soak for 4-8 hours.

2 Drain the beans and rinse them. Measure the beans again in a measuring jug. Put them into a casserole that will take 4.5 L [8 pt].

3 Peel and chop the onions roughly. Peel and halve the garlic cloves. Add these to the beans in the casserole.

4 Measure the unsalted stock and cover the beans with twice their volume in liquid.

5 Add the bay leaf and bring the beans to the boil. Lower the heat, cover and simmer for 1 hour.

6 Meanwhile prepare the meat. Cut the belly of pork into 2.5 cm [1"] slices down through the slice. Cut up the lamb into bite-sized pieces. Skin and chop the salami into thick rings.

7 Drain the beans, onions, garlic and bay leaf into a colander. Reserve the liquor.

8 Heat the oven to 150°C [300°F] gas mark 2.

9 Season the beans generously with salt and pepper.

10 Put a layer of beans into the bottom of the casserole.

11 Put the pork in a layer over the beans and cover with a second layer of beans.

12 Layer the lamb over the beans, with the bouquet garni in the middle. Cover with another layer of beans.

13 Turn the canned tomatoes into a jug and break them up with a fork. Add a little stock, stir and then pour over the beans.

14 Put the salami in the next layer and finish with a layer of beans.

15 Put a little stock into the measuring jug and add the tomato paste. Stir to mix and then add to the cassoulet. If necessary, add more stock to bring liquid level up to the top of the beans.

16 Mix the breadcrumbs with the oregano and thyme. Sprinkle half

A selection of cassoulet ingredients.

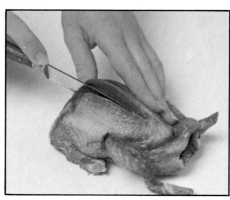

To take the breast off a pigeon, make a neat slit along the breast bone, cutting down vertically close to the bone.

the herbed breadcrumbs over the beans in a thick, even layer. Reserve the remaining breadcrumbs.

17 Put the cassoulet in the oven, uncovered, and cook for 3 hours, until the crust is golden. Check the liquid level from time to time, adding more of the reserved stock if it seems at all dry. (If wished, cooking may be stopped at this point and resumed later.)

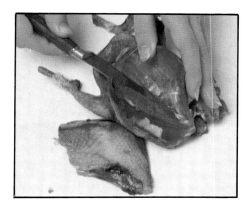

Turn the blade to follow the line of the ribs and take off the whole breast in one piece. Repeat on the other side.

18 With a large spoon, push the crust on top of the cassoulet down into the beans. Add a little extra stock at this point to bring the liquid level in line with the top of the crust.

19 Sprinkle the remaining herbed breadcrumbs on top and return the cassoulet to the oven. Cook for a further 30 minutes. (If cooking was interrupted at step 17 and the cassoulet is now being re-heated from cold, cook for a minimum of 1 hour.) Further cooking of up to 2 hours will not spoil this dish.

OTHER CASSOULETS
Salt pork cassoulet
Use 350 g [¾ lb] salt pork instead of belly of pork. Use lamb as before, but omit the salami. Use a 225 g [½ lb] of cervalas or a boiling ring of pure pork sausage instead; slice it into rough chunks. Alternatively, use sliced chorizos or cabanos which are dried sausages. These do not need to be pre-fried or blanched to stiffen them, because they will be cooked in the cassoulet liquid.

Breast of lamb cassoulet
Buy 900 g [2 lb] breast of lamb. Cut it into riblets, as shown on pages 104–105, and take out the bones. Use the lamb with 225 g [½ lb] salt pork or 225 g [½ lb] bacon. This can be in rashers or the cheaper bacon scraps sold by some supermarkets and butchers. The amount of fatty meat is reduced because the lamb is much fattier. Use 225 g [½ lb] cabanos, or salami if you are unable to obtain cabanos.

Bacon cassoulet
A ham bone makes excellent stock for beans but these are rarely seen. Try instead a knuckle-end of a forehock of bacon, available in supermarkets. You will need a 900 g [2 lb] one to allow for bone and skin. Blanch the bacon first, unless the cure is mild. Omit the pork and reduce the amount of lamb down to 350 g [¾ lb].

The method will differ slightly because the knuckle is cooked whole in the centre of the beans. Omit the first breadcrumb crust altogether. When you remove the casserole from the oven for the first time, remove the knuckle from the beans with a perforated spoon on to a plate. Remove the skin and bone and

discard them. Chop the meat into rough chunks and cut the fat up more finely. Return these two to the pan. Stir and add the crust (see step 16— use half the given quantity of breadcrumbs) and proceed to cook for the last hour. The crust on this cassoulet will be less substantial.

Pigeon cassoulet
For a special-occasion cassoulet, use game. This is not a wicked waste of luxury food, but a way of making 2 pigeons feed 8 people. Omit the lamb from the recipe. Only the breasts of the pigeons (which have 90 per cent of the meat) are used. Remove the pigeon breasts and reserve. Use the carcasses to make a stock, (without salt). Strain this and then use it to cook the beans in step 4. The advantage of this is that your guests do not have to struggle with small bones. Cut the pigeon breasts into small pieces and layer the meat in the middle layer as described in the recipe. Salt pork—use 350 g [¾ lb]— and 225 g [½ lb] chorizos or cabanos (which are cheaper than salami) combine well with pigeons.

Duck cassoulet
A duck can be substituted for pigeon, for another party cassoulet. Buy one ready boned or, if you are boning it yourself, use the bones to make saltless stock. This is used to cook the beans in the same way as described in the previous variation. Cut the duck into bite-sized pieces and layer this as before. As ducks tend to be rather fatty, reduce the amount of salt pork to 225 g [½ lb]. Use 100 g [¼ lb] of salami, so as not to overpower the delicate flavour of the duck. For added flavour, roughly chop and add the contents of a small can of red pimentos.

Small-size cassoulet
Cassoulet is not really a dish for cooking in small quantities, because of the long cooking time and the variety of ingredients. Here, however, is a cassoulet for a family of four which will fit into a 3.4 L [6 pt] casserole. Use 175 g [6 oz] salt belly of pork with 225 g [½ lb] boned lamb and 100 g [¼ lb] chorizos or cabanos. Check the liquid level in the pot from time to time, as a small potful is liable to reduce more quickly than a larger one. Cooking at the first stage can be reduced slightly to 1½ hours, though the second stage is the same.

Norwegian cream

◧◧◧ *This is a delicious variation on the more usual type of baked custard but is richer and more eggy than, for instance, crème caramel. For a fruitier contrast to the custard, buy a luxurious apricot conserve in place of the jam to act as a base. This cream dessert looks its prettiest cooked in individual soufflé dishes, but if you do not have any, use a small ovenproof dish instead. Improvise a bain-marie with a roasting tin of boiling water.*

When served after a filling dish such as cassoulet, this cream is enough for eight. After a less filling meal, it would serve 6 and boudoir fingers would be a nice accompaniment.

SERVES 6-8
425 ml [¾ pt] milk
vanilla pod
75 ml [5 tablespoons] apricot jam or conserve
4 medium-sized eggs
15 ml [1 tablespoon] caster sugar
150 ml [5 fl oz] thick cream
3 squares of dessert chocolate

1 Pour the milk into a heavy-based pan and add the vanilla pod. Place the pan over a medium heat and bring to scalding point. Remove from heat, cover and leave to infuse for 30 minutes.

2 Heat the oven to 160°C [325°F] gas mark 3.

3 Spread the jam on the bottom of individual soufflé or ramekin dishes or on to one large one.

4 Separate one of the eggs. Reserve the white and put the yolk in a large mixing bowl. Add the 3 whole eggs to the yolk.

5 Cream the eggs with the sugar. Gradually blend in the cooled flavoured milk, stirring with a wooden spoon.

6 Prepare a bain-marie. Pour in boiling water to half the depth of the ramekins or the dish you have chosen.

7 Strain through a sieve into the soufflé dish(es), pouring carefully to avoid dislodging the jam. Cover the bain-marie with foil. Bake for about 40 minutes.

8 At the end of the cooking time, check that the custard is ready by inserting the point of a knife and watching to see that this leaves a visible mark. (If not, cover the bain-marie again and return to the oven). Then remove from the oven, uncover and leave to cool.

9 When completely cold, cover again and chill in the refrigerator.

10 Shortly before serving, whisk the cream until it stands in soft peaks.

11 In a separate dry clean bowl, whip the reserved egg white until stiff.

12 Using a metal spoon, lightly fold the cream into the egg white.

13 Spread the cream mixture on top of the chilled custard.

14 Grate the chocolate and sprinkle carefully over the top of the cream to decorate.

Summer fork supper for eight

After a day out, bring your friends home to supper and make it a party. Here is a sensational meal for the occasion, it is tailor-made for informality. There is an original crunchy hors d'oeuvre, a magnificent one-pot paella and a rich cheesecake with which to end the festivities. The menu is planned to leave you free most of the day and yet still produce a big stylish supper.

Menu

Summer-style
crudités with a
yoghurt dip

Party paella

Champion
chocolate
cheesecake

Coffee

To drink: Mateus rosé

There are occasions when you want to be out—with friends at a wedding, a day at the races or in the country—and yet know that on your return you can entertain at home with the minimum of fuss. This menu is designed for just such an occasion, providing a good meal without your being involved in last-minute preparations which could spoil your relaxing day.

The first thing when planning to entertain after being out all day is to set your sights away from a formal, sit-down dinner and towards a meal that can be eaten as informally as possible.

As for the food—you want something exotic, tasty and suitable for a party, and yet at the same time simple enough to be prepared ahead of time and/or when seven hungry guests are actually with you—and waiting! The main course is hot because the chances are that the food you consumed during the day was cold—especially so if you have been out on

a picnic. The perfect solution is a paella: a one-pot dish, served hot, which is gorgeous to look at and to eat. The party paella on the menu contains a mixture of chicken and shellfish, including mussels, with rice dyed a marvellous yellow with turmeric or, ideally, saffron. Peas, tomatoes and red and green peppers assist in giving a positive panorama of colour.

Paella is a Spanish classic from Valencia. It started life as a dish that contained various meats mixed in with the rice, chicken and typical Spanish vegetables, but gradually the meats were replaced by shellfish. Today a paella in Spain might contain squid, lobster or even chorizo sausage. It remains an adaptable dish into which the cook can toss an assortment of good things from the larder.

For a fork supper, paella can stand alone; but if you were serving it at a sit-down dinner, accompaniments of crusty French bread and lettuce and cress salad would probably be welcome.

To precede the paella, you require something that will keep your guests occupied for a nice long time while you slip away—at any rate intermittently—to attend to your paella pan. An excellent solution is to serve crudités—raw vegetables served with a separate dip. Crudités are a friendly, free-for-all hors d'oeuvre and take the place of nuts and olives, but are obviously more substantial. They are always an unusual choice and therefore a talking point which will get your party going.

The summer-style crudités listed on the menu include baby carrots; firm, tasty mushrooms; crunchy radishes; cool, cool cucumber and celery, if you wish, all to be savoured with a yoghurt dip. Alternative crudités are strips of red and green peppers, leaves of endive or chicory, and spring onions.

GETTING ORGANIZED
For big, formal parties like the drinks party featured on page 213, hostesses are often prepared to start work as much as four or five days beforehand, but not so for the light informal supper such as this menu has in mind. The day before seems quite soon enough for getting organized for such an event. The one exception, though, should be the base for the

cheesecake. It needs to be absolutely firm before any filling goes on top. So it is worth making the biscuit-crumb base a couple of days in advance—a 15-minute job at the most.

The day after, do all the necessary shopping, except for the shellfish. If at all practical, pick up the mussels, prawns and shrimps on the morning itself. Shellfish go off quickly causing dire stomach upsets; so the fresher you can transport yours home, the better. When you get in from your shopping jaunt, make the filling for the cheesecake and store it in the refrigerator.

On the big day you have about 2½ hours' work to do in the morning. This means that if you are planning a day out, you will need to get an early start. Send someone else to collect the shellfish while you decorate the cheesecake. Then make the yoghurt dip. Once that is dealt with, you can give your full attention to the lengthy process of preparing the ingredients for the paella. It isn't difficult but the cook needs peace and concentration—something to be said in favour of an early morning start. Finally prepare the vegetables for the summer-style crudités. They won't come to any harm for being left, providing you pack them loosely in polythene in the salad section of the refrigerator. However, do not cut up the cucumber until you are ready to serve the crudités. Then make sure that someone has remembered to put the wine in the refrigerator to chill.

When you return in the evening, leave your man to take guests' drinks orders while you nip out to get the crudités arranged on a dish. Serve these in the living room and leave your guests to play. Meanwhile, like Cinderella, you return to the kitchen to get the paella under way. It will be a full hour between unlocking the front door and serving your paella; but don't worry—your guests will barely notice the wait. They will be far too busy enjoying the crudités. And, unlike Cinderella, there is an interval of 20 minutes marked on the timetable when you can join them and get something to eat and drink yourself.

The final 10 minutes will be hectic. There are the plates to warm, the table to lay and the finishing touches to be added to the paella. Never mind—when your guests see and taste the fruit of your labour, every moment you spent will seem more than worthwhile.

THE DRINKS

Mateus rosé with its sweet sparkle is the choice for this menu because a rosé wine is of sufficiently strong flavour to complement the prawns and shrimps without overriding the more subtle taste of the chicken and mussels. Any rosé would do, of course, but Mateus is a famous party wine—and just the sight of its prettily shaped bottle will put your guests in the right mood. Also, sparkling rosés are comparatively rare; but this one is so popular it will be stocked by practically any wine-merchant you choose to buy from.

If you do not wish to serve aperitifs you could serve the Mateus with the crudités also. Alternatively, an Amontillado sherry might be pleasant.

Finish the meal with fresh coffee, together with brandy or liqueurs or any other after-dinner drinks.

SHOPPING CHECKLIST

The most important purchase for this menu is the shellfish. You need a wet-fish shop—and a fairly enterprising one, too. Not many fish shops stock mussels as a matter of course, and many—even if they do sell prawns—stock frozen peeled ones. Unpeeled prawns are preferable, if available. Bottled mussels in a jar will have a vinegary taste which will do nothing for the paella. So a few days in advance do locate a suitable fishmonger and give him a firm order—paid for in advance if necessary. And if you possibly can, arrange to collect your fresh shellfish on the morning itself.

In the UK shellfish are still sold by 'pint' measure, meaning the number of shellfish that can be scooped into a pint-sized jug.

Thus in the list of paella ingredients you will find a 'quart' of mussels and prawns and a 'pint' of

Countdown timetable

2 DAYS BEFORE THE MEAL
Champion chocolate cheesecake: check that ingredients for biscuit-crumb base are in stock and then make the base—steps 1-3.

THE DAY BEFORE THE MEAL
Do the shopping.
Champion chocolate cheesecake: make the filling and refrigerate—steps 4-14.

ON THE DAY
In the morning
Party paella: if possible, collect ordered shellfish.
Champion chocolate cheesecake: unmould and decorate—steps 15-16.
Yoghurt dip: make, cover and keep in a cool place—steps 1-2.
Party paella: boil the chicken, shell the shellfish and make stock, reduced to the correct amount—steps 1-10.
Summer-style crudités: prepare, dry and wrap loosely in polythene. Store in the salad box of the refrigerator—steps 1-4.

Put wine to chill.

1 hour before the meal
Yoghurt dip: check seasoning and transfer to serving dish—step 3.
Crudités: cut up cucumber and arrange vegetables on the serving dish—steps 5-6.
Serve the pre-dinner drinks and the summer-style crudités.
Party paella: heat oil in the paella pan, prepare and fry peppers, onion and garlic; and add rice—steps 11-14.

30 minutes before the meal
Uncork the wine.
Party paella: add the stock, skinned tomato, shellfish and saffron (if using) to the pan, cover with foil and cook for 20 minutes—steps 15-18.

10 minutes before the meal
Put plates to warm; also serving dish for paella if required.
Party paella: add peppers, peas and unshelled prawns to paella pan and cook for a further 5-10 minutes—steps 19-20.
Set the buffet table.
Party paella: serve—step 21.

Summer-style crudités

Crudité means 'raw' in French and in culinary terms describes the raw vegetables that are served as an aperitif course with a creamy dip. It is the perfect choice for a summer party, when palates fancy something cold and refreshing, and the season's crop of vegetables are at their best. At a fork supper, serve the crudités with the welcoming drinks, ahead of the rest of the meal. Supply one central bowl of dip and invite guests to help themselves. This is one occasion when it is polite to use your fingers!

shrimps. Equivalent metric measures—in weight—are given alongside. If using frozen you will need 225–275 g [8–10 oz] prawns and 120–150 g [4–5 oz] shrimps.

While you're at the fishmongers, you may be able to pick up the packet of frozen peas you need and even, possibly, the 4 chicken joints. It could save you a visit to another shop.

Along with a good fishmonger, this menu also calls for a delicatessen in order to find the necessary turmeric or saffron and Parmesan.

Your dairy order is brief but costly. You want 3 medium-sized eggs for the cheesecake filling. Then the cheesecake also demands 350 g [¾ lb] of cottage cheese, and 150 ml [¼ pt] of thick cream. Buy 275 ml [½ pt] of yoghurt for the dip. Avoid thin yoghurt as it will be messy, and when you open the yoghurt pour off any liquid in the carton.

Greengrocery needs are multitudinous. A visit to the market would make sense.
●450 g [1 lb] baby carrots—a bunch, well scrubbed, would look particularly attractive for the crudités dish

●1 large cucumber
●225 g [½ lb] radishes
●225 g [½ lb] mushrooms—these must be firm and dry for eating raw
●a head of celery (optional)
●a large green pepper—make sure it is shiny and in peak condition
●a large red pepper
●2 Spanish onions—that is for the genuine article but if Spanish onions are not around buy 450 g [1 lb] of other onions
●bulb of garlic
●700 g [1½ lb] of ripe tomatoes
●a large orange and a lemon.
●2 fresh herbs, such as chives, basil, tarragon or parsley for the dip.

Finally there are just a few groceries: caster sugar, cooking oil, gelatine, 350 g [¾ lb] long-grain rice and chocolate for the cheesecake. Remember that you will need at least 40 g [1½ oz] of your 65 g [2½ oz] chocolate ahead of your main shopping in order to make the cheesecake base. The base also takes 175 g [6 oz] of digestive biscuits and 40 g [1½ oz] of butter. Check your supplies—you need bay leaves, mustard and Tabasco.

SERVES 8

450 g [1 lb] new carrots
225 g [½ lb] radishes
225 g [½ lb] mushrooms
1 head of celery (optional)
1 large cucumber

1 Top and tail and scrub the carrots.

2 Top and tail and rinse the radishes.

3 Wipe the mushrooms and trim off the ends of the stalks, leaving most of the stalk intact.

4 Wash the celery, if using, and cut into slices.

5 Top and tail the cucumber and cut off some of the peel. Quarter by dividing into 2 both lengthways and widthways. Cut each quarter into 4 long strips.

6 Arrange the different crudités in groups around the dip.

Yoghurt dip

This dip makes a tangy accompaniment for raw vegetables. Make sure it is sufficiently thick to hold its shape on a crudité without dripping on to clothes and carpet! Dried herbs are not suitable for this dip. If you are limited to parsley stir in some mayonnaise or French mustard.

SERVES 8

275 ml [½ pt] yoghurt
30 ml [2 tablespoons] freshly chopped herbs, such as basil, chives, tarragon or parsley
salt and black pepper
dash of Tabasco sauce
25 g [1 oz] grated Parmesan cheese
30 ml [2 tablespoons] French mustard

1 Pour any liquid off the yoghurt. Stir in remaining ingredients.

2 Chill until required.

3 Check seasoning, transfer to a serving dish and serve.

Party paella

This traditional one-pot Spanish dish gets its name from the heavy iron frying-pan with two handles in which it is customarily cooked and served. In the absence of a proper paella, use a frying-pan, sauté pan or a wide-bottomed flameproof casserole. However, note that whatever you use it must be large enough to contain 1.4 litres [2½ pt] of stock plus the large quantity of rice in addition to the chicken, shellfish and vegetables. If necessary, divide your ingredients into two pans and cook side by side.

The result is a pretty and colourful party dish, which looks and tastes just as good cold. Saffron is one of the main ingredients of a true paella because of its unique flavour and rich yellow colour. But in this recipe it has been listed as an alternative as it is expensive. Instead turmeric can be used for colouring, although, it must be admitted, the flavour is not quite the same.

SERVES 8
4 chicken joints
15 ml [1 tablespoon] turmeric
    or 4 ml [¾ teaspoon]
    powdered saffron
2 large bay leaves
500 g [1 quart] prawns in
    their shells
225 g [1 pt] shrimps in
    their shells
1 kg [1 quart] mussels in their
    shells
salt
freshly ground black pepper
cooking oil
1 large green pepper
1 large red pepper
2 Spanish onions
4 garlic cloves
350 g [¾ lb] long-grain rice
700 g [1½ lb] tomatoes
125 g [¼ lb] frozen peas

1 Put the chicken joints in a pan. Add the turmeric. If using saffron, dissolve the powder in 15 ml [1 tablespoon] of boiling water but do not add to the pan at this stage.

2 Cover the chicken joints with water and add the bay leaves. Bring the water to the boil, cover and simmer for 25 minutes.

3 When the time is up, take out the chicken joints and discard the bay leaves. Reserve the stock.

4 Shell half the prawns and all the shrimps, reserving the shells for making the stock.

5 Rinse the mussels to remove grit and if any of the mussel shells are open, given them a sharp tap with the back of a knife. If they do not close, discard them—as this will mean they are dead. Pull away beards, scape off encrustations and scrub shells thoroughly under cold running water. Put the prepared mussels in a saucepan. Cover with water and boil rapidly until they open.

6 Reserving the mussel stock, remove the mussels from the pan and remove top shell. Discard any that have remained closed.

7 Strain the mussel stock through a fine sieve to catch any sand or grit.

8 Skin the chicken and shred the flesh from the bones. Reserve these bones.

9 Measure both the mussel stock and the reserved chicken stock into a large pan and make up to 1.7 L [3 pt] with water. Add the re-

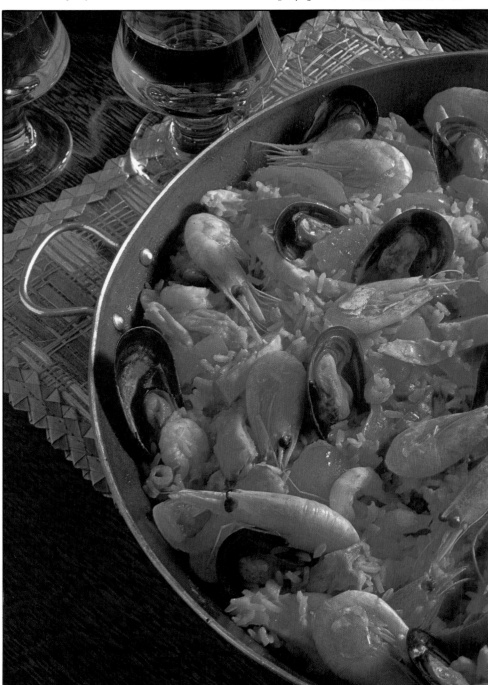

served chicken bones and prawn and shrimp shells to the pan.

10 Boil rapidly until the liquid in the pan has reduced to 1.4 L [2½ pt]. Taste and season with salt and black pepper if necessary.

11 Take the dish in which the paella is to be cooked and cover the bottom with oil. Place over a moderate heat.

12 Rinse, quarter and de-seed the peppers. Cut across into 6 mm [¼″] wide strips. Fry gently in the oil for

2-3 minutes. Take out and reserve.

13 Peel and chop the onion and garlic finely. Fry in the same oil until soft.

14 Pour in the rice and turn over and over in the oil to heat through.

15 Strain the hot reduced stock into the paella pan and add the shredded chicken meat. Stir until the mixture is bubbling.

16 Lower the heat and continue stirring until the rice begins to absorb the stock.

17 Meanwhile scald the tomatoes in a pan of boiling water for 1 minute in order to skin them. Then chop roughly, de-seeding where possible.

18 Stir the chopped tomato into the paella. Add the shelled prawns, shrimps and mussels. If using saffron, add the infused powder at this stage too. Cover the paella pan tightly with foil. Turn to the lowest possible heat and cook gently, without disturbing, for 20 minutes.

19 When the time is up, stir the paella. Add the reserved peppers and the peas and stir again.

20 Strew the remaining prawns (unshelled) over the top. Re-cover tightly with foil and cook for a further 5-10 minutes. By this time the rice should have absorbed all the liquid but still be firm.

21 Serve hot from a paella pan or, if cooking in a substitute pan, transfer to one or two large, warmed serving dishes before taking to the table.

Champion chocolate cheesecake

⊠⊠⊠ *This uncooked cheesecake uses a basic soufflé mixture for its filling. Cheese is added before the gelatine is stirred in. Allow the base to set completely before adding the filling. This will take about 5 hours or, if desired, the base can be left in the refrigerator for a couple of days.*

If you haven't got a loose-bottomed cake tin, then line an ordinary cake tin with overhanging foil which will do the job just as well.

SERVES 8
For the base:
175 g [6 oz] digestive biscuits
40 g [1½ oz] butter
40 g [1½ oz] chocolate

For the filling:
3 medium-sized eggs
75 g [3 oz] caster sugar
1 large orange
half a lemon
350 g [¾ lb] cottage cheese
20 ml [4 teaspoons] gelatine
150 ml [¼ pt] thick cream

For the decoration:
25 g [1 oz] chocolate

1 First make the base. Crush the biscuits finely.

2 Melt the butter and chocolate together over a gentle heat. Off the heat, stir in the biscuits until evenly coated in chocolate.

3 Press the mixture into the base of an 18 cm [7"] loose-bottomed cake tin. Chill until firm.

4 Start the filling. Separate the eggs and place the yolks in a basin with the sugar. Whisk until thick and creamy.

5 Grate the rind from the orange and the lemon into the egg mixture.

6 Sieve the cottage cheese into the mixture.

7 Squeeze the juice from the orange and lemon into a small saucepan.

8 Sprinkle the gelatine over the fruit juices. Allow to soften for 5 minutes.

9 Place the pan over a very low heat and leave until the liquid is clear—about 3 minutes.

10 Meanwhile beat the egg and cheese mixture in the bowl until it is smooth.

11 Pour in the dissolved gelatine and fruit juice in a thin stream, stirring all the time.

12 Whip the cream until it just holds its shape. Fold into the mixture.

13 Whisk the egg whites until stiff. Fold into the cheesecake mixture using a metal spoon.

14 Spoon the filling over the chocolate biscuit-crumb base. Refrigerate for several hours or overnight if preferred.

15 When firm, unmould on to a serving plate.

16 Melt the chocolate in a basin over hot water. Use to fill a greaseproof piping bag. Drizzle chocolate in a decorative pattern over the cheesecake. Allow to set before serving.

Late-night supper for four

The cinema and theatre always seem to start too early for inviting friends to a proper relaxing dinner beforehand, and to finish too late for any of us to have the appetite to face a big meal afterwards. This menu has been carefully planned with a late hour in mind. It is very much a supper, rather than a fully fledged dinner, because few people want to eat a heavy meal at night after an evening out, whether they've been to a show or drinks at the pub. The food is light and tempting and exciting enough to provide a happy ending to your night out. All the courses are cold and will be waiting for you when you get home, so nothing can spoil if you stay out longer than you originally intended.

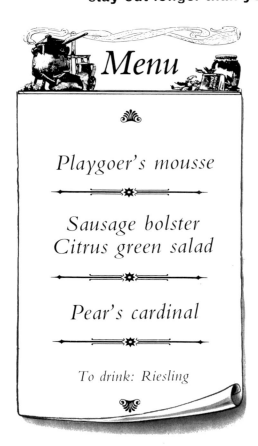

Menu

Playgoer's mousse

Sausage bolster
Citrus green salad

Pear's cardinal

To drink: Riesling

GETTING ORGANIZED

The good news about catering for a late-night supper party is that everything is done before you go out, so you can relax and enjoy your evening with your friends. If this is to be a Saturday night out, you have all day to make advance preparations. Alternatively, most of the meal can be prepared the evening before.

The not-so-good news is that when your guests finally arrive you will be with them, so there is no opportunity for any last minute catching up in the kitchen. However if you stick to the timetable there will only be a few jobs left to do on your return, and they will only take a few minutes. This is important as in all probability you will be a little tired and very hungry and 11 pm is no time to start cooking, so the sooner you can sit down to eat the better.

You will almost be able to complete the first course in the morning (or the night before).

Decorate the mousses with 'caviare' and cover them before going out for the evening. The easiest way to cover them is to invert a cereal bowl over the side-plate so that it does not touch the mousse or disturb the decorations. If you have no suitable bowls, cover the mousse with foil, raising it in the centre so that it does not touch the mousse.

Uncover the mousses when you arrive home and serve with brown bread rolls and pats of butter.

The oranges and vinaigrette for the salad can also be prepared in advance. The oranges can be refrigerated and the vinaigrette left in a cool place. Be sure to give the vinaigrette a brisk stir before dressing the salad—it will have separated with standing.

The sausage bolster is completely cooked in advance. Wrap in foil and store it in the refrigerator. All you will have to do on your return is to slice it up and arrange it on a plate with a few sprigs of parsley around it for a garnish.

The pears and their sauce can both be made in advance but not brought together—the sauce tends to soak into the pears if it is added too far in advance. Pouring the sauce only takes a few seconds between courses.

Remember that you will be arriving at the same time as your guests so tidy up the room beforehand when you lay the table. Leave yourself a few minutes before you finally go out for last minute plumping the cushions, pulling the curtains and putting ready the glasses for the wine.

In cold weather it is well worth leaving on some form of heating at a low setting. Coming home to cold food and cold drink in a cold house is not very welcoming.

SPECIAL EQUIPMENT

The only special equipment needed here is small cocotte dishes—individual portions for each diner look elegant. However if you do not own cocottes, make one mousse in a 12.5-15 cm [5-6"] gratin dish or shallow stainless steel bowl. Decorate the top with a ring of four butterflies.

PRE-DINNER DRINKS

Unless it is a perishingly cold night, in which case you might be in dire need of a warming whisky and ginger wine after the journey, the best plan is to forget about aperitifs as such. You will probably have had a few drinks during the evening anyway. Instead of an aperitif serve the wine you plan to have with supper.

Don't forget that you will need to buy a larger bottle than usual—a litre size should be adequate for modest drinkers. Choose a white wine in order to blend with the distinctive flavours of both the first and main courses. It should be sufficiently dry to go both with the rich mousses yet at the same time be sweet enough to be drunk as an aperitif on its own. A medium Riesling would be an ideal compromise. This is best served chilled so put it in the refrigerator before you go out.

SHOPPING CHECKLIST

Red salmon caviare or red lumpfish roe are available from delicatessens and some enterprising fishmongers.

Salmon caviare is more expensive but its globules are larger and therefore look more decorative. Red lumpfish roe is cheaper and more easily obtainable.

The consommé used for the mousse must be of the concentrated kind or it will not set to a firm gel. This is usually clearly marked on the tin. Do not dilute it or you will turn it into a soup instead of a jelly. Buy cream cheese that is firm and foil wrapped. Do not buy a soft cream cheese that is runny.

The citrus salad requires an endive, that attractive curly lettuce. If you are unable to obtain endive, buy chicory or, failing that, an ordinary lettuce, but the flavour of lettuce will not go quite so well with the orange.

Check that you have butter, parsley and cucumber for decorating, and buy brown rolls to go with the mousse.

Vanilla pod has a finer flavour than vanilla essence (which is an extract made from the pod). The pod is dried off after use and is used again. Most good grocers and delicatessens stock them.

Countdown timetable

THE DAY BEFORE

Do the shopping.
The programme in the morning may be done the night before if wished.

ON THE DAY

In the morning
Playgoer's mousse: make the main part of the mousse and chill—steps 1-5.
Sausage bolster: make it—steps 1-21. Leave to cool, then wrap in foil and place in the refrigerator.

In the afternoon
Pears cardinal: poach the pears. Cover and leave in the syrup in the refrigerator. Make the raspberry purée topping—steps 1-10. Cover and leave in the refrigerator and lay the table. Tidy the rooms to be used.
Playgoer's mousse: decorate the top of each mousse with a butterfly and add consommé. Reserve in the refrigerator—steps 6-12.

45 minutes before going out
Citrus green salad: prepare by segmenting the oranges and making the vinaigrette—steps 1-6.
Playgoer's mousse: decorate each mousse with 'caviare'. Cover with foil or an upturned cereal bowl. Reserve in the refrigerator—steps 13-14.
Have a last minute tidy round, put out the glasses and place the wine in the refrigerator.

On returning home
Pour out the wine and give the guests a glass.
Citrus green salad: assemble and dress—steps 7-9.
Sausage bolster: cut into slices—step 22.
Playgoer's mousse: uncover the mousses and serve with brown rolls and butter.
Pears cardinal: drain and put on a serving dish and pour on the purée—steps 11-13.

Playgoer's mousse

Although these mousses are very small they are also very rich so a little goes a long way. If you do not have individual cocotte or soufflé dishes, make one large mousse and decorate this on top.

Accompany the mousses with fresh brown rolls and butter so that guests can help themselves.

SERVES 4
125 ml [4 fl oz] concentrated consommé
5 ml [1 teaspoon] curry powder
100 g [¼ lb] full fat cream cheese
half a cucumber for garnish
2 midget pickled gherkins
50 g [2 oz] red caviare or red lumpfish roe

1 If the consommé has gelled in the tin, turn it into a small pan and heat until it is thin.

2 Remove the consommé from the heat and measure a generous 60 ml [4 tablespoons] into a cup and reserve for decoration.

3 Add the curry powder to the remaining consommé in the pan and stir to mix. Allow this to cool.

4 Blend the cool reserved consommé into the cheese until smooth and creamy. You can do this in a liquidizer or in a bowl beating it with a fork. In a liquidizer blend at high speed for 3 seconds.

5 Pour the cheese mixture into 4 cocottes. Place these in the coldest part of the refrigerator to allow the mousses to solidify.

6 Cut 2 thin slices of cucumber, then cut each slice into 4 triangles.

7 Remove the cocottes from the refrigerator and check that the mousse is sufficiently set to bear the decorations without these sinking. If the mousse still seems too liquid, put the cocottes into the ice box for 10 minutes.

8 To decorate, make a cucumber butterfly on top of the cheese in each cocotte. Use 2 cucumber triangles to make the wings. Lower them carefully on to the consommé in each dish.

9 To make the bodies of the butterflies, split the gherkins in half

lengthways. Blot them well on kitchen paper to remove all vinegar. Then lay them carefully between the cucumber wings, skin side upward. Press the gherkins slightly into the mouse so that they do not protrude too much.

10 If the reserved consommé has gelled, put this into a small pan and heat it until liquid. Set aside to cool for a few minutes.

11 Spoon 15 ml [1 tablespoon] of consommé on top of the decoration in one cocotte. Tilt the little dish in your hand to allow the consommé to run round the decoration, but do not be so energetic that the decoration dislodges. Repeat with others.

12 Cover each mousse with foil and reserve in the refrigerator, for the consommé top to set.

13 Garnish each mousse round the edge with the red caviare.

14 Cover each mousse with an inverted cereal bowl so that the decorations do not get damaged. Alternatively, cover lightly with foil. Reserve in the refrigerator until required then serve with brown bread and butter.

Citrus green salad

⊠ *This salad has a sharp and refreshing flavour to contrast pleasantly with the rich taste of the sausage-meat. If wished, a mixture of orange and pink grapefruit segments may be used instead of limes or lemon. Chicory or cabbage lettuce could be used instead of endive.*

SERVES 4
1 medium-sized curly endive
2 oranges
2 limes or 1 lemon
salt and pepper
60 ml [4 tablespoons] olive oil
a few stuffed green olives

1 Remove any ragged outer leaves from the endive, wash, drain and place in a polythene bag in the refrigerator to crisp.

2 Remove all the skin and pith from the oranges, standing them on a plate to prevent loss of juice. Divide into segments and set aside.

3 Squeeze the juice from the orange membranes into a bowl or jug. Add any juice from the plate.

4 Squeeze the juice from the limes or lemon into the bowl with the orange juice.

5 Add the salt and pepper and stir with a fork to dissolve the salt. Add the oil and mix well with a fork.

6 Tear the crisped endive leaves into pieces as you pile them into a salad bowl. Add the orange segments.

7 Add the stuffed olives to the salad.

8 Toss with citrus vinaigrette just before serving.

Sausage bolster

⊠⊠⊠ *The sausage bolster is eaten cold. There is no need to grease the baking tray when making it because the sausage-meat contains enough fat to prevent the pastry from sticking. Adding extra grease would make the bolster fry. If you are unable to obtain sausage-meat, remove the skin from pork sausages and use them instead.*

The pastry is sealed with beaten egg to help make a secure seam which will not come open during cooking.

SERVES 4
225 g [½ lb] shortcrust pastry
350 g [¾ lb] pork sausage-meat
2 medium-sized onions
3 ripe tomatoes
5 fresh sage leaves or 10 ml [2 teaspoons] dried sage
salt
freshly ground black pepper
1 medium-sized egg

1 Make or buy the shortcrust pastry.

2 Heat the oven to 220°C [425°F] gas mark 7.

3 If time permits, wrap the pastry in polythene and leave in the refrigerator for 30 minutes.

4 Remove the pastry from the refrigerator, unwrap and leave to stand for a further 15 minutes.

5 Meanwhile, place the sausage-meat in a bowl.

6 Peel and chop the onions and skin and chop the tomatoes. Add them to the bowl.

7 If using fresh sage leaves, snip finely into the bowl using scissors. Dried sage can be added direct.

8 Mix all ingredients together until well blended. Season to taste.

9 Turn the pastry on to a lightly floured board and roll out to an oblong sized 30 × 25 cm [12 × 10"].

10 Using the rolling pin, lift the pastry on to a baking sheet, and then unroll, positioning it in the centre.

11 Place the sausage-meat mixture in the middle of the pastry and form to a long roll shape with your hands so that it leaves a margin of 6.5 cm [2½"] at each side and 2.5 cm [1"] at the top and bottom. If you flour your hands first this will make the shaping easier.

12 Break the egg into a bowl and beat with a fork.

13 Brush the margins of the pastry with some of the beaten egg.

Sausage bolster accompanied by a citrus green salad is a tasty main course for a late supper after an evening out.

14 Bring the 2 long edges of the pastry together and press lightly to seal.

15 Fold the join to one side so that it lies flat.

16 Pinch the ends of the roll firmly to seal.

17 Push the roll over so that the join is underneath, and re-position the bolster in the centre of the tray.

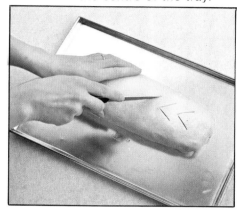

18 Using a sharp knife, make a series of V-shaped cuts in the top of the roll so that steam can escape during cooking.

19 Brush with the remaining beaten egg and cook in the centre of the oven for 10 minutes.

20 Then lower the heat to 190°C [375°F] gas mark 5 and cook for a further 20 minutes until golden brown.

21 Allow the bolster to cool. When cold, wrap in foil and chill for at least 2 hours, or until required, in the refrigerator.

22 Just before serving, cut off the pinched ends and discard. Cut the roll into 2.5 cm [1"] thick slices.

Pears cardinal

The pears in this classic pudding are described as cardinal because they are cloaked in red, like a cardinal's cloak. Frozen raspberries may be used for the sauce. Choose a pan that is the right size for the pears, that is, one in which they will just fit lying down and the liquid will come half-way up their sides. Try the pan for size before you peel the pears.

SERVES 4
4 large cooking pears
100 g [¼ lb] caster sugar
1 vanilla pod
a squeeze of lemon juice
450 g [1 lb] raspberries
60 ml [4 tablespoons] icing sugar

1 Put the sugar in a heavy-based pan and add 275 ml [½ pt] water. Stir.

2 Place the pan over medium heat and bring to the boil, stirring. Allow to boil rapidly for at least 2 minutes.

3 Peel the pears, leaving the stalks intact.

4 As soon as the syrup has boiled remove from the heat. Add the vanilla pod and a squeeze of lemon juice. Carefully lower the pears into the pan using a draining spoon. Lay them head to tail.

5 Cover and poach at a gentle simmer for 30 minutes or until the pears are tender. Occasionally spoon the liquid over tops of the pears and re-cover.

6 When cooked, remove pears temporarily and reduce syrup to half by boiling rapidly for 2 minutes. Replace the pears, cover and leave in a cool place until the pears are cold. Spoon the liquid over the pears periodically so that they are moist and flavourful.

7 Discard any mouldy raspberries. Wash remaining berries by putting them into a colander and lowering into a bowlful of water. This prevents bruising.

8 Drain the raspberries well then turn them on to kitchen paper to absorb excess water.

9 Sift the icing sugar into a bowl. Do this first so that you do not have to wash the sieve before puréeing the berries.

10 Push the raspberries through the sieve on to the sugar. Stir well to mix.

11 Just before serving, lift the cold pears carefully out of the syrup using a draining spoon. Stand them in one large or four individual serving dishes.

12 Remove the vanilla pod from the syrup. Pour a spoonful or two of the syrup over each pear.

13 Pour the raspberry purée over each pear.

Special Occasion Menus

Budget dinner for six

The main drawback to inviting friends to dinner is that it can take a big bite out of your housekeeping budget and, in these lean times, that could be enough to put you off entertaining for months. But you can entertain with style without breaking the bank, as this menu proves. The meal is for six because not only is it more fun to have two couples round at once but, frankly, it also works out cheaper—one dinner party will entertain two sets of friends.

Menu

❧

Oeufs durs soubise with hot bread rolls

---❖---

Whiting Spencer Tracy Carottes à la nivernaise

---❖---

Danish peasant girl with a veil

---❖---

To drink: tomato juice, followed by any low-priced white table wine such as Italian Soave

ENTERTAINING ON A TIGHT BUDGET

When entertaining without much money to spend, every course must be chosen with economy in mind, but with this menu none will look or taste cheap. The secret is to use simple and inexpensive ingredients and to cook and serve them with flair.

Begin the dinner with an egg dish served with a super sauce to get the meal off to a satisfying start. The main course is stuffed whiting, a much under-rated but delicious fish, accompanied by a glamorous carrot dish. The dessert bears only a little resemblance to plain stewed apple, as it is made glorious with cinnamon crumble, chocolate and cream.

Serving rolls with both the first and main course makes the food go further.

GETTING ORGANIZED

The hors d'oeuvre and the dessert for this meal are prepared in advance while the main course can be prepared in under two hours, making it suitable for a hostess who has to get dinner ready after coming home from work. If you are a working person, it might be wise to get up a little earlier in the morning and set the dinner table after breakfast.

Stuff the whiting before the guests arrive. For really tasty results, fish should be eaten the moment cooking is finished, so be particularly careful about timing here. Start cooking the fish about 10 minutes before you plan to sit down to eat and turn the fish when you serve the first course. If guests linger over the first course longer than expected, nip into the kitchen, turn the grill to its lowest setting, and lower the pan so the fish will keep for a further five minutes.

Serve the wine when you bring out the main course; the onions in the first course are rather strong.

The dessert is made in advance, but the topping is best added just before the meal.

Countdown timetable

THE EVENING BEFORE OR MORNING

Danish peasant girl with a veil: make the dessert and leave covered in the refrigerator. Grate the chocolate and reserve—steps 1-9.
Oeufs durs soubise: prepare the eggs and accompanying onion sauce—steps 1-7.

IN THE MORNING

Lay the table.
Put the tomato juice in the refrigerator to chill and check that ice-cube trays are filled.
Buy the fish, bread rolls and remaining ingredients.

1¾ hours before

Prepare pre-dinner drinks tray.
Whiting Spencer Tracy: prepare and stuff the fish—steps 1-9. Cover loosely and reserve in the refrigerator until the guests have arrived and you are ready to start cooking. If you bought the fish ready gutted, there is no need to start preparing until 1½ hours before.
Oeufs durs soubise: shell and divide the eggs, put on individual plates, coat with sauce and garnish—steps 8-11.

1 hour before

Carottes à la nivernaise: prepare the carrots—steps 1-7.

20 minutes before

Heat the grill to moderate and put the serving dishes and plates in the warmer.
Whiting Spencer Tracy: start cooking—steps 11-13.
Carottes à la nivernaise: start cooking the carrots—steps 8-13.
Danish peasant girl with a veil: top with cream and grated chocolate—step 10.
Heat the bread rolls.

2 minutes before

Whiting Spencer Tracy: turn the fish just before you start eating the first course—step 14. If the fish is ready before you are, move the grill pan down and turn the grill to its lowest setting. The fish will keep quite well for a further 5 minutes.

SHOPPING CHECKLIST

The most important item on your shopping list is undoubtedly the whiting. Buy it on the day just to make absolutely certain it is fresh but order it in advance to be sure of getting it. If you ask the fishmonger, he will do all the gutting for you and this will save time on the preparation.

A selection of rolls (say, bridge rolls and wholemeal rolls) look attractive and give your guests a choice—a good party touch at little extra cost. The table will look that much more inviting, too, if you roll the butter into balls, make curls or use butter moulds to stamp the butter into pretty shapes.

Don't forget the cream for the dessert. Save one spoonful for the sauce for the eggs.

Finally, be sure to supply yourself with plenty of greaseproof paper or kitchen foil to cover dishes while they are waiting in the refrigerator. This will prevent them absorbing other food flavours.

DRINKS

Pre-dinner spirits are impractical when funds are low. A jumbo-sized can of tomato juice makes an excellent alternative to the more expensive aperitifs. Chill it in the refrigerator and pour it into an attractive glass jug. Bring it in grandly on a tray with six smart tumblers, Worcestershire sauce, salt and pepper, plenty of ice cubes, lemon slices and a long-handled spoon to stir it with. Serve with panache and certainly without apology. You'll find it makes a refreshing change.

For a wine to go with dinner, this is an occasion to economize on quality rather than quantity. Both the fish and carrots have quite a robust flavour, so a slight roughness about the taste of the wine won't be noticed too much. What would matter is if your guests found themselves with nothing left to drink before the meal is over. This might well kill the party mood and bring a tone of austerity to the occasion, so buy plenty.

Oeufs durs soubise

This cold dish of hard-boiled eggs, wrapped in a creamy onion sauce, makes a satisfying start to a meal. This economical version of a traditional recipe is based on milk rather than stock, so very little cream is added at the end. Top of the milk can be used for slightly thinning the cold sauce and giving it an extra creamy appearance.

The quantities given would also make a hot main course for a simple supper for three people; soft boil the eggs instead of hard boiling them and time them to be peeled and ready when the sauce is done.

SERVES 6
6 eggs
225 g [8 oz] onions
400 ml [¾ pt] milk
salt and pepper
40 g [1½ oz] butter
40 g [1½ oz] flour
pinch of nutmeg
15 ml [1 tablespoon] thick cream
30 ml [2 tablespoons] top of the milk
10 ml [2 teaspoons] freshly chopped parsley
5 ml [1 teaspoon] paprika

1 Peel the onions and chop them finely.

2 Put the eggs into a small pan, cover with water and bring to the boil. Cook for 10 minutes. Arrest cooking by plunging the eggs into cold water.

3 Meanwhile put the milk into a milk pan and add the onions, salt and pepper. Bring slowly to the boil, then simmer for 15 minutes.

4 Press the onions through a sieve into a bowl or blend in a liquidizer.

5 Melt the butter in a clean heavy-based pan. Remove from heat and add the flour. Return to the heat and blend the flour into the butter, stirring. Cook for a minute.

6 Remove from heat and add a little of the onion and milk purée to the flour and stir to a smooth paste. Add the rest of the liquid and

return to the heat.

7 Bring to the boil, stirring all the time, then simmer for 5 minutes to cook the flour. Add the nutmeg. Remove from the heat and set aside to cool.

8 Shell the hard-boiled eggs and cut them in half lengthways with a sharp knife.

9 Place the eggs, face down, in individual soup bowls or on side-plates.

10 Add the thick and thin cream to the cold sauce and stir it in. Spoon the sauce over the eggs.

11 Garnish each egg with parsley and paprika. Reserve in the refrigerator until needed.

Whiting Spencer Tracy

Film star Spencer Tracy is credited with inventing this dish. Whiting is rather a neglected fish nowadays which is a pity because it is almost always cheap and makes really delicious dishes. Here the sharp flavour of the stuffing contrasts pleasantly with the flavour of the fish. You can gut the fish yourself or ask the fishmonger to do it for you. If you do this at home, be sure to keep the heads and other trimmings for stock. During grilling turn the fish with a fish slice and a round-bladed knife. Tongs do not provide enough support and the fish is likely to break.

SERVES 6
6 medium-sized whiting
1 large orange
1 small onion
2 slices wholemeal bread
30 ml [2 tablespoons] freshly
     chopped parsley
1 lemon
salt
freshly ground black pepper
50 g [2 oz] butter

1 Using a serrated knife, scrape the fish skin to dislodge loose scales. Cut off the fins using kitchen scissors.

2 Make a slit along the underside of the fish and pull out the innards, working from tail to head.

3 Rinse the inside of the fish under cold running water and pat dry with a kitchen towel.

4 Peel the orange and cut the segments free from the membrane, keeping it on a plate or grooved board to avoid loss of juice. Chop roughly and place the juice and flesh in a bowl. Discard pips and pith.

5 Peel and finely chop the onion. Add to the bowl.

6 Reduce the bread to crumbs, chop the parsley. Squeeze the remaining juice from the orange membrane.

7 Add these ingredients to the bowl. Season to taste then mix with a fork until well blended.

8 Make 2-3 diagonal cuts in the flesh along each side of the fish.

9 Divide the stuffing equally between the fish, pushing it into the cavity where the innards were. Do not overstuff.

10 Heat the grill to moderate.

11 Melt the butter in a heavy-based pan over low heat. Do not allow to brown.

12 Sprinkle each fish on both sides with salt, rubbing in the salt with your fingertips. Then brush with melted butter.

13 Place the fish under the grill about 10 cm [4"] away from the heat. Grill for 10 minutes.

14 Turn carefully with a fish slice and a round-bladed knife to avoid breaking, then cook for a further 10 minutes on the second side.

Carottes à la nivernaise

This regional French dish of glazed carrots is particularly suited to the large old carrots of the end of the season, before the new carrots appear. Old carrots often weigh 225 g [½ lb] each. The centre is hard and woody and this is pared away, so you must buy extra weight to allow for this. Use the trimmings for soup or stock. For a party shape surrounding carrot flesh.

SERVES 6
1.15 kg [2½ lb] old carrots
100 g [¼ lb] onions
salt

22 ml [1½ tablespoons] sugar
75 g [3 oz] butter
60 ml [4 tablespoons] beef stock
freshly ground black pepper

1 Peel and finely chop the onion.

2 Top and tail the carrots and peel them very thinly with a swivel-bladed potato peeler.

3 Cut each carrot lengthways into 4 pieces.

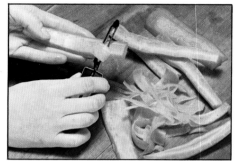

4 Pare away the hard yellow core from each piece of carrot. Then cut each piece into lengths approximately 2.5 cm [1″] long.

5 Melt the butter in a heavy-based 22.5 cm [9″] saucepan and add the onions. Cover and heat slowly for 15 minutes over low heat. Shake or stir the pan occasionally to prevent burning or sticking.

6 Meanwhile shape the carrots. Holding one trimmed carrot length between finger and thumb, work round it swiftly with the potato peeler, removing the square corners and giving it a shape something like an almond.

7 Shape all the carrot pieces in the same way. Reserve all the carrot chips and the cores for soup.

8 Bring to the boil 850 ml [1½ pt] water in a medium-sized saucepan and add the salt and sugar.

9 Add the carrots, cover and lower the heat. Cook for 6 minutes until parboiled (until almost tender but not cooked through).

10 Drain the carrots in a colander, than add them to the onion pan. Turn them over until thoroughly covered with butter.

11 Add the beef stock and cook, uncovered, over a low heat for a further 3 minutes, shaking the pan occasionally to prevent the carrots sticking.

12 When the beef stock has nearly all disappeared, and the carrots are tender but not breaking up, they are ready.

13 Grind over the carrots a generous quantity of black pepper. Transfer to a warmed serving dish ready to be served.

Danish peasant girl with a veil

⊠⊠ *When frying the crumbs for this dish, it is essential to use a heavy-based pan and to keep the heat really low to prevent the butter from burning. A smaller amount of sugar than usual is used when stewing the apples, because more is mixed with the crumbs.*

SERVES 6
700 g [1½ lb] cooking apples
5 ml [1 teaspoon] lemon juice
40 g [1½ oz] granulated sugar or
   15 ml [1 tablespoon] honey
4 thick slices brown bread
100 g [¼ lb] soft brown sugar
15 ml [1 tablespoon] ground
   cinnamon
75 g [3 oz] butter
150 ml [¼ pt] thick cream
50 g [2 oz] plain dessert
   chocolate

1 Peel, core and thinly slice the apples.

2 Put the fruit in a heavy-based pan with the lemon juice, sugar or honey and 45 ml [3 tablespoons] cold water.

3 Cover, place over low heat and stew for 25 minutes or until the fruit is tender, stirring from time to time.

4 Meanwhile, cut the crusts off the bread and reduce the slices to breadcrumbs using a grater or liquidizer.

5 Melt the butter in a heavy-based pan over low heat. When it is sizzling, add the crumbs and fry gently until brown and crisp, stirring from time to time.

6 Sprinkle the brown sugar and cinnamon over the crumbs. Remove the pan from the heat and stir to mix the ingredients.

7 In a glass serving dish, layer the cooked fruit and crumbs, ending with a layer of crumbs. Set aside to cool.

8 Then cover the dish and put in the refrigerator until quite cold (about 1 hour).

9 Grate the chocolate.

10 Pour the cream over the top of the dish and sprinkle over the chocolate just before serving.

Romantic dinner for two

Ever since Eve gave Adam that memorable apple, women have been tempting men with exciting things to eat. To celebrate a birthday, an engagement or a wedding anniversary, or to impress on a new friend that there is more to you than just a pretty face, you may want to light the candles and give an intimate little dinner just for two. That's why this menu has a first course and a pudding that can be made in advance, and a main course that can be cooked whenever the two of you are ready for it. Steak is always a favourite with men and the dish featured here has just enough touches of the exotic to give a festive feeling.

Menu

Celery soup
amandine hot melba
toast

Tournedos Mirabeau
Fringed button
mushrooms
Petits pois à la
Française

Melon surprise

*To drink: champagne
throughout or, martinis before
dinner then a burgundy such as
Nuits St Georges*

GETTING ORGANIZED

When there are only two of you— and that's the whole point of a romantic dinner—then there's nobody else around to entertain your guests while you're in the kitchen. This menu and timetable have been deliberately worked out so that the main preparation is done before the chosen man makes his appearance and, when he does, all that's left is to pour a pair of delicious-looking drinks and sit down and talk, confident in the knowledge that the pudding is ready and the soup can appear within minutes of wanting it.

You'll notice that the timetable gives you a whole uninterrupted hour to spend on your appearance. The occasion would lose its point if the hostess had to greet her guest with her hair still in rollers because she could not leave her cooking in the last vital hour.

You will have to vanish for a bit after the soup to grill the spectacular tournedos—steak can never be pre-cooked successfully—but, even if

Countdown timetable

THE DAY BEFORE

Fill the ice-cube trays with water and put in the freezing compartment.
Tidy and clean the rooms your guest will see.
Clean the cutlery and polish the glasses.
Do the main shopping.
Celery soup amandine: make the soup—steps 1-4. Cool. When cold, cover and reserve in the refrigerator.
Melba toast: make the toast—steps 1-5. When cold put in an airtight tin.
Choose your mood music, dusting the records if necessary.
If serving champagne on ice, after 5 hours empty the cube trays into a plastic bag. Tie it and return to the freezer. Refill the ice cube trays and place them in the freezer to make more ice. Repeat if necessary.

ON THE DAY

4 hours before the meal
Fetch the ordered tournedos from the butcher.
Melon surprise: reserving ice needed for cooler, crush ice cubes and re-freeze. Prepare the melon and fill with ginger—steps 1-4.
Arrange the table centre flowers. Lay the table, not forgetting the candles.
Prepare the coffee tray.

2½ hours before the meal
Tournedos Mirabeau: make the anchovy butter. Prepare the canapés— steps 1-7. Reserve in a plastic bag.
Celery soup amandine: toast the almonds—step 5.
Petits pois à la Française: prepare the peas—steps 1-3.

1½ hours before the meal
Have a relaxing hot bath, dress and make yourself beautiful.

30 minutes before the meal
Put glasses for the pre-dinner drinks (with the Martini if you are serving this) in the sitting area.
Turn the record-player on and the dining-room lights down low.
Put the soup bowls, plates, serving and vegetable dishes in the plate warmer.
Put ice cubes and champagne bottle in wine cooler and half fill with cold water. Reserve in refrigerator.
Fringed button mushrooms: prepare— steps 1-3.
Petits pois à la Française: if using fresh peas for the petits pois, cook now—steps 4-5.
Tournedos Mirabeau: fry the canapés—steps 8-11. Place on kitchen paper, cover and leave in a cool oven at 70°C [150°F] gas mark ¼.

your man likes his meat really well done, you won't be missing for more than ten minutes. Don't pop back during that period to make sure he is happy—a conversation will start and you could forget your timing, your steaks could be black and your dinner spoiled. While you're missing, he can pour the wine, drink it, listen to the music and think about you.

The day before the dinner, don't forget to clean and tidy up the rooms he will see. It could spoil a beautiful image he has of you if, while he idles, he strikes dust upon the shelves. The table is the centre of interest and is well worth, say, a small bowl of roses, but don't overdo the flowers. And don't forget that men are very fussy when it comes to glasses; make sure you've polished them well. But these are all jobs for doing hours ahead of time. With the countdown timetable there's no need to rush

anything. This is a magnificent meal which deserves to be savoured and relaxed over. Follow your timetable religiously and it will be.

SPECIAL PARTY DRINKS

Don't automatically rule out champagne as too expensive. Of course it is expensive but, on an occasion like this, if you have no suitable aperitifs in your cupboard already, it may save buying two bottles (one for before-dinner drinks and another of wine) which together could mean the same outlay as one bottle of champagne. The popping of that cork and the rush of bubbles give a wonderful air of excitement to the occasion and mark the evening as special. Give the bottle to your man to open, but have the glasses close by when he does.

The second big advantage of champagne is that you can drink it as an aperitif and then right through the

5 minutes before the meal
Petits pois à la Française: if using frozen peas, cook now with the other ingredients, then put in the serving dish. If using fresh peas, strain and put in the vegetable dish—step 6. Cover and place in the oven.
Tournedos Mirabeau: turn on the grill to the highest setting, brush the tournedos with oil—steps 11-12.
Melba toast: put under the grill to toast quickly for a minute until brown.
Celery soup amandine: reheat the soup up gently. Add the cream, scatter over the almonds and serve—steps 6-7.

Between the soup and main courses
Tournedos Mirabeau: grill the steaks to your liking—steps 13-14.
Fringed button mushrooms: 4 minutes before the steaks are due to be ready, put under the grill—step 4.
Tournedos Mirabeau: warm the anchovy butter, place the cooked tournedos on the canapés, garnish and serve—steps 15-19.

Between the main course and dessert
Melon surprise: spoon in the ice-cream. Serve on a bed of crushed ice—steps 5-6.

meal, even with red meat.
Put champagne into the refrigerator (lay it on its side near the top) as soon as you get it home. Ideally it should chill for a good 24 hours. If you can borrow a wine cooler, serve the champagne on ice.
If the occasion does not merit champagne, you will want a suitable aperitif. Martini is 30 per cent alcohol and so will give the evening a good start. For a cocktail in small glasses, choose the sweeter red martini, sometimes called 'Italian' or 'rosso'.
With the main course serve a bottle of burgundy: Nuits St Georges is very well known, a red Mâcon would be rather cheaper. If red wine is cold it will give off less of its flavour so, when you get it home, stand burgundy in a warm room to bring it to room temperature—leave it for several hours. The wine is then called 'chambré'.

SHOPPING CHECKLIST
If you decide to splurge on champagne, buy the real thing—French champagne—rather than any substitute. Sugar is added to champagne after it is made, so even 'medium' champagne is rather sweet. As you are planning to drink it with meat, look for one with 'dry' or 'extra dry' on the label.
If you are going to buy burgundy, remember to check that you have a corkscrew which works properly and does not go in for infuriating tricks such as splitting the cork or becoming wedged in the bottle.
Make sure you have enough unsliced bread. This will do for both the melba toast and for the canapés, with a little extra to allow for any accidents.
Check that you have garlic. The thought of including garlic in a menu for a romantic dinner may worry you: it need not. If both of you are eating it then it will not be offensive to either. But if the thought nags you, include a small bunch of parsley in your shopping list. When later you go out to make the coffee, chew some parsley stalks to clear your breath.
Buy your almonds ready-flaked to prevent the risk of frayed fingernails. Unless you own an olive stoner, buy stoned olives: they look messy as a garnish when stones are removed by other methods.
Ask the butcher to bard (wrap round a thin sheet of pork fat) the tournedos for you, but pick them up as near the evening as you can manage. Order them in advance and don't skimp on the thickness. If you are going to worry about expense it would be better to choose something simpler in the first place, or to eat cornflakes the next night, than to start economizing at this stage.
An Ogen melon, which is small and sweet, is the best choice, but if you can't find one buy a small honeydew. The essential thing is to be sure it is ripe: test by pressing its end. It may seem extravagant to buy a whole jar of stem ginger just for the syrup, but you will have a lot of ginger left over for other exciting recipes.

SPECIAL EQUIPMENT
The anchovy butter is most easily prepared in a mortar with a pestle. However, if you do not own one, use a fork and crush the anchovies in a small bowl.
A long stemmed sundae spoon is very useful for fishing the pips out of the melon.

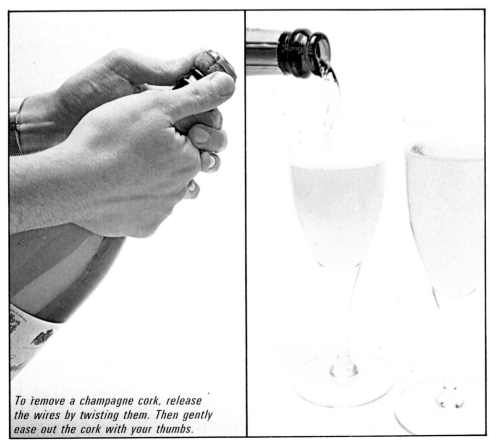

To remove a champagne cork, release the wires by twisting them. Then gently ease out the cork with your thumbs.

Celery soup amandine

Celery makes one of the best of all purée of vegetable soups. Its delicate flavour and pale colour are enhanced by a swirl of cream and the crunchy topping of almonds. Serve it with crisp melba toast.

SERVES 2
225 g [½lb] celery
25 g [1 oz] butter
salt
freshly ground black pepper
250 ml [½ pt] white stock
sprig of parsley
15 g [½ oz] flaked almonds
250 ml [½ pt] milk
30 ml [2 tablespoons] thin cream

1 Wash and chop celery, removing any tough stringy parts.

2 Melt the butter in a heavy-based saucepan and sweat the celery for 10 minutes, shaking the pan occasionally.

3 Season and pour on the white stock. Add the parsley. Bring to simmering point, cover and simmer for 20 minutes or until celery is quite tender. Add the milk.

4 Reduce contents of pan to a purée using a sieve, vegetable mill or liquidizer. If using a liquidizer, sieve afterwards to remove any fibres.

5 Heat a heavy-based frying pan for a minute over moderate heat. Pop in the flaked almonds and toast them for about a minute until brown, shaking the pan to keep them turning. Do not let them overcook. Reserve until needed.

6 Return soup to the saucepan. Reheat gently.

7 Pour into soup bowls and dribble a spoonful of cream into each one. Garnish with the browned almonds.

Melba toast

This very thin toast is dried through completely and has no crumb inside. It makes an admirable contrast to the smooth soup. Melba toast can be served either hot, straight from the grill, or cold.

SERVES 2
2 thin slices white bread, about 6 mm [¼″] thick

1 Heat grill to high.

2 Remove the crusts from the bread.

3 Toast the bread lightly on both sides.

4 Lay the toast on a flat surface and, holding it firmly down with one hand, carefully split the toast through the middle with a bread knife.

5 Grill the uncooked surfaces for almost 1 minute until they are crisp and curled.

Tournedos Mirabeau

These sophisticated French steaks allow you to enjoy the rich flavour of freshly grilled fillet steak, sharpened by the anchovy and black olive garnish. The crisply fried canapés underneath provide a pleasing contrast in texture, as well as catching the meat juices when the steak is cut.

The anchovy butter should be made ahead and reserved in the refrigerator, to be served warm with the steaks.

SERVES 2
2 tournedos, 4 cm [1½″] thick
30 ml [2 tablespoons] butter

For the anchovy butter:
25 g [1 oz] butter
10 ml [2 teaspoons] anchovy essence
4 anchovy fillets
freshly ground black pepper
half a garlic clove

For the canapés:
2 slices day-old bread, 1 cm [⅓″] thick
30 ml [2 tablespoons] oil
50 g [2 oz] butter

For the garnish:
4 anchovy fillets
bunch of watercress
2 large black olives

1 To make the anchovy butter, put the butter, which should be at room temperature, in a small bowl and beat it with a fork until creamy. Add the anchovy essence and beat until incorporated.

2 Drain all the oil from a can of anchovies. Choose 4 good-looking fillets for the garnish. Split them lengthways and reserve.

3 Place 4 more fillets in a mortar. Pound with a pestle until a smooth paste is formed. Alternatively, mash in a small bowl with a fork until smooth.

4 Incorporate the anchovy paste into the butter.

5 Peel the garlic and crush using either salt and a round-bladed knife or a garlic crusher.

6 Incorporate garlic and pepper into the butter and mix thoroughly. Reserve, covered, in the refrigerator.

7 To shape the canapés, cut a circle from each slice of bread approximately the same size as the tournedos with a plain or fluted cutter. Alternatively, place a coffee cup on the bread and cut round that with a sharp knife.

8 Melt the butter and oil in a heavy-based frying pan over medium heat. When the fat is foaming, fry the canapés for up to 3 minutes on each side or until they are crisp and golden.

9 Drain the canapés on absorbent kitchen paper.

10 Place a layer of absorbent kitchen paper in a serving dish. Place the canapés in the dish, cover and leave in a cool oven heated to 70°C [150°F] gas mark $\frac{1}{4}$ until needed.

11 Heat the grill until very hot.

12 Meanwhile melt the butter in a small pan and brush the tournedos liberally with it.

13 Grill the steaks close to the grill for 1 minute on each side to seal the cut surfaces.

14 Lower heat or pan and continue cooking for 2 minutes on each side for rare steaks, 4 minutes for well-done.

15 Wash the watercress and remove any coarse stems or yellow leaves.

Tournedos Mirabeau, named after a French revolutionary leader, contrasts fillet steak with the sharpness of anchovies and olives.

16 Put the anchovy butter in a small pan and place over a moderate heat for 1 minute or until it is half melted and warmed.

17 Remove the serving dish from the oven. Lift out the kitchen paper, re-arrange the canapés and place one tournedos on top of each.

18 Arrange a lattice pattern of 4 anchovy strips on the top of each tournedos. Place a black olive in the middle. Garnish with the watercress and serve immediately.

19 Transfer the anchovy butter to a small jug or sauce-boat and pass it separately.

Fringed button mushrooms

Clever cutting gives these grilled mushrooms a party appearance.

SERVES 2
100 g [¼ lb] small button mushrooms
15 g [½ oz] butter

1 Wipe the mushrooms and trim off any earthy stalks.

2 With scissors, snip round the edge of the mushroom caps to give a fringed effect.

3 Melt the butter in a small pan and brush over the mushrooms.

4 Four minutes before the tournedos are due to finish cooking, put the mushrooms under the grill. Grill for four minutes.

Petits pois à la Francaise

This is a good way to tenderize slightly tough end-of-season peas or give frozen peas a personal touch. It is also an ideal way to use up the outer leaves of a lettuce, the heart of which is being used for making a salad. For an out-of-season version of this recipe use frozen peas and pearl onions instead of fresh peas and spring onions. Use 125 ml [4 fl oz] water and simmer ingredients for 5 minutes only.

SERVES 2
700 g [¾ lb] peas, shelled weight
4 lettuce leaves
3 spring onions
salt
large sprig of parsley and of mint
15 g [½ oz] butter

1 Shell the peas.

2 Wash and shred the lettuce leaves. Trim the spring onions and cut in half.

3 Tie the parsley and mint together with a long piece of thread.

4 In a medium-sized saucepan bring 150 ml [¼ pt] lightly salted water to the boil.

5 Add the peas, lettuce, onions and herbs to the pan and simmer, covered, for 25 minutes, or until almost all the liquid has been absorbed by the peas and they are quite tender.

6 Drain, discarding the herbs, and turn into a warm serving dish. Dot with the butter.

Melon surprise

◻◼◻ *This unusual fruit dish has a*
◼◼◼ *surprise in the filling—spicy*
ginger with cooling ice-cream.

SERVES 2
1 Ogen melon
150 ml [¼ pt] ginger syrup
15 ml [1 tablespoon] chopped
   ginger
120 ml [8 tablespoons] vanilla
   ice-cream
2 trays of ice

1 Crush ice for the melon by putting ice-cubes into a polythene bag and hammering it with a hammer or rolling pin. Tie up the bag and replace it in the freezer compartment of the refrigerator until needed.

2 Using a sharp knife, cut a plug 5 cm [2"] in diameter from the top of the melon so that you can see throught to the seed section. Set this plug aside.

To crush ice cubes, hammer them in a plastic bag; refreeze them in the bag.

3 Using a long handled spoon, remove the seeds and filaments from the centre of the melon, lifting out carefully through the hole at the top.

4 Chop the ginger finely and spoon, with the ginger syrup, into the melon. Replace the plug. Chill the melon in the refrigerator, while the

Cut downward into the melon to remove the plug, then spoon out the seeds.

ginger soaks into the melon flesh.

5 When ready to eat, remove the plug and spoon in the ice-cream.

6 Serve melon in style on a bed of crushed ice. To serve, cut it open from top to bottom so that both halves contain a portion of ginger and ice-cream.

Special occasion dinner party for six

On a special occasion every hostess wants her party to be a great success, so it is more sensible to choose a classic menu, and to produce it really well, than to attempt too ambitious dishes which you might feel a bit anxious about, or which could go wrong. Atmosphere is as important to a party as good food and drink. You want the occasion to be relaxed and happy, and you want to be able to talk to your guests rather than have a last minute flap in the kitchen. Use first-class ingredients, cook them to perfection and this simple menu should provide a delicious meal and an evening to remember.

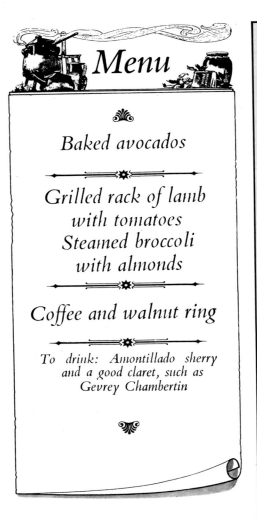

Menu

❧

Baked avocados

━━━✵━━━

*Grilled rack of lamb
with tomatoes
Steamed broccoli
with almonds*

━━━✵━━━

Coffee and walnut ring

━━━✵━━━

*To drink: Amontillado sherry
and a good claret, such as
Gevrey Chambertin*

❧

Countdown timetable

THE DAY BEFORE

Coffee and walnut ring: bake and decorate – steps 1–20.
Wash or polish your china, cutlery and glass.

ON THE DAY

Do any special shopping early in the day.
Grilled rack of lamb: prepare the meat – steps 1–4.
Baked avocados: prepare the stuffing – steps 1–7.
Lay the table, arrange flowers and prepare the drinks and, if possible, the coffee trays.

1 hour before the meal

Baked avocados: halve the avocados and stuff them – steps 9–11.
Heat the grill.

$\frac{3}{4}$ hour before the meal

Warm the oven.
Grilled rack of lamb: put the meat under the grill, basting regularly – steps 6–8.

$\frac{1}{2}$ hour before the meal

Baked avocados: put them in the oven – step 12.
Steamed broccoli with almonds: prepare the broccoli – steps 1–2.
Place the plates, serving dish and vegetable dish in the plate warmer.

10 minutes before the meal

Steamed broccoli with almonds: melt the butter – step 3.
Grilled rack of lamb: prepare the tomatoes and grill – step 9.

5 minutes before the meal

Steamed broccoli with almonds: put the broccoli to steam – step 4.
Grilled rack of lamb: turn the meat and tomatoes on to a serving dish and put on frills. Put in the oven and turn the heat off – step 10.
Baked avocados: remove from the oven and serve.

Between courses

Steamed broccoli with almonds: turn on to a serving dish. Foam the butter, add to it the almonds and pour over the broccoli – steps 5–7.

GETTING ORGANIZED

The more preparations you can do in advance the less chance there is of a last minute panic.

Our menu and timetable are deliberately planned to leave you comparatively few and simple jobs to do on the evening itself, so you will have time to enjoy a relaxing hot bath beforehand and get into the party mood.

The coffee and walnut ring can be completed the day before. The meat and the avocado stuffing can be prepared early on the same day. Both the first course and the cake are rather rich, so a clean, fresh-tasting main course is provided to balance the meal.

Remember that china which you don't often use may need washing before putting on the table, and glasses may need polishing, and so may the table. These are more jobs that can be done the day before.

On the day itself allow plenty of time for table laying. If the room is free, lay the table early in the day. If you are going to lay the table at the beginning of the actual evening, allow extra time if you want to arrange flowers.

Put the glasses for the pre-dinner drinks on a separate tray with the bottles and any extras, such as salted peanuts and ashtrays, and put it in the sitting area. If you can prepare the after-dinner coffee things and put them out of the way on a second tray, so much the better.

PRE-DINNER DRINKS

Sherry is the perfect pre-dinner drink and, unlike many patent aperitifs that clash with it, enhances the food that follows. Spanish sherry is undoubtedly the best, and one in the middle of the range, between sweet and dry, such as amontillado is likely to suit most tastes.

The first course of the dinner planned here is too spicy to go well with the wine, so you can ask your guests to bring their sherry glasses to the table when the meal is served.

SHOPPING CHECKLIST

If you haven't time to make your own cutlet frills, you can buy these at the paper goods section of most department stores.

You will need two cutlets for each person, so choose two meaty best ends of neck of lamb, each with six cutlets.

Buy the best quality home-produced meat for a party and do not be tempted to buy cheaper imported meat for this recipe. Ask the butcher to skin the meat and to chine it for easier serving, but to keep each rack in one piece. Make sure he does not cut through the end of the cutlet bones, otherwise they will be too short to decorate.

SPECIAL EQUIPMENT

For the cake you require a 20–22.5 cm [8–9″] ring mould. If you are buying this, look for one which you can turn out easily. Alternatively, an ordinary shallow cake tin of 17.5 cm [7″] diameter will do.

Baked avocados

⧗ *This is an unusual hot first course – usually avocados are served raw. Baked avocados are easy to make and the stuffing can be prepared well in advance of the meal.*

SERVES 6
3 avocado pears
4 medium-sized eggs
75 g [3 oz] salami
125 g [¼ lb] fresh white bread
3.5 ml [¾ teaspoon] mustard powder
7.5 ml [1½ teaspoons] curry powder
75 g [3 oz] butter
125 ml [4 fl oz] milk
salt
freshly ground black pepper
lemon juice

1 Hard-boil the eggs. When cooked, shell and put them in a bowl of cold water.

2 Reduce the bread to crumbs using a liquidizer or cheese grater.

3 Reserve three-quarters of the crumbs for the stuffing, and put the remainder on a baking sheet in the bottom of the oven, 140 C [275 F] gas mark 1 for 10 minutes, or until toasted.

4 Using a sharp knife, nick the salami skin along the length of the sausage and peel away the skin. Chop it into small dice and put it into a mixing bowl.

5 Drain, dry and chop the eggs and add them to the bowl.

6 Melt half the butter in a heavy-based pan and pour into the mixing bowl.

7 Add the mustard powder, curry powder, the milk and a little salt and pepper, and mix to blend well. Cover the bowl and put it aside.

8 Heat the oven to 190°C [375°F] gas mark 5.

9 Halve and stone the avocados.

Brush the cut surfaces with lemon juice to prevent discolouration.

10 Butter a baking dish and put the avocados into it. Fill the hollows with the stuffing and press it down well with the back of a spoon.

11 Sprinkle each top with toasted breadcrumbs and dot with remaining butter.

12 Cook for 25 minutes, or until the tops are well browned.

Baked avocados are hot and spicy, and this is an unusual way to serve them. Add lemon wedges to squeeze over them.

Grilled rack of lamb with tomatoes

⧖ *In principle, meat is best prepared immediately before cooking, but you can do it earlier in the day or get the butcher to do it for you. As the cut surfaces are small, it won't lose much flavour.*

Remember to baste occasionally during cooking and to cook the fat side last, so that the joint goes to the table golden and sizzling.

SERVES 6
**2 best ends of neck of lamb,
    each of 6 cutlets
75 g [3 oz] butter
6 large tomatoes
12 paper cutlet frills
salt and pepper**

1 Cut down 5 cm [2″] between the top of each cutlet bone and remove the intervening meat. Set this aside for use in stock.

2 Scrape away any shreds of meat or fat covering the bones. The end result should give a comb effect.

3 Lay the meat fat side up. Using the tip of a sharp knife, make light diagonal cuts across the fat.

4 Now make cuts in the opposite direction, so that a diamond pattern is formed.

5 Heat the grill until very hot.

6 Rub the lamb fat with 40 g [1½ oz] of the butter.

7 Place the meat under the grill and cook for 5 minutes on each side.

8 Reduce heat or move grill away from it. Cook, basting occasionally, for a further 15 minutes on each side for medium rare, 20 minutes on each side for well-done.

9 Five minutes before the meat is ready, prepare the tomatoes: melt the remaining butter in a pan, cut the tomatoes in half, brush the cut sides with butter and place under the grill.

10 Place the meat on a serving dish with the diamond side uppermost. Decorate each cutlet bone with a frill. Arrange the tomatoes in a circle around the meat.

To carve the meat, cut down between each cutlet bone. Hold the end of the bone if this makes cutting easier – the cutlet frill is there to keep your fingers clean. Arrange on the plate with two cutlets overlapping and the tomatoes in the curve.

Steamed broccoli with almonds

Steaming will help this delicate vegetable to keep its shape. The almonds add a touch of luxury and enhance its flavour. When heating the almonds, it is important to brown them over a low heat in a heavy-based pan. If the butter gets too hot, it will turn black and spoil the almonds.

SERVES 6
900 g [2 lb] broccoli spears
50 g [2 oz] butter
70 g [3 oz] flaked almonds
salt and pepper

1 Wash the broccoli, remove the leaves and trim off any woody-looking ends.

2 Half fill a saucepan with water and bring it to the boil.

3 Melt the butter in a heavy-based saucepan over low heat.

4 Place the broccoli in a steamer over the boiling water. Cover and cook for 10 minutes, or until the stalks are tender.

5 Just before serving, re-heat the butter until it is hot and add the almonds.

6 The butter will foam up. Cook the almonds for about 60 seconds, shaking the pan so that they brown evenly.

7 Turn the cooked broccoli into a serving dish. Sprinkle with salt and pepper and pour the almond butter on top.

Coffee and walnut ring

⧗⧗ *This delicious cake can be completely prepared in advance. The ring mould adds to its decorative appearance but you can cook the cake in a 17.5 cm [7"] cake tin, in which case allow 10 extra minutes cooking time. You can use broken walnut pieces for the filling but you need walnut halves for decorating.*

SERVES 8–10

100 g [$\frac{1}{4}$ lb] soft margarine
100 g [$\frac{1}{4}$ lb] caster sugar
2 eggs
100 g [$\frac{1}{4}$ lb] self-raising flour
5 ml [1 teaspoon] baking powder
15 ml [1 tablespoon] instant coffee
15 ml [1 tablespoon] milk

For the filling:
40 g [1$\frac{1}{2}$ oz] butter at room temperature
125 g [$\frac{1}{4}$ lb] icing sugar
20 ml [2 teaspoons] instant coffee
40 ml [4 teaspoons] milk
40 g [2 oz] walnut pieces

For the fudge icing:
50 g [2 oz] soft margarine or butter at room temperature
450 g [1 lb] icing sugar
30 ml [2 tablespoons] instant coffee
90 ml [6 tablespoons] milk
walnut halves for decorating

1 Heat the oven to 160°C [325°F] gas mark 3.

2 Grease a 20–22.5 cm [8–9"] ring mould, line it with greaseproof paper and grease the paper.

3 Put the milk into a cup and stir in the coffee until it dissolves.

4 Sieve the flour and baking powder together into a large warm mixing bowl.

5 Add the margarine and sugar to the bowl. Break in the eggs and add the coffee mixture. Beat with a wooden spoon for 2–3 minutes until glossy and light.

6 Turn the cake mixture into the mould, being careful to distribute it evenly around the ring.

7 Bake for 35–45 minutes.

8 Take the cake out of the oven, cool for 3 minutes, then turn out on to a wire cake rack. Leave for a minimum of 1$\frac{1}{2}$ hours until cold.

9 Chop the broken walnuts with a sharp knife until reduced to small and even pieces.

10 Make the filling. Dissolve the instant coffee in the milk.

11 Sieve the icing sugar into a bowl.

12 Add the butter, coffee mixture and nuts. Beat together for 2–3 minutes until well-mixed.

13 Cut the cake in half by pushing the knife through to the middle. Keep the knife steady and turn the cake.

14 Invert the bottom half of the cake, and spread the filling on the firm, browned side – the crumbs-side would stick to your knife. Sandwich the cake together again.

15 Make the icing. Dissolve the instant coffee in the milk.

16 Half fill a saucepan with water and place a trivet or scone-cutter in it, and stand a mixing basin on top. Set to heat.

17 When the water is simmering sieve the icing sugar into the basin.

18 Add the margarine (or butter) and coffee mixture, beat until the mixture is smooth.

19 Pour icing over the cake and smooth with a palette knife.

20 Stud with a ring of walnut halves before the icing sets.

Guests are bound to want second helpings of this delicious fudge-covered cake, and there's plenty of it so you can spoil them with generous portions.

A meal without meat for four

A vegetarian coming for dinner throws the average hostess into confusion. How can you even begin to think up a menu if there is no fish or meat to plan it round? Here is one answer to the problem—with a hot stuffed tomato for hors d'oeuvre, an onion and cheese flan with an unusual base of leaves for a main course, and a fruit meringue for dessert. It is a lovely, wholesome meal and you do not have to be a vegetarian to appreciate it.

Menu

Mushroom-stuffed tomatoes

Alsatian cabbage flan
Baked potato croquettes
with Tomato sauce

Apples in snow

To drink: lager or a Moselle

There is an innate fear in most meat-lovers that if they cut out their beloved chops and bacon they will suffer nutritionally. Everyone knows that meat and fish are rich sources of protein which the body needs to maintain and repair its cells. Without animal fats to plan round, you must eat with a little care and include other protein-rich food, such as pulses (beans of various sorts) and nuts, or the eggs and dairy produce used here. Potatoes and bread also contain protein in useful amounts.

Nutrition is only half the story. There is little inspiration in a meat-less meal if it is tasteless and soggy. This menu has a colourful Mediterranean starter of tomatoes stuffed with mushrooms, parsley and garlic. The main course is a creamy Alsatian flan to give the meal a centrepiece, full of flavourful onions with the tang of mustard and cheese. It is served with potato croquettes for a crisp contrast, accompanied by their own tomato sauce (use fresh or drained canned tomatoes).

The pudding is a classic one of stuffed apples covered with a little meringue—inexpensive but, because of its meringue topping, always something special.

This menu is in no way extravagant and is therefore suitable for a lunch or family meal. Because of its pleasant progression of tastes, how-ever, it is sufficiently attractive to serve at dinner to guests, vegetarian or otherwise.

Countdown timetable

During the morning or the day before
Make breadcrumbs, if necessary.
Apples in snow: make totally, cool and leave in refrigerator—steps 1-10.

2 hours before the meal
Mushroom-stuffed tomatoes: make tomato shells, salt inside and leave to drain—steps 1-2.
Tomato sauce: skin and de-seed tomatoes if fresh or drain if canned.
Baked potato croquettes: peel the potatoes and simmer—steps 1-3.

1¼ hours before the meal
Baked potato croquettes: make the potato purée—steps 4-5.

1 hour before the meal
Alsatian cabbage flan: prepare the onions and start cooking—steps 1-2.
Heat the oven to 200°C [400°F] gas mark 6—step 3.
Tomato sauce: purée tomatoes with 30 ml [2 tablespoons] stock. Season.
Baked potato croquettes: make the croquettes—steps 6-9.

Apples in snow: remove from the refrigerator to room temperature.

35 minutes before the meal
Alsatian cabbage flan: blanch the cabbage leaves, prepare the filling and make the flan—steps 4-10.

25 minutes before the meal
Alsatian cabbage flan: put in oven—step 11.
Mushroom-stuffed tomatoes: make the filling and stuff—steps 4-9.

15 minutes before the meal
Mushroom-stuffed tomatoes: put in oven on lower shelf—step 10.
Baked potato croquettes: dot with butter and put in oven—step 10.
Tomato sauce: gently heat tomato purée in a heavy-based pan but be careful not to boil. Keep warm.

Between first and main course
Alsation cabbage flan: garnish and serve—step 12.
Baked potato croquettes: garnish and serve—step 11.

GETTING ORGANIZED
For a contrast of a cold sweet after two hot courses, it is necessary to cook the apples in snow completely in advance—earlier in the day, or even the previous day. On the evening itself you will need 2 hours for cooking supper.

Many cooks, out at work all day, prefer to do everything possible well before an evening's entertaining and to leave precious minutes free on the evening itself. The tomato shells for the hors d'oeuvre can be prepared in advance up to step 2, and tomato sauce can be made completely. The potato for making the croquettes can be prepared earlier in the day up to stage 4, or even, if you know you will be pressed for time later, up to stage 9, and kept in the refrigerator ready for baking.

The insides of the tomatoes are used for a sauce to accompany the croquettes, but an additional 400 g [14 oz] can is needed to augment the quantity. On the evening itself you will then have to prepare the stuffing and fill the tomatoes and make the flan.

The oven is economically used to cook the starter as well as the whole of the main course. Once you have got these dishes into the oven you know your evening's work is almost done. The tomatoes would normally be baked at a rather lower heat than the one used here. Therefore arrange the oven shelves above and below the centre before you heat it and cook the tomatoes on the lower shelf.

Dried breadcrumbs can economi-cally be made out of those crusts that tend to accumulate uneaten in the bottom of the bread tin, if not removed.

SHOPPING CHECKLIST
This vegetarian menu definitely does not involve you in shopping from specialist health food shops. There is no ingredient that is particularly exotic—all are household familiars.

In the dairy department you will want half a dozen medium-sized

eggs. The pudding is economically designed to use the whites which are left over from the potatoes in the main course. All the vegetable dishes contain butter, so buy a 225 g [½ lb] packet. The main course requires 275 ml [½ pt] sour cream. If you cannot get this—normally available from supermarkets—make some at home by adding 10 ml [2 teaspoons] vinegar or lemon juice to 275 ml [½ pt] thin cream. Make sure you also have a bottle of creamy milk.

Check that you have flour and enough sugar. A 400 g [14 oz] can of tomatoes is needed for the sauce. For the filling for the apples buy 100 g [¼ lb] pressed dates. Pressed dates (which are stoneless) are a good deal cheaper than the luxury dessert dates often sold by greengrocers. Check that you have dry mustard, cayenne pepper, nutmeg, dried thyme and a bay leaf.

From the greengrocer you will need a cabbage with large loose outer leaves such as Savoy or Primo. The rest of the cabbage can be used for a weekday supper. Buy 450 g [1 lb] tomatoes, 900 g [2 lb] onions, 450 g [1 lb] potatoes, 100 g [¼ lb] mushrooms, a lemon and a bunch of parsley and

check that you have garlic in the house. Last of all you will need 4 big beautiful cooking apples for the dessert. Choose the apples individually, rather than buying a fixed weight of assorted sizes.

Mushroom-stuffed tomatoes

Succulent, hot, baked tomatoes always make a cheerful start to a meal. The tops and the insides of the tomatoes can be used for tomato sauce to save wastage.

If the tomatoes are to be cooked in the oven on their own without other dishes, bake them at 180°C [350°F] gas mark 4 for 20 minutes.

SERVES 4
4 medium-sized tomatoes
salt and pepper
50 g [2 oz] white bread
30 ml [2 tablespoons] lemon juice
30 ml [2 tablespoons] freshly chopped parsley
1 garlic clove
50 g [2 oz] mushrooms
25 g [1 oz] butter

1 Slice off the top of each tomato. Using a small spoon, scoop out the core and seeds from the cavity. Reserve the pulp and lids for another dish.

2 Salt the inside of the tomato shells and turn them upside down on a plate for 30 minutes to drain.

3 Turn oven to 200°C [400°F] gas mark 6.

4 Grate the bread into crumbs and put into a bowl. Add a squeeze of lemon juice and the chopped parsley.

5 Peel and chop the garlic clove. Slice then chop the mushrooms.

6 Melt the butter in a frying-pan and toss the garlic and mushrooms over a low heat for 2 minutes until the mushrooms have softened.

7 Add the mushroom mixture to the bread in the bowl. Season with salt and pepper.

8 Rinse the tomato shells and pat dry with paper. Divide the stuffing

equally between the four shells and pile into the tomatoes.

9 Grease a gratin dish (or use 4 individual cocottes) and put tomatoes in the dish.

10 Bake for 15 minutes.

Alsatian cabbage flan

This flan is based on the famous French Alsatian flan, which has a creamy onion filling, but instead of pastry, a lining of cabbage leaves is used (or use blanched spinach leaves). This makes the dish both economical and light enough to serve to anyone who is watching their waistline. For the lining, you will need the large outer leaves from a green winter, Savoy or Primo cabbage.

SERVES 4
700 g [1½ lb] onions
50 g [2 oz] butter
6-8 large green cabbage leaves
3 medium-sized eggs
275 ml [½ pt] sour cream
100 g [¼ lb] Cheddar cheese
5 ml [1 teaspoon] dry mustard
salt and pepper
5 ml [1 teaspoon] cooking oil
paprika

1 Skin and finely chop the onion. If peeling a large quantity of onions makes your eyes run, peel the onions under a tap of running water. Slice the onions finely.

2 Melt the butter in a large, heavy-based frying-pan. Add the onions and cook over very low heat for 25 minutes. Stir them from time to time so that the top slices go to the bottom. At the end of this time they should be soft and golden coloured.

3 Heat the oven to 200°C [400°F] gas mark 6.

4 Trim away any very coarse central stalks from the cabbage leaves.

5 Bring a large pan of salted water to the boil. Blanch the cabbage leaves for 2 minutes. Remove from the water and drain on kitchen paper.

6 Break the eggs into a bowl and beat lightly with a fork. Add the sour cream and stir to mix.

7 Grate the cheese and add it to the cream mixture in the bowl. Add the mustard powder and season generously to taste.

8 Beat the cream and egg mixture into the onions.

9 Brush a 22.5 cm [9"] flan tin or gratin dish with oil. Use the cabbage leaves to line the tin, arranging them with the stalks at the edge of the flan tin or dish until bottom and sides are covered. Trim off edges if necessary.

10 Place the onion filling in the lined tin and level off with a spatula.

11 Bake in the centre of the oven for 30 minutes.

12 Sprinkle with paprika and serve hot, cutting the flan into wedges.

Baked potato croquettes

A change from boiled and mashed, these baked potatoes from Austria have a crispy finish. They may be deep-

fried but in this recipe they are baked in the oven. This dish may be made from left-over cold mashed potato (and is a pleasant and economical way of using it up) but is best made from specially prepared potato. These croquettes are prepared by the same egg and crumbing technique used for escalopes of veal or pork. This quantity makes 6-7 croquettes each for four. Serve with tomato sauce.

SERVES 4
450 g [1 lb] potatoes
salt and pepper
65-75 g [2½-3 oz] butter
2 yolks, used separately
30 ml [2 tablespoons] top of
   the milk plus 30 ml [2
   tablespoons] milk
pinch of nutmeg
pinch of cayenne pepper
50-75 g [2-3 oz] dried
   breadcrumbs
parsley sprigs to garnish

1 Peel the potatoes and cut medium-sized potatoes in half, large ones into quarters.

2 Prepare a pan of boiling water. Salt it and simmer the potatoes for 15 minutes until just cooked but not mushy.

3 Turn the potatoes into a colander and drain.

4 Put 25 g [1 oz] of the butter in the bottom of the warm saucepan. If you have a vegetable mill, purée the potatoes back into the sauce-pan. Otherwise mash the potatoes very thoroughly in the pan, using a potato masher, taking care to eliminate all lumps.

5 Add one egg yolk, seasonings, the top of the milk, nutmeg and cayenne and stir to mix. Allow the potato to cool slightly.

6 Using lightly floured hands, and a lightly floured work surface as well if you wish, roll a heaped serving spoonful of potato into a sausage shape. This should be bullet shaped, about 4 cm [1½"] long and 2 cm [¾"] thick. If you find it easier, roll out a long sausage on the work surface and cut it into 4 cm [1½"] lengths with a knife. Continue until all the potato has been turned into croquettes.

7 Put the second egg yolk on a saucer. Add the remaining milk and beat together with a fork to mix. Arrange a plate with the browned breadcrumbs close by.

8 Roll each croquette first in the egg liquid to cover then in the crumbs to coat it. Tap each end of the croquette lightly on the plate to ensure that the ends are coated and to maintain the shape.

9 Use some of the butter to grease a gratin dish big enough to hold 24 or so croquettes, or use a swiss roll tin. Arrange the croquettes in rows and dot each one with a little of the remaining butter.

10 Bake on the top shelf of the oven for 20 minutes.

11 If baked on a swiss roll tin, transfer to a warmed vegetable dish. Garnish with parsley sprigs and serve.

Apples in snow

☒ *This festive-looking dessert is actually simple to make and inexpensive as well. On an occasion when you wish to add a touch of luxury, serve a chocolate or apricot sauce round the edge of the meringue. For this menu, the sweet is cold as a contrast to the other two hot courses;* *but apples in snow is equally nice hot. Pears or peaches can be served in the same way.*

SERVES 4
4 large cooking apples
125 g [¼ lb] granulated sugar
7.5 ml [½ tablespoon] butter
100 g [¼ lb] pressed dates
2 egg whites
pinch of salt
125 g [¼ lb] caster sugar

1 Put 550 ml [1 pt] water into a pan and bring to the boil. Add the sugar and boil hard for 2 minutes to make a syrup.

2 Peel and core the apples and poach in the syrup over a very gentle heat for 10–15 minutes, turning and basting frequently.

3 Heat the oven to 200°C [400°F] gas mark 6.

4 Mash the butter with a fork in the bowl. Chop the dates finely and add to the bowl. Mix in, adding a spoonful of syrup if necessary to make the mixture adhere.

5 Drain the apples and arrange in a fireproof dish. Fill the centres with the date mixture.

6 Place the whites in a clean dry bowl.

7 Whisk with a small pinch of salt, until the egg white stands up in stiff peaks.

8 Add half of the caster sugar and whisk slowly for 3 minutes. Then fold in the rest.

9 Pile the meringue over the apples, using the handle of a spoon to rough the top into peaks.

10 Bake in the centre of the oven for 10 minutes. Serve hot or allow to cool for a cold sweet.

Celebration dinner for eight

Here is a special menu to enjoy on a celebratory occasion when you want to splash out a little and do things in style. It is not the cheapest of menus but, considering how impressive looking and memorably delicious the dishes are, you will agree that it is good value.

PUTTING ON THE STYLE

A home-produced cut of beef suitable for roasting is definitely in the luxury price bracket these days. So, when you buy one, you want to serve it with maximum style to make the occasion memorable.

This menu is carefully planned around a roast fore rib to provide a distinctly impressive meal, but one that is not so rich as to make guests reach into their pockets in search of indigestion tablets. Colours, textures and flavours balance each other well.

The first course is a refreshing purée soup which makes cunning use of convenience foods to produce ritzy results with a decidedly home-made flavour. It is quick to prepare and could be made the day before. Serve it with grissini (crisp breadsticks).

For the beef, an unusual and trouble-free method of roasting is introduced which makes it ideal for entertaining. The rich flavour of the meat is complemented by a robust sauce and, to offset this, the vege-

tables are deliberately plain (this is an occasion to omit tossing the vegetables in butter). And a bonus for the cook—the joint is a large one so leftovers should provide you with an excellent roast beef salad on the following day.

Flaming fruit kebabs end the meal with a dramatic flourish: fresh fruity flavours, heightened by flaming with brandy and accompanied by a spiced cream, the richness of which is tempered by the inclusion of sour cream.

Menu

Instant iced tomato soup with grissini

❈

No-roast beef with shallot sauce
Newly minted potatoes and mange-tout

❈

Flaming fruit kebabs with cinnamon orange cream

❈

To drink: dry sherry before dinner and to accompany the soup; a good claret, such as Margaux or St Julien, to serve with the main course

DECORATING THE TABLE

As every woman knows, candle-light is the most flattering light there is. However, tall candlesticks, like big flower arrangements, can screen guests from each other and divide the dinner-table.

A dish of floating candles is low enough to avoid creating such a barrier; it looks very pretty and is rather unusual. Use one large, shallow glass dish half filled with water and place it in the centre of the table. Alternatively, use finger-bowls, placing one beside each guest, to create small pools of soft light all round the table. If your budget allows, float a few flowers on the surface of the water together with the candles.

SHOPPING CHECKLIST

Order the fore rib in advance from a butcher who hangs his meat well, and ask him to bone and roll it for you. The final weight should be 2.25 kg [5 lb].

Check that you have black and

Countdown timetable

ON THE DAY

3 hours 20 minutes before the meal
No-roast beef with shallot sauce: heat oven, prepare meat—steps 1-3.
Flaming fruit kebabs: whip cream, prepare fruit and chill—steps 1-7.

2 hours 45 minutes before the meal
No-roast beef with shallot sauce: roast joint, start sauce—steps 4-7.
Instant iced tomato soup: make soup and chill together with soup cups—steps 1-8.

2 hours before the meal
No-roast beef with shallot sauce: switch off oven, continue making sauce—steps 8-10.
Flaming fruit kebabs: skewer and wrap the fruit, measure liquor—steps 8-11.
Lay table, drinks and coffee trays. Decant wine and leave at room temperature.

30 minutes before the meal
Newly minted potatoes and mange-tout: prepare vegetables—steps 1-2.
Put plates, dishes and sauce-boat (if

using) to warm. Put cream and grissini in dining-room.

20 minutes before the meal
Newly minted potatoes and mange-tout: cook potatoes, chop mint—steps 3-5.

5 minutes before the meal
Instant iced tomato soup: dry cups, garnish soup and take into dining room—step 9.
Light candles.

2 minutes before the meal
No-roast beef with shallot sauce: add meat drippings to sauce, reheat sauce and joint, switching oven to 260°C [500°F] gas mark 10—steps 11-13.
Newly minted potatoes and mange-tout: add mange-tout to steamer—step 6.

Between first and main course
Newly minted potatoes and mange-tout: dish and season—step 7.
No-roast beef with shallot sauce: dish joint, add cream to sauce and pour over or put into sauce-boat—step 14.
Flaming fruit kebabs: switch oven to 190°C [375°F] gas mark 5 and start cooking—step 12.

Between main course and dessert
Flaming fruit kebabs: dish and flame with liqueur—steps 13-15.

white peppercorns, ground cinnamon, thyme, claret, sherry, a miniature bottle of brandy and plenty of foil (wide rolls are best for wrapping the kebabs).

Go to a delicatessen or Italian grocer for grissini and large pitted (stoneless) prunes.

You will need a total of 275 ml [½ pt] thick cream (a few spoonfuls for the shallot sauce and the remainder for the cinnamon orange cream), 425 ml [¾ pt] sour cream (a few spoonfuls for the cinnamon orange cream and the rest for the soup) and 150 ml [¼ pt] plain yoghurt.

It is worth paying a little extra for really small new potatoes (they look so pretty) and mange-tout (large ones can be stringy), and for fruit that is in prime condition. You will also need shallots or pickling onions (the latter are cheaper), garlic and a bunch of mint.

Finally, floating candles can be bought from department stores. Buy flowers with simple blossoms and a box of matches to light the candles and ignite the kebabs.

SPECIAL EQUIPMENT

You will need a large steamer to cook the vegetables, and eight 17.5-20 cm [7-8"] skewers for the kebabs. These must be plain metal ones (fancy handles made of other materials might buckle, melt or burn in the heat of the oven).

A liquidizer is used to purée the soup but you could use a sieve instead—although the soup would not be quite so instant.

A bain-marie or double-boiler is used to reheat the sauce. If you don't own one, improvise by standing a covered bowl on a trivet in a saucepan half filled with water.

Instant iced tomato soup

⊠ *The subtle flavour of this prettily coloured soup will lead diners to believe that you must have spent many hours in the kitchen creaming it. In fact, it takes only a matter of minutes and is marvellously easy to prepare.*

For best results, chill the tomatoes, sour cream and yoghurt for at least four hours before making the soup. This is a successful alternative to chilling the soup after it has been made. For a professional touch, chill the soup cups too. To do this, put a few ice cubes into each cup and place the cups in the refrigerator. Empty out the ice and dry the cups just before serving. Plain white soup cups show off the soup best.

Always use canned whole tomatoes: tomato juice would make preparation even more speedy but the resulting soup would be very thin.

SERVES 8
1.25 kg [2¾ lb] canned tomatoes
350 ml [12 fl oz] sour cream
150 ml [¼ pt] plain yoghurt
1 garlic clove
salt
1 large lemon
25 g [1 oz] caster sugar
freshly ground white pepper
sprigs of mint

1 Peel and chop the garlic. Using the back of the knife, crush it with some salt. Put it into a soup tureen or large mixing bowl.

2 Stir the sour cream until it is smooth and creamy, then turn it into the soup tureen or bowl.

3 Stir the yoghurt in the same way. Add three quarters of it to the tureen and blend to mix thoroughly with the sour cream and garlic.

4 Turn the canned tomatoes and their juices into a liquidizer and blend until reduced to a purée.

5 To remove the tomato seeds, pass the purée through a nylon sieve (metal would taint the flavour) into the tureen. Do this in batches, pressing down on the tomatoes with a vegetable press or the back

of a wooden spoon. Rinse the tomato seeds out of the sieve between batches.

6 Squeeze the lemon and add 45 ml [3 tablespoons] juice to the soup.

7 Add the caster sugar and a good grinding of white pepper (black pepper would speckle the soup and spoil its appearance). Mix well with a wooden spoon and taste. Add more lemon juice, sugar, salt and/or pepper if wished.

8 If not serving immediately, cover the soup and refrigerate. (This soup can safely be kept in the refrigerator for 24 hours or more.)

9 Stir the soup before serving and dribble the remaining yoghurt over the surface, pouring it over the back of a spoon as though adding cream to coffee.

OR half stir the yoghurt into the soup to create a marbled effect. Garnish with sprigs of mint.

No-roast beef with shallot sauce

▨▨▨ *If you like rare beef, here is a real treat: pink, succulent meat with a richly crusted surface and a robust accompanying sauce. The unusual roasting method given here is ideal for joints of beef weighing 2.25 kg [5 lb] or more after boning, but is unsuitable for smaller joints. It is essential that the correct oven temperature is reached before the meat is put into the oven; the joint is roasted for 9 minutes per 450 g [1 lb] then left in the oven for 2 hours with the heat switched off. Do not open the door during this time.*

SERVES 8

2.25 kg [5 lb] boned and rolled fore rib of beef
40 g [1½ oz] dripping
2.5 ml [½ teaspoon] dried thyme
salt and pepper
16 shallots or small pickling onions
50 g [2 oz] butter
200 ml [7 fl oz] red wine
60 ml [4 tablespoons] French mustard
90 ml [6 tablespoons] thick cream

1 Switch the oven to 260°C [500°F] gas mark 10. Allow 30 minutes to reach the correct temperature—some ovens may require a little longer.

2 Meanwhile prepare the meat. Sprinkle your work surface with the thyme and some salt and pepper. Roll the joint in the mixture to coat the surface fat. Do not season the cut surfaces of the meat.

3 Spread the dripping over the entire surface of the joint, and put the joint on a rack in a roasting tin.

4 When the correct oven temperature is reached, put the tin on the centre shelf and roast the beef for 45 minutes.

5 Meanwhile start preparing the sauce. Chop the shallots finely.

6 Melt the butter in a heavy-based saucepan. Add the shallots and shake the pan to coat them evenly with the fat.

7 Cover the pan and sweat for 20-25 minutes.

8 Switch off the oven as soon as roasting time is up but leave the joint inside the oven for a further two hours. Do not, on any account, open the oven door during this time.

9 When the shallots are softened, pour on the wine, increase heat and bring to the boil. Boil for 4 minutes or until the wine has reduced to a few spoonfuls.

10 Remove the pan from the heat, stir in the mustard plus a generous seasoning of salt and freshly ground black pepper. Then transfer the sauce to the upper part of a double boiler or a heatproof bowl and set aside.

14 Turn the hot joint on to a warmed serving dish. Stir the cream into the sauce and serve in a sauce-boat. If wished the beef may be carved in the kitchen and sauce poured over the slices on the serving dish before serving.

Newly minted potatoes and mange-tout

This is a simple but excellent summery vegetable dish. The vegetables are open steamed in the same pan, the mange-tout being added later as they cook relatively quickly. If serving as an accompaniment to a plainly cooked meat dish, toss the vegetables in butter just before serving.

SERVES 8
900 g [2 lb] new potatoes
700 g [1½ lb] mange-tout peas
a few sprigs of mint
salt and pepper

1 Scrub the potatoes but do not peel them. Place them in a steamer basket.

2 Top and tail the mange-tout and set aside.

3 Choose a pan into which the steamer fits snugly. Put some water into the pan, but not so much as will touch the base of the steamer basket. Bring to the boil over medium heat.

4 Add the steamer basket containing the potatoes, cover the pan with a well-fitting lid and reduce heat so that the water simmers gently.

5 Meanwhile chop the mint finely.

6 When the potatoes have been steaming for 20 minutes, put the mange-tout on top of them and continue cooking for a further 10 minutes.

7 Turn the cooked vegetables into a warmed serving dish, sprinkle with salt, freshly ground black pepper and the chopped mint. Toss lightly and serve immediately.

11 When the two hours are up, take the joint out of the oven. Carefully pour off surplus fat. Scrape the meat drippings from the base of the roasting tin and add them to the sauce.

12 If the joint is still hot, it can be served straight away. But most ovens do not retain their heat that well: the chances are that the beef is somewhat tepid and requires reheating to be eaten at its best. So

return the joint to the roasting tin and put it back in the oven. Switch the heat to 260°C [500°F] gas mark 10 again and leave for 10-15 minutes—this will raise the temperature of the beef without affecting its rareness.

13 Meanwhile reheat the sauce in the boiler top or covered bowl placed over a pan of gently simmering water. (Do not warm the sauce on direct heat.)

Flaming fruit kebabs with cinnamon orange cream

⊠⊠ *Use pitted (stoneless) prunes, firm bananas and ripe dessert fruit for this dish.*

The instructions in step 12 apply only when cooking the kebabs in conjunction with the no-roast beef given in this menu. When following the recipe in other circumstances, preheat the oven to 200°C [400°F] gas mark 6, then bake the kebabs for 10-15 minutes. Alternatively, grill the kebabs for 5-10 minutes under medium heat, in which case no foil is needed but the fruit should be turned and basted occasionally with melted butter.

For economy's sake the brandy and cream could be omitted. Instead, warm the macerating liquor and pour it over the kebabs just before serving.

SERVES 8
200 ml [7 fl oz] thick cream
90 ml [6 tablespoons] sour cream
15 ml [1 tablespoon] icing sugar
15 ml [3 teaspoons] ground cinnamon
1 large orange
1 large lemon
60 ml [4 tablespoons] soft brown sugar
16 large pitted prunes or 8 dessert plums

8 apricots or small peaches
2 small dessert pears
4 large, firm bananas
45 ml [3 tablespoons] brandy

1 Grate the orange zest and reserve.

2 Lightly whip cream to the soft stage. Sift icing sugar. Add the sour cream, sifted icing sugar, reserved orange zest and 5 ml [1 teaspoon] cinnamon, folding them in gently. Transfer to a sauce-boat, cover and chill.

3 If using prunes, put them in a small pan, pour on boiling water, cover and simmer for 10 minutes. Then set the covered pan aside for 40 minutes.

4 Squeeze the orange and lemon juice into a large mixing bowl. Stir in the sugar and remaining ground cinnamon.

5 If using peaches, plunge them in boiling water for 1 minute, drain and refresh. Skin, halve, stone and put into the mixing bowl.

6 Halve and stone apricots and plums if used. Peel, quarter and core pears. Peel bananas and cut each into four pieces. Add to the fruit bowl.

7 Toss the fruit lightly with your hands to coat all over, cover the bowl and refrigerate for one hour to allow full flavours to be absorbed—this is called macerating.

8 Drain prunes and macerated fruit (serve liquor for a delicious fruity drink) and thread on to metal skewers. Each kebab should include a piece of banana, apricot or peach, prune or plum, pear, prune or plum, apricot or peach and banana in that order.

9 Lay the kebabs in a single layer in the centre of a very large double-thick sheet of foil (there is no need to grease the foil). Fold the sides and ends of the foil over the top and crimp firmly to seal the parcel. (Take care to prevent the skewer points from piercing the foil.)

10 Lay the parcel in a large ovenproof dish (do not use a baking sheet) and chill until required.

11 Measure the brandy into a small pan and set aside.

12 Switch the oven to 190°C [375°F] gas mark 5 and immediately put the ovenproof dish containing the kebab parcel into the oven. Cook for 20-25 minutes.

13 Using an oven cloth, unwrap the kebabs and lay them directly in the ovenproof dish.

14 Put the brandy pan over medium heat.

15 Carry the kebab dish into the dining-room. Pour the warmed brandy over the fruit and immediately set it alight. Serve as soon as the flames have died down.

A grand dinner party for six

Here is a menu for a really special night, with the sort of dishes usually seen only at the best restaurants. The food is far from cheap, but still a fraction of the price you would pay eating out. It is a meal truly worthy of the advanced cook, yet— thanks to the simple recipe instructions and timetable on the following pages— within the grasp of every hostess. And your guests? They'll still be talking about this dinner a year from now!

Menu

Prosciutto with melon

Fruits de mer (Shellfish with a duchesse potato border)

Cauliflower and French beans à la grecque

Nègre en chemise (Cold chocolate soufflé)

To drink: St Clement's cocktail beforehand, and a white burgundy such as Chassagne Montrachet with the meal.

Just occasionally, dinner needs to be something really great: when the boss is invited for example, or your tenth wedding anniversary arrives, or old friends return from foreign parts after years of absence. It is on such a night that you really want to push the boat out. Expense becomes a secondary consideration and glamorous, glorious food is the first priority. With this sort of date in mind, the main course of this menu is one of those magnificent shellfish cocktails in a delicious creamy wine sauce, served surrounded by ornamental piped duchesse potato. It is the kind of dish that head waiters display to diners with huge ceremony before serving. Do the same—boast about your 'fruits de mer'; show it off. Guests will remember it for years.

Because fish has such a delicate taste the fruits de mer—literally translated means fruits of the sea—is served without an accompanying vegetable or side salad. Instead, a cold vegetable course of cauliflower, beans and tomato in a vinaigrette is brought in afterwards. This will refresh the palate before the extremely rich soufflé dessert. Nègre en chemise has been described as the nearest thing to eating a bar of dark chocolate known to the cook. As you will see from the recipe, it is a steamed soufflé which is unmoulded when cold—quite different from the hot baked soufflés that must be served immediately. To achieve the correct shape, it should be cooked in a tall, tapering bowl of 1.7 L [3 pt] capacity. If your pudding bowl is short and fat,

perhaps you could substitute a metal measuring jug.

With so much rich, fancy food on the menu, the starter course needs to be fresh, cold and plain—and what better choice than melon with Parma ham? Raw ham costs so much it is automatically a rarity of the dinner-table and thus a treat, but if cut paper-thin, as this dish demands, you get the 6 slices you need for 100 g [¼ lb]. Melon makes a popular accompaniment, and a ripe honeydew or cantaloupe is the best choice.

GETTING ORGANIZED

When giving such a special dinner party, it would be heartbreaking if one of your pairs of guests could not make it; so obviously the first thing to

Countdown timetable

THE WEEK BEFORE
Issue the invitations.
Order shellfish.

THE DAY BEFORE
Do the shopping, except for shellfish.
Make the fish stock. Strain it and reduce to 150 ml [¼ pt].
Nègre en chemise: make and store in the refrigerator—steps 1-10.
Cauliflower and French beans à la grecque: make and chill in the refrigerator—steps 1-8.
Tidy dining room. Arrange flowers.

ON THE DAY
In the morning
Buy the shellfish.
Chill the wine.
Fruits de mer: clean the mussels—step 1.

In the afternoon
Fruits de mer: prepare the shellfish and fish and reserve in the refrigerator—steps 2-3.
Set the table.
Prosciutto with melon: prepare and slice the melon, cover with Parma ham—steps 1-2.
Nègre en chemise: whip the cream and add sherry, and pour over the soufflé—step 11.

3 hours before the meal
Fruits de mer: peel and cook the potatoes, cream them and pipe the duchesse border onto the serving plate—steps 4-6.
St Clement's cocktail: mix spirit and fruit juice in cocktail shaker and leave in the refrigerator—steps 1-3.
Prosciutto with melon: arrange portions on small plates, and set round table.

2 hours before the meal
Fruits de mer: start cooking the mussels and shell them—steps 7-9 and 11.
Heat the oven to 160°C [325°F] gas mark 3—step 10.
1 hour free to get self ready.

40 minutes before the meal
St Clement's cocktail: whisk the egg white and add—step 4.
Greet the guests with a drink.

30 minutes before the meal
Fruits de mer: Put the serving plate into the oven to reheat the duchesse potato and to brown the edges—step 12.
Cook the rest of the fish and make the velouté sauce—steps 13-17.

10 minutes before the meal
·Turn the oven to low and put in the main course plates to warm.
Fruits de mer: add the fish to the sauce, add the extra seasonings and transfer to serving plate. Cover and reserve in oven—steps 18-21.
Light the candles on the table and sit down to the prosciutto with melon.

do is to issue firm invitations for your big night. Eight for 8:30 is probably the most popular time for a dinner party, giving you half an hour for cocktails.

Also in the preceding week, order the fish. Mussels and scallops are particularly hard to find in some areas, even when in season, and should be bought fresh on the day.

If the worst does come to the worst, and you cannot get the shellfish when all is planned and guests invited, you could substitute another main course. To fit between the proscuitto with melon starter and the rich dessert of nègre en chemise, you could serve tournedos Mirabeau (see pages 123–125). This is an expensive meat dish, but, after all, the menu is planned for a special occasion. If you do decide to substitute the steaks, you may feel the need for some potatoes. A basic duchesse mixture piped into shapes on a baking sheet and baked in a moderate oven until just lightly browned and heated through, would be a good accompaniment for succulent steaks.

The day before the party, do all the shopping with the exception of the shellfish—risky if not purchased fresh on the day itself. Then make the fish stock. If you have a freezer, it is a good idea to have fish stock in there as a matter of course; just as you would probably keep beef and chicken stock constantly on hand. Dozens of fish dishes are hugely improved by a proper stock base, but it is a bore to boil up fish heads and trimmings etc too frequently. So here is one instance where batch cooking really pays off.

The nègre en chemise can be made totally in advance, which is comforting. It's nice to know on the eve of a party that at least one course is ready and waiting for the morrow. The vegetables can be made in advance and improve by having time to absorb the dressing.

If you wish, the day before, too, you can tidy up the eating area and arrange the flowers. For a party as grand as this one, table flowers are almost obligatory. Whether you choose to do these two jobs the day before or on the morning will probably depend on (a) whether you are a working girl and accordingly when you are at home, and (b) whether you have a young family who are likely to mess the room up again if there is an ensuing interval!

As the timetable stands, the party morning is very easy-going. You collect the shellfish, put the wine and ice to chill and do the mucky, fiddly job of cleaning the mussels. There is plenty of time for having your hair done and so on.

After lunch there is a number of small jobs. Prepare all the shellfish—but do not cook it. Prepare the first course by de-seeding and slicing the melon—two thin slices for each guest—and arrange ham over the portions. Leave the slices on a big plate in the refrigerator covered with cling film.

Whip the sherry into the cream and pour this on to the top of the chocolate soufflé to make the 'chemise'. This can then be put on the sideboard, ready to serve later.

With a dinner as grand as this one, it would be a shame to serve the fruits de mer at less than their very best. For this reason you will have to be in the kitchen for the last half-hour, with only a few minutes off to greet your guests on their arrival. The duchesse potato border of the fruits de mer, however, can be done ahead, and reheated, without anyone noticing; this is scheduled for the first job at 5 o'clock when cooking starts in earnest. You could, however, make the potato border in the afternoon, if it would add to your sense of security. The potato is then reheated nearer the dinner hour.

Before you disappear to decorate yourself in honour of the occasion, mix the cocktail base unless, of course, you are relying on your man to do it for you. Transfer the melon slices to individual plates at each place setting, and you can go off knowing that the first two items on the agenda are ready and waiting.

When you return to the kitchen you have an hour for the main course. Shellfish only need the briefest cooking, but you have also to make the rich velouté sauce. Half way through you must put the potato in the oven to reheat.

Turn down the oven 10 minutes before the meal, when you put the plates to warm. Cover the fruits de mer in their velouté sauce with buttered greaseproof paper to prevent a skin forming while your guests are enjoying their first course. Then light your candles and invite your guests to the table.

THE DRINKS

With such a magnificent spread, this is the occasion for a good French wine. The menu card therefore suggests a vintage white burgundy like Chassagne Montrachet: superb and dry. To keep six people topped up for two courses—the fruits de mer and the cold vegetable dish which follows it—you must buy two bottles.

In place of the usual shorts—gin and vermouths, vodka and fruit juices etc—why not make a proper Thirties cocktail in true silver shaker (or glass jug if you do not possess a shaker)? The St Clement's cocktail contains all the usual spirits to satisfy sophisticates, but the clever addition of citrus fruit and egg white also make it light enough to tempt more hesitant brethren. Its subtle, refreshing taste seems almost innocuous. It isn't—but your guests will not discover that until far too late!

St.Clement's cocktail

This festive drink looks its most impressive served from a silver cocktail shaker. But because this particular cocktail—in true James Bond fashion—is stirred, not shaken, this is certainly not essential. A glass jug will serve equally well. Do not add the whisked egg white until the last minute.

SERVES 6
5 parts gin
1 part Cointreau
3 parts sweetened orange juice
2 lemons
1 egg white

1 Place a few ice cubes in the cocktail shaker or serving jug.

2 Using the same measure to ensure correct proportions (a cocktail glass makes a convenient measure), pour in the gin, Cointreau and canned or bottled orange juice.

3 Squeeze the lemons and add the juice to the cocktail. Mix well.

4 Whisk the egg white thoroughly and add to the cocktail. Mix again and serve.

Fruits de mer

◨◨ Here is a spectacular main course for a special dinner party. The fruits of the sea are a mixture of shellfish: mussels, prawns, and scallops, They are served in a rich cream and wine velouté sauce which is as velvety as its name. Since comparatively few shellfish are able to supply the right taste and mood, it is unnecessarily extravagant to use them exclusively. That is why this recipe cunningly bulks them out with cubes of far less expensive monkfish.

The fish are cooked in a mixture of white vermouth, mussel liquor and fish stock, reduced to give the strongest possible flavour. For fish stock, simmer white fish trimmings, sliced onion, celery and juice of half a lemon in 1 L [2 pt] water for 20–30 minutes. Strain the stock and discard all the bones. Then boil the strained stock over high heat until reduced by half.

Note that white pepper, not black, is used as seasoning to avoid getting dark flecks in the finished creamy gold dish.

Creamed potato is piped round the outside of the serving plate to form an elaborate 'shell'.

If using raw prawns, cook with the scallops at step 13.

SERVES 6
2 kg [2 quart] mussels
350 g [12 oz] Mediterranean or Pacific prawns in their shells
6 small scallops
450 g [1 lb] monkfish fillet
150 ml [$\frac{1}{4}$ pt] dry white vermouth
275 ml [$\frac{1}{2}$ pt] fish stock reduced to 150 ml [$\frac{1}{4}$ pt]

For the duchesse potato border:
900 g [2 lb] old potatoes
50 g [2 oz] butter
1 medium-sized egg
salt
freshly ground white pepper

For the velouté sauce:
40 g [1$\frac{1}{2}$ oz] butter
40 g [1$\frac{1}{2}$ oz] flour
1 large egg yolk
45 ml [3 tablespoons] thick cream
salt
freshly ground white pepper
2.5 ml [$\frac{1}{2}$ teaspoon] lemon juice

For finishing the dish:
125 ml [4 fl oz] thick cream
freshly ground white pepper
salt
lemon juice
30 ml [2 tablespoons] chopped
**   parsley**
1 lemon cut into 6 wedges

1 Discard any mussels which do not close on being tapped with the back of a knife—they are dead. From the remaining closed mussels, pull away beards, scrape off any encrustations and scrub shells thoroughly under cold running water.

2 Peel the prawns. Cut the scallops from their half shells (if applicable). Discard any black pieces adhering to them and the tough skin which joins them to the shells. Rinse under cold running water to remove every trace of sand. Pat dry and then separate the coral from their whites and slice each white disc across into two.

3 Cut the monkfish into 2.5 cm [1″] cubes, removing all trace of skin. Reserve all the prepared shellfish.

4 Start preparing the potatoes. Peel and put them to boil.

5 Drain the cooked potatoes and cream them as described on page 132, omitting the milk.

6 Place the creamed potatoes into a piping bag with a size 8 nozzle. Pipe a double border around the edge of an ovenproof serving plate. Reserve. (If not cooking ahead put in pre-heated oven.)

7 Start cooking the shellfish. Pour the vermouth into a large pan and bring to the boil. Add the mussels, cover and shake gently over a fierce heat for about 2 minutes.

8 When the mussels open, boil for 1 further minute and then remove them with a draining spoon and reserve. Discard any mussels which remain closed—these are bad.

9 Strain the cooking liquor through a muslin-lined sieve into a bowl, to remove all traces of sand and shell. Return the strained liquor to the pan and reserve.

10 Heat oven to 160°C [325°F] gas mark 3, if reheating potato.

11 When the mussels are cool enough to handle, shell them over a plate in order to catch any remaining liquor. Strain this through the muslin and add to the pan. Reserve the shelled mussels on a plate and discard the empty shells.

12 Put the serving plate in the oven, in order to warm the potato and brown the edges.

13 Add the reduced fish stock to the vermouth and mussel stock and bring this to the boil. Add the white discs of the scallops, cover the pan and simmer very gently for 2 minutes. Turn all the fish.

14 Add the cubes of monkfish to the pan. Cook for a further minute, then add the corals from the scallops and cook for a final minute.

15 Remove the fish and scallops from the liquor with a perforated spoon to a warm plate. Check the quantity of liquid and, if necessary, boil down to 425 ml [¾ pt].

16 Now make the velouté sauce. Put the butter in a new pan and add the flour to make a roux. Cook for 1 minute. Stir in the hot, reduced fish stock. Cook over a low heat, stirring all the time.

17 Blend together the egg yolk and cream in a separate bowl. Add to the sauce, whisking. Season with salt and pepper and lemon juice. Return the sauce to boiling point.

18 Add all the reserved fish to the velouté sauce and heat through in the sauce, stirring gently.

19 Add the extra cream. Taste and correct flavouring if necessary. (If keeping hot, cover with buttered greaseproof paper. Leave on lowest possible heat.)

20 Pour the fruits of the sea into the centre of the hot duchesse potato, making sure that some of the pink prawn and corals are visible on the surface. Scatter chopped parsley over the surface.

21 Add lemon wedges and serve.

Cauliflower and French beans à la grecque

This is an unusual and reasonably priced cold vegetable hors d'oeuvre. It is an ideal choice to precede, or even follow, a hot, rich main course, especially if that main dish is not accompanied by a green vegetable.

SERVES 6
1 small cauliflower
450 g [1 lb] French beans

90 ml [6 tablespoons] olive oil
1 Spanish onion
150 ml [¼ pt] dry white wine
freshly ground black pepper
1 bouquet garni
12 coriander seeds
1 garlic clove
225 g [½ lb] tomatoes
salt
half a lemon
12 black olives, stoned
30 ml [2 tablespoons] chopped
parsley

1 Rinse the cauliflower and break into florets; rinse the beans and top and tail. Peel and finely chop the onion. The vegetables should be in attractive pieces.

2 Heat 30 ml [2 tablespoons] of the oil in a heavy pan and sauté the onion—about 5 minutes.

3 Remove the pan from the heat. Add the wine, pepper, bouquet garni and coriander seeds.

4 Peel and crush the garlic and add to the pan. Concassé the tomatoes (skin, de-seed and chop coarsely) and add the flesh to the pan. Add prepared cauliflower and French beans. Mix all ingredients well.

5 Bring to the boil and season to taste with salt. Cook over a moderate heat for 10 minutes, stirring occasionally. The sauce is in-

tended to reduce, but if it evaporates too fast, top up with extra water.

6 When the cooking time is up, remove from the heat, extract bouquet garni and then leave the hors d'oeuvre to cool.

7 When mixture is cold, stir in remaining olive oil. Squeeze the lemon and add lemon juice and extra seasoning to taste.

8 Arrange cauliflower and beans in a serving dish with the sauce. Dot with the olives and garnish with parsley. Chill in the refrigerator until ready to serve.

Nègre en chemise

⧖⧖ *This is a classic from Vienna: a chocolate soufflé, unmoulded from a bowl and served cold. The nègre of the title is the tall smooth black shape of the soufflé, his chemise (or night shirt) the white cream which is poured over it. This famous dessert is more like a mousse than a traditional cold soufflé, and it is denser than either. This is partly due to the different proportions of the ingredients, but is*

mainly because the soufflé is cooked and then allowed to cool—and it is steamed rather than baked. Unlike the hot soufflé dessert that is cooked while diners wait in anxious anticipation, this one is made ahead of time and is guaranteed not to let the cook down.

Because it tends to have a rather dry consistency, it is always served with pouring cream. Add a little sherry to the cream if you fear it may otherwise make your meal too rich. Rum or Cointreau could be substituted for the Grand Marnier if preferred.

SERVES 6 GENEROUSLY

225 g [½ lb] cooking chocolate
2.5 ml [½ teaspoon] instant coffee powder
30 ml [2 tablespoons] Grand Marnier
6 large-sized eggs
175 g [6 oz] sugar
175 g [6 oz] butter
pinch of salt or cream of tartar

For the cream topping:
150 ml [5 fl oz] thick cream
30 ml [2 tablespoons] sherry

For serving:
150 ml [5 fl oz] thin cream in a serving jug

1 Break the chocolate into a bowl.

2 Dissolve the coffee powder in 45 ml [3 tablespoons] of hot water and add to the chocolate. Add the Grand Marnier.

3 Place the bowl over a pan of hot water on a very low heat. Stir until the chocolate has melted. Reserve.

4 Separate the eggs, placing the whites in a large clean bowl and yolks in a small bowl.

5 Beat the yolks with the sugar and the butter until creamy. Add to the melted chocolate. Leave until the mixture has cooled.

6 Whisk the egg whites with the salt or cream of tartar until very stiff. Fold in the chocolate mixture.

7 Butter a 1.7 L [3 pt] tall pudding bowl. Pour in the mixture and make a slight hollow in the centre with the back of a spoon. Cover the top of the mould tightly with foil or a pudding cloth.

8 Place the bowl in a pan with water reaching halfway up the sides. Bring the water to the boil, cover pan and leave to steam for 1½ hours. Top up with extra water during cooking if necessary.

9 When the soufflé is firm, remove from the pan and leave to cool.

10 Unmould on to a serving plate.

11 Lightly whip the cream, add the sherry and pour over the soufflé. Serve with a jug of cream.

Dinner party for family or close friends

Here is a tasty, colourful and well balanced meal which is just right for family or friends. Recipes are based on elementary cooking techniques such as boiling eggs, grilling pork, making a leafy green salad and making biscuit crust so you can test your skills in the context of a full menu. You'll also find out elements and supplementary information—how to thread skewers for grilling, how to cook perfect rice and how to make a warm salad dressing. There is a reminder checklist on ingredients and equipment, and an easy-to-follow count-down timetable—all designed to help you plan and cook the meal so that everything is ready on time, without fuss or rush.

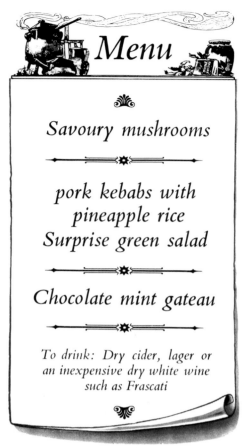

Menu

❧

Savoury mushrooms

———◆———�֎———◆———

*pork kebabs with
pineapple rice
Surprise green salad*

———◆———✖———◆———

Chocolate mint gateau

———◆———✖———◆———

*To drink: Dry cider, lager or
an inexpensive dry white wine
such as Frascati*

❧

A WELL-BALANCED MEAL
There's a temptation to produce several elaborate dishes for a party. The results may look impressive but they often prove too rich to enjoy.

The menu given here is well balanced, including a good variety of colour and textures for maximum eye and appetite appeal, and only one creamy dish—so your guests will feel fêted but not overpowered. It is a practical menu too: first course and dessert can be made in advance so you won't be too hectic on party night.

SHOPPING CHECKLIST
The best way to avoid a last minute dash to the shops for something you have forgotten is to go through the recipes well in advance. Check your storecupboard, larder and fridge, tick off those ingredients you already have and write the remainder on a shopping list. The only ingredient you may have difficulty getting is sesame seeds: go to a delicatessen or health food shop if they are unobtainable at your supermarket.

SPECIAL EQUIPMENT
It's a good idea to check recipes for

Countdown timetable

THE DAY BEFORE
Savoury mushrooms: prepare and marinade the mushrooms—steps 1-6.
Chocolate mint gâteau: make the three cereal crust layers—steps 1–6.

ON THE DAY

2½ hours before the meal
Savoury mushrooms: complete dish —steps 7-16, cover with foil and put in a cool place until needed.

1½ hours before the meal
Surprise green salad: prepare chicory or endive—step 1.
Chocolate mint gâteau: assemble and complete the gâteau steps 7–11. Place in a large plastic bag and refrigerate until needed.

¾ hour before the meal
Pork kebabs: prepare kebabs and prepare basting sauce—steps 1–6.
Surprise green salad: put salad in bowl and toast sesame seeds—steps 2-5. Cover the salad with a damp tea towel and put in a cool place.

25 mins before the meal
Pork kebabs: start cooking—step 7.
Pineapple rice: start cooking rice— steps 8-9.
Put the dinner plates and serving dishes in a heated plate drawer or

low oven to warm—120°C [250°F] gas mark ½.

10 mins before the meal
Pineapple rice: test rice and turn onto a serving dish if cooked—steps 10-11. Place cooked kebabs on top, cover and keep warm until needed—step 12.

5 mins before the meal
Surprise green salad: prepare dressing—step 6. Pour into a jug, stand in a bowl or pan of hot water and cover until needed.

Between first and main courses
Surprise green salad: season, stir dressing briskly and pour over salad —step 7.

equipment too. In this menu, most of the necessary equipment is very straightforward. The only special equipment is kebab skewers. You will need four long or eight short skewers. Flat stainless steel skewers with pointed ends are best. Failing this, butchers will sometimes give away or sell very cheaply the 'corkscrew' skewers they use for holding meat together. If your skewers have fancy wooden or plastic handles, remember to keep the handles well away from the heat during cooking.

PLANNING AHEAD
Following this timetable should help

you avoid any last minute panic, so you can relax and enjoy your own party. The only job to be done between courses is the dressing of the salad.

The timings can of course be adapted to suit your needs. For instance, if you are busy the day before the meal but free in the morning, you can do the 'day before' stages then. If you feel that it will take you a longer or shorter time than allocated for the preparation of some of the dishes, adjust the timings accordingly. Cooking times obviously cannot be changed, so any alteration in timing must be in the preparation stages.

Savoury mushrooms

△△△ *Use medium-sized open-type or cap mushrooms for this dish as these allow enough room for the stuffing. Do not peel the mushrooms—much of their flavour lies in the skin. A gentle wipe with a damp cloth will remove any dirt.*

Use a glass or earthenware dish to marinate the mushrooms as these materials will not absorb the taste of the marinade.

SERVES 4
8 medium-sized open or cap mushrooms
salt and freshly ground black pepper
pinch of dry mustard
pinch of caster sugar
30 ml [2 tablespoons] wine vinegar
60 ml [4 tablespoons] corn or olive oil
3 eggs
15 ml [1 tablespoon] chopped fresh chives or parsley
25 g [1 oz] stale white bread
15 ml [1 tablespoon] sour cream

1. Wipe the mushrooms with a clean damp cloth.

2. Using a sharp knife, trim off the stalks level with mushroom caps. Wrap and reserve stalks.

3. Place the mushrooms in a single layer, gills facing upward, in a shallow glass or earthenware dish.

4. Put salt and freshly ground black pepper, dry mustard and sugar in a cup or screw-top jar. Pour on the vinegar and stir briskly with a fork to blend.

5. Add the oil and stir briskly until well mixed, or screw the top firmly on the jar and shake.

This recipe transforms everyday ingredients into an original and delicious appetizer.

6. Pour the marinade over the mushrooms, cover the dish with foil and leave in a cool place for 4-8 hours, spooning the mixture over the mushrooms occasionally.

7. Hard-boil the eggs, plunge into cold water to arrest cooking and shell. Store in a bowl of cold water until needed.

8. Chop the reserved mushroom stalks and chives or parsley. A quick and easy way to do this is to place the ingredients in a cup and snip with kitchen scissors.

9. Break the bread into pieces and rub against the fine holes of a cheese grater to make crumbs. Alternatively, make the crumbs in a liquidizer, following manufacturer's instructions.

10. Dry the hard-boiled eggs, halve and remove yolks with a teaspoon. Sieve yolks and chop whites finely.

11. In a small bowl, mix together the chopped mushroom stalks, herbs, eggs and breadcrumbs. Season to taste with salt and pepper.

12. Carefully transfer the mushrooms on to a serving dish, using a spoon and fork to lift them.

13. Add any marinade that has not been absorbed by the mushrooms to the egg mixture and mix together with a fork.

14. Mix in the sour cream and adjust seasoning if necessary.

15. Using a teaspoon, divide the stuffing between the mushrooms, mounding it in the centre of each cap.

16. Garnish with sprigs of watercress or parsley.

Pork kebabs with pineapple rice

You will need four long or eight short skewers for this recipe. When threading the meat and fruit on to skewers, be sure not to pack the ingredients too tightly together, or the heat will not be able to penetrate and cook the pork properly.

Because pork fillet is very lean meat it has a tendency to dry out, so brush generously with the basting sauce before grilling and baste the meat frequently during cooking.

Many people are a little frightened about cooking rice but it's really very simple to achieve delicious fluffy rice if you use the pre-fluffed long grain variety—and you must resist the temptation to lift the lid or stir the rice during cooking. Removing the lid allows steam to escape and lowers the cooking temperature, which could spoil the rice. Stirring makes the rice sticky. Pre-fluffed long grain rice, properly cooked, will separate of its own accord during cooking and there is no need to rinse it before or after cooking.

SERVES 4
450 g [1 lb] pork fillet
8 thin rashers streaky bacon
225 g [½ lb] fresh or canned
  pineapple pieces
a little olive or cooking oil
225 g [½ lb] long grain rice
5 ml [1 teaspoon] salt
25 g [1 oz] butter

For the basting sauce:
30 ml [2 tablespoons] olive oil
15 ml [1 tablespoon] mustard
30 ml [2 tablespoons] clear
  honey
25 g [1 oz] soft brown sugar
15 ml [1 tablespoon] lemon
  juice

1 Using a sharp knife, cut the pork fillet into 16 pieces of equal size.

2 Using kitchen scissors, cut off and discard the bacon rind and any bones. Cut the bacon rashers in half, stretch with the back of a knife and roll up.

3 Drain the pineapple. Set 16 pieces to one side and reserve remainder. Pour away or drink the juice.

4 Brush each kebab skewer liberally with oil. Thread each with pieces of bacon, pork and pineapple in sequence.

5 Heat the grill, with grid and grill pan in position.

6 Meanwhile, put all the ingredients for the basting sauce into a small saucepan and heat gently, stirring, until dissolved and blended.

7 Brush the grid with oil, lay the kebabs on the grid, brush with the baste and grill under fierce heat for 1 minute or so on each side. Reduce heat to medium or lower the pan and continue grilling for 12-16 minutes, turning the skewers and basting frequently.

8 Meanwhile, prepare the rice. Put rice, salt and 575 ml [1 pt] cold water into a large saucepan. Bring to the boil and stir once.

9 Immediately reduce the heat as low as possible. Cover the pan and simmer for 15 minutes without removing the lid or stirring.

10 Test the rice by biting a few grains. If not quite tender, or if the liquid is not completely absorbed, replace the lid and cook for a few minutes longer.

11 Remove the pan from the heat, turn the rice into a warm serving dish

and toss gently (fluff) with a fork. Stir in remaining pineapple pieces and the butter.

12 Place the cooked kebabs on the bed of rice and pour over any sauce and juices from the grill pan. Cover the dish with foil and keep warm in an oven heated to 120 C [250 F] gas mark ½ until needed—preferably not more than 30 minutes.

Push a kebab off its skewer and on to your plate before eating. Use a fork to do this and put the empty skewer back on the serving dish.

Surprise green salad

⧗ *The surprising thing about this salad is that the delicious butter and sesame seed dressing is warm. Don't pour on the dressing until you are ready to serve the salad—if added too soon the butter will solidify. To keep the dressing warm until needed, pour into a jug, stand in a bowl of hot water and cover the bowl and jug with foil.*

SERVES 4

4 medium-sized heads of chicory or 1 endive
3 spring onions
15 ml [1 tablespoon] sesame seeds
50 g [2 oz] butter
salt and freshly ground black pepper

1 Using a sharp knife, cut a thin slice from the base of each head of chicory. Remove the core using a sharp knife or apple corer and discard. Pull away any bruised or brown outer leaves and discard. Gently separate the leaves and wash in cold water. Shake lightly and dry carefully in a tea towel, salad spinner or basket. Wrap leaves gently in a fresh, dry tea towel and put the towel into a polythene bag in the crisper drawer of the refrigerator for 30–60 minutes. If using endive, remove the stalk and separate the leaves, discarding any that are bruised or brown. Wash and crisp as for chicory.

2 Put the leaves of chicory or endive into the salad bowl.

3 Cut the bottom (root end) off the spring onions and trim away about 10 cm [4"] of the green tops.

Remove transparent outer skin and slice thinly.

4 Drop the onions into the centre of the salad bowl.

5 Toast the sesame seeds. To do this, put the sesame seeds in a small frying pan (add no fat) and cook, stirring over medium heat until lightly browned.

6 Add the butter to the pan, allow to melt then cook over medium heat until foaming and browned.

7 Add salt and pepper to the salad and toss lightly. Pour over the warm dressing and toss lightly using salad servers. Serve immediately.

The aroma of honey-mustard basting sauce is enough to rouse most appetites—and the succulent, tenderness of kebabs is well-balanced by nutty-textured rice and a crisp salad.

Chocolate mint gâteau

▨▨▨ *Cream-filled cakes can be difficult and messy to cut, especially if the cake is a crisp one like this cereal crust gâteau. To make cutting easier, the top two layers of the gâteau are divided into portions before being allowed to set. To make sure the two layers are divided into equal portions, cut two circles of greaseproof paper the same size as the inside base of the flan rings. Using a compass, divide into six equal portions. Place the greaseproof patterns on top of the two cereal crust bases to be cut into portions. Using a sharp knife, cut through both paper and cereal crust, then peel away the paper.*

SERVES 4-6
175 g [6 oz] puffed rice
75 g [4 oz] chocolate
15 g [½ oz] butter
275 ml [½ pt] whipped cream
peppermint essence
green food colouring
mint leaves or geranium
leaves to decorate

1 Melt chocolate in a bowl placed on a trivet in a heavy-based pan containing gently boiling water.

2 Place puffed rice in a bowl. Pour on melted chocolate and mix well with a metal spoon.

3 Use the butter to grease the bases of three 18 cm [7″] flan rings.

4 Press puffed rice and chocolate into base only of the flan rings, making a layer about 6 mm [¼″] thick.

5 Using a sharp knife and grease-proof patterns, cut two of the lined bases into six portions. Leave the third base whole.

6 Place each flan tin in a polythene bag, seal and refrigerate for 5 hours, or overnight.

A creamy, prettily decorated gâteau ends the meal with a rich flourish.

7 Remove flan bases from the rings.

8 Add three drops peppermint essence and two drops green food colouring to whipped cream. Mix well with a spoon so that the cream is an even, pale green colour.

9 Spread half the cream over the whole flan base. Arrange six slices of flan base in a circle on top.

10 Spread the remaining cream on top. Place the final six flan slices on top of this, so that cream shows between them.

11 Decorate the gâteau with fresh mint or geranium leaves.

Menus from Overseas

A Russian meal for six

Give your friends a feast worthy of the old Imperial Tsars—with caviare, deep-fried chicken and a spectacular cheesecake finale . . . all preceded by plenty of vodka, of course. Let guests discover that Russian cuisine can be as exciting as a Salyut space mission, as romantic as the Bolshoi ballet, and as memorable as Red Square on May day—without even setting foot out of England.

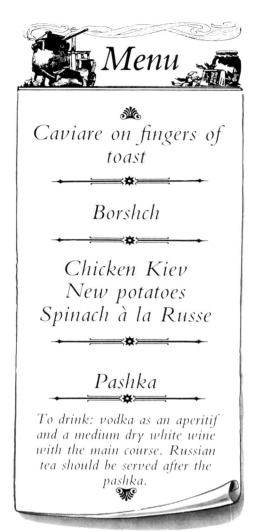

Tourists about to visit the USSR for the first time enquire nervously: 'But is the food good or is it dreadfully stodgy?'

The answer cannot be a simple yes or no: for how can you generalize about a country that covers 8½ million square miles? The climate and the terrain differ wildly and so does the food.

In the Siberian north, the food is heavy to keep out the bitter cold—root vegetables and 'pelmeni' (meat dumplings) abound. But down in the south with its mystical names like Tashkent and Samarkand, you are in Central Asia, where the food will be almost Middle Eastern, with rice and kebab dishes.

This menu starts, rather obviously, with caviare from the Caspian Sea. Caviare is a great luxury over here, and even in Russia is rare enough to be regarded as a delicacy. It isn't imperative to the meal but if you can afford it, it will offer an exciting opener. Alternatively, lumpfish roe (which is mock caviare) could be used as a cheaper substitute.

The caviare is followed by a beetroot soup, borshch, an East European soup that in Russia can be anything from a sparkling consommé to a hearty peasant dish packed with vegetables. The version given here strikes a happy medium which is ideal for Western tastes.

The main course on the menu is named after the city of Kiev, capital of the Ukraine and one of Europe's oldest and most beautiful cities. Deep-fried chicken with a 'surprise' melted butter and garlic centre, chicken Kiev is a Russian treat well known in restaurants around the world.

The chicken is accompanied by plain potatoes and spinach—typical Russian favourites, easy to obtain elsewhere in the world.

The menu finishes with pashka: a rich cheesecake from the plains west of Moscow. In culinary terms, Russia is the land of soured cream, unsalted butter and a multitude of cheeses. For example, there is a famous national dish called 'blini', which is a pancake filled with cottage cheese and dried fruit. Pashka contains cream cheese, unsalted butter and thick cream (not soured in this particular recipe). It is very rich indeed and was originally made at Easter—as a relief, no doubt, from the strictures of Lent. It has no pastry or biscuit-crumb base, so it is possible that a few of your guests will take one look and refuse it as 'sickly'. If so, produce plain digestive or shortbread biscuits as an accompaniment to persuade them to change their minds.

GETTING ORGANIZED

This meal is a fairly relaxed affair for the cook. The pashka is started one day before the party so that it can drain. The soup can be made the day before so that all you need do is reheat and add soured cream before serving. This means that on the day you can concentrate on the main course—a good idea when serving something like chicken Kiev which needs care to succeed.

In the morning, you can prepare the chicken and make the garlic butter filling. After chilling the butter until firm (about 1½ hours), you can stuff the chicken pieces, egg and crumb them, then leave them firming in the refrigerator until required. Remember, with deep frying, the longer you leave the coated food to

firm, the better the results are likely to be.

The potatoes can be cooked in their skins—always a delicious way with tender new potatoes and especially good when there is garlic butter from the chicken Kiev to bathe them in. Spinach is quick to prepare too, so you can leave this until just before cooking time. If you are serving the caviare hors d'oeuvres, prepare these in the afternoon, leaving you a few relaxed hours before its time to head for the kitchen.

This is the sort of meal where you can invite your guests about an hour before you intend to eat. That will give you some 30 minutes with them in the living room, handing round the caviare snacks, before you have to disappear to the kitchen. For as you will see from the timetable, once you start your final cooking bout, there's no stopping.

SHOPPING CHECKLIST

There is nothing on your shopping list for this menu that cannot be bought a couple of days beforehand. The most important item is, of course, the chicken pieces. If you are really absolutely useless with a knife, then either ask your butcher to bone and prepare your chicken (or turkey) pieces or buy chicken (or turkey) breast fillets. They won't look so traditional, more like football shapes than mock chicken legs, but if they spare your nerves and temper, then they are worth it.

For the caviare or lumpfish roe (if you are including it) you will probably need a good delicatessen. There are many different types of caviare ranging from the most expensive—Beluga—to lumpfish caviare.

From then on, your shopping is amazingly ordinary for such an exceptional meal. Starting with the greengrocer, you need about 900 g [2 lb] of new potatoes and 1.4 kg [3 lb] of spinach. For the borshch you will require a quarter of small cabbage, a medium onion and 350 g [¾ lb] of beetroot. Many market stalls and greengrocers sell pre-cooked beet which is a great time saver. The soup also takes the juice of a lemon; but buy 3 because you need the lemon juice and rind of another in the chicken Kiev and the third sliced into wedges for garnishing it. Check that the last garlic you bought is still sporting 4 sound medium-sized

Countdown timetable

TWO DAYS BEFORE
Do the shopping.

THE DAY BEFORE
Pashka: make the cheesecake mixture and put in mould in the refrigerator—steps 1-9.
Borshch: make the soup—steps 1-8. Store covered in the refrigerator until required.

ON THE DAY
In the morning
Chicken Kiev: bone chicken if necessary and beat flat. Prepare the lemon garlic butter and chill in the refrigerator—steps 1-5.
Put the white wine in the refrigerator to chill.
Chicken Kiev: assemble—steps 5-11.

In the afternoon
Caviare: make toast and leave to cool.

Pashka: unmould the cheesecake and decorate—steps 10-11.
Caviare: cut the toast into fingers and spread on caviare. Cover with cling film and store in the refrigerator. Set the table.

60 minutes before the meal
Serve your guests with vodka aperitifs and caviare on toast.

30 minutes before the meal
Spinach à la Russe: wash—step 1.
New Potatoes: scrub—step 1.
Chicken Kiev: heat oil and deep fry the first batch of chicken—steps 12-13.

15 minutes before the meal
Chicken Kiev: transfer the cooked first batch of chicken to the oven to keep warm and fry the second batch—step 14. When cooked, place in a low oven with the other pieces that are already cooked.

New potatoes: place in boiling salted water and set over low heat.
Spinach à la Russe: place in a steamer over pan of potatoes—steps 1-2. Place serving dishes in warming drawer.
Borshch: this needs to be reheated slowly. Add swirls of soured cream. Serve—steps 9-10.

Between first and main courses
Spinach à la Russe: transfer to heated vegetable dish. Add soured cream and toss—step 3.
New potatoes: transfer to heated vegetable dish.
Chicken Kiev: transfer to heated serving dish. Garnish with lemon wedges and parsley—step 15.

After dinner
Make Russian tea and serve it to give an unusual and refreshing finish to the meal.

---

cloves—for the chicken Kiev. Finally buy a good supply of fresh parsley to go into the chicken Kiev, you also want to reserve a few sprigs whole for garnishing the serving plate.

Moving on to the dairy department, you need a total of 250 g [9 oz] of unsalted butter for the chicken Kiev and the pashka. You also need a little butter for the soup.

The Russians use a lot of soured cream and in this menu it occurs in the soup and in the spinach. Don't worry about having it in both courses. The amount used is small—you need less than 150 ml [¼ pt]—so it is scarcely noticeable. The pashka also takes a lot of cream cheese—350 g [¾ lb] to be precise. This is usually cheaper bought over the delicatessen counter than pre-packed from a supermarket. You also need 150 ml [¼ pt] thick cream. Buy from the dairy half a dozen medium-sized eggs for egg and crumbing the chicken and for the pashka.

Your grocery list starts with an ordinary white loaf. Buy it at this stage because slightly stale bread is much better for toast and for making breadcrumbs.

Check that you have in stock both granulated and caster sugar, salt, oil for frying, flour, caraway seeds, chicken stock, and all the cake decoration

bits and pieces you need for the pashka: vanilla essence, mixed peel, raisins, glacé cherries, almonds and a few extra nuts for decorating.

SPECIAL EQUIPMENT
You cannot deep fry anything—and that includes the chicken Kiev—without a deep fat fryer and a basket, and preferably a thermometer too for measuring the temperature of the oil. It is certainly worth investing in a thermometer if you deep fry food regularly.

The other special equipment you need to concern yourself with for this menu is required for the pashka. Obviously it is technically possible to set this cheesecake in any mould, but one of the things that makes pashka so special is its peculiarly different and instantly recognizable shape—tall and narrow. You could, of course, hunt around and try and buy a mould specially but, apart from the expense, the chances of your finding such a thing are remote. For this reason the recipe introduction suggests you make do with a terracotta flowerpot. This is an ideal shape and, what's more, it has a drainage hole in the base through which any remaining whey can ooze. Apart from the mould, you need clean muslin for

straining and 'weights' for pressing the mixture down. Cans of food make excellent heavy weights.

THE DRINKS
It is no myth that the Russians like vodka; to them, no party's a party without at least one bottle of the stuff on generous offer. In fact their government thinks they drink too much of it and since the 1950's there has been an official campaign to promote wine drinking. Good vodka is the nearest thing to pure alcohol that a distiller can produce. He might begin with grain, potatoes or even wood shavings, but in the end he will be left with a powerful blend of alcohol and water. For the sake of authenticity, it is worth buying a bottle of genuine Russian vodka rather than the slightly less fearsome local brands. Go to a good off-licence and ask for a real Russian vodka. Serve it ice cold with a slice of lemon as an aperitif and accompaniment to the caviare or lumpfish roe, if you are serving it.

It is unlikely that many of your guests will be bold enough to take the vodka neat in true Russian tradition, so you'd better be prepared to offer some mixers to go with it—tonic, lime cordial or tomato juice perhaps. And don't be too censorious if the odd faint heart requests a small sherry instead. But here's hoping that at least one or two of your guests will shout a loud 'Zdrovya!' and down their glassful with a flourish. Who knows—if they really get going, you may have to restrain them from breaking the empty glasses in the hearth!

For a table wine, a medium-dry white would be nice with the chicken. Russian wine is seldom exported to the West, so you will probably have to make do with an East European equivalent. Hungarian wines are often good, or a Yugoslav Riesling

would be a reliable choice.

Whatever you do buy, you'd better have at least two litre bottles to serve 6; don't forget you'll be needing some to flavour the borshch.

After dinner, wheel in Russian tea—again unlikely to be the genuine Russian article made in a samovar; but at least it can be lemon tea without milk, served in handsome glass tumblers.

Borshch

This is the famous Russian soup based on beetroot. This particular recipe is for hot borshch, although in the height of summer cold borshch is equally popular. When borshch is served chilled, it usually contains a larger proportion of soured cream than that used here.

SERVES 6
350 g [¾ lb] uncooked beetroot
quarter of small cabbage
salt
1 medium onion
25 g [1 oz] butter
850 ml [1½ pt] chicken stock
5 ml [1 teaspoon] caraway
seeds
5 ml [1 teaspoon] sugar
freshly ground black pepper
juice of 1 lemon
60 ml [4 tablespoons] dry
white wine
30 ml [2 tablespoons] soured
cream

1 Cook the beetroot in boiling salted water for 1½ hours until tender. Cool, then slip off skins.

2 Shred the cabbage finely.

3 Bring 275 ml [½ pt] salted water to the boil in a pan. Add the cabbage. Cover the pan and simmer for 8 minutes.

4 Skin and chop the onion.

5 Melt the butter in a large pan and fry the onion until tender but not coloured—about 5 minutes.

6 Grate the beetroot and reserve any juice.

7 Pour the chicken stock on to the onions and bring to the boil.

8 Add the cabbage and its cooking water, the grated beetroot with its juice, the caraway seeds, sugar and salt and black pepper to taste. Simmer for 10 minutes, removing any scum from the surface with a slotted spoon or stock skimmer.

9 Add the lemon juice and the wine and bring to the boil. Check seasoning.

10 Pour into a warm soup tureen, or individual soup bowls and add swirls of soured cream.

Spinach à la Russe

Steaming spinach saves both energy and the juices of this delicious green vegetable, as you can cook it over another vegetable. When steaming spinach, be sure to turn the leaves from time to time so that they cook evenly.

SERVES 6
1.4 kg [3 lb] spinach
salt
60 ml [4 tablespoons] soured cream

1 Wash the spinach in two waters and shake to remove excess moisture. Place in a steamer over a pan of just boiling water. Add salt and cover, or sweat in a covered saucepan.

2 Cook for 3-5 minutes, turning from time to time.

3 Transfer to a heated vegetable dish. Add sour cream and freshly ground black pepper. Toss and serve.

Chicken Kiev

◨◨◨ *The secrets of perfect chicken Kiev come in chilling the centre thoroughly beforehand, so that it melts gradually throughout the frying process; in using fresh, home-made breadcrumbs and not the ready-made ones to which busy restaurants so often resort; and in heating the oil to the exact temperature specified, in order that both the breadcrumb coating and the chicken within are fried to perfection and no more. If the oil is too hot, the outside browns while the chicken inside is still half raw; if the oil is not hot enough, it soaks right through the coating making the dish soggy.*

The infallible way of achieving the right oil temperature is by using a thermometer, unless you have an electric controlled-temperature deep frier.

For a stylish finished effect, bone chicken portions but do it in such a way that the end of the leg bone is left attached. If desired, this can be covered with a paper frill at the serving stage. For this effect, buy chicken portions made up of the leg and a piece of breast.

SERVES 6
6 chicken portions, weighing about 125-175 g [4-6 oz] each with bone
175 g [6 oz] unsalted softened butter
1 lemon
salt
freshly ground black pepper
4 garlic cloves
45 ml [3 tablespoons] freshly chopped parsley
30 ml [2 tablespoons] plain flour
freshly ground black pepper
4 medium eggs
275 g [10 oz] fresh white breadcrumbs
oil for deep frying

For the garnish:
lemon wedges
sprigs of parsley

1 Use a sharp knife to bone the chicken portions, leaving the small bone at the end of the leg attached to each of the pieces. Boning is not essential but, as well as improving appearance, it makes eating easier.

2 Place the butter in a bowl. Grate three-quarters of the zest off the lemon into it. Beat the butter and lemon zest together.

3 Squeeze the lemon and add the juice slowly to the butter mixture, beating all the time. Mix in the seasoning.

4 Skin and crush the garlic and add to the bowl. Add the parsley and stir well.

5 Transfer the butter mixture to a sheet of greaseproof paper. Form into a roll and chill in the refrigerator for at least 1 hour.

6 When the butter is firm, divide it into six. Take the prepared chicken portions and place a piece of the butter in the centre of each piece of chicken. Roll the chicken up round the butter and secure with a cocktail stick.

7 Season the flour and put in a polythene bag.

8 Beat the eggs and pour on to a large plate.

9 Tip the breadcrumbs into another polythene bag.

10 Lightly coat each piece of chicken by tossing in the bag of seasoned flour, then brush with beaten egg and finally toss in the breadcrumbs.

11 Repeat coating process. Chill in the refrigerator until required.

12 In a deep fat fryer, heat the oil to 180°C [350°F], or until it will brown a cube of bread in 60 seconds.

13 Place 3 of the chilled, coated chicken portions in the frying basket and lower into the oil. Fry for 15 minutes, until golden brown.

14 Take the basket out of the fat, remove cocktail sticks and transfer the chicken pieces to absorbent kitchen paper to drain, and then keep warm in a low oven while the other 3 chicken pieces are fried.

15 Arrange fried chicken pieces on a warm serving plate and garnish with lemon wedges and sprigs of parsley.

Pashka

XXX *This is a Russian cheesecake, traditionally eaten at Easter. In Russia it is made in a special tall pashka mould, but similar results can be obtained by using a large well-washed terracotta flowerpot. The cream cheese mixture is strained through muslin to remove excess liquid so that the resulting cheesecake is firm. If you cannot obtain muslin, a double thickness dishcloth can be used. Make sure that the butter is soft before you begin. Choose your favourite nuts for decorating the pashka and use glacé cherries to add colour.*

SERVES 6

350 g [¾ lb] full fat cream cheese

50 g [2 oz] softened unsalted butter

1 medium-sized egg yolk

40 g [1½ oz] caster sugar

60 ml [4 tablespoons] thick cream

1.5 ml [¼ teaspoon] vanilla essence

40 g [1½ oz] mixed peel

40 g [1½ oz] almonds

40 g [1½ oz] small raisins

For the decoration:

15 g [½ oz] glacé cherries

15 g [½ oz] nuts

1 Beat the butter in a mixing bowl until soft then beat in the cream cheese with a wooden spoon or electric whisk.

2 Place the egg yolk and sugar in a bowl and whisk until thick and creamy in colour.

3 Pour the cream into a small heavy-based saucepan. Add the vanilla and warm over a low heat to blood temperature.

4 Pour the heated cream into the egg yolk mixture, beating continuously with a wooden spoon.

5 Put the bowl over a saucepan quarter full with simmering water and cook for 5 minutes, stirring continuously, until thickened slightly.

6 Remove the bowl from the saucepan and stir in the mixed peel. Allow the mixture to cool, stirring frequently.

7 Roughly chop the almonds and fold them into the cream cheese mixture together with the raisins and cooled cream and egg yolk mixture.

8 Line a dry, cool, medium-sized flowerpot with a piece of muslin and spoon the mixture into it.

9 Cover the mixture with another piece of muslin, a small plate and a weight. Place flowerpot on a wire rack on top of a tray. Leave in the refrigerator for 8 hours or overnight.

10 Remove the weight, plate and top piece of muslin and unmould the pashka on to a serving plate.

11 Carefully remove the rest of the muslin. Roughly chop cherries and nuts and sprinkle over and serve.

A meal of Middle Eastern delights for six

Turkey—land of mystery, hot nights and sensational food. Borrow a couple of her time-honoured dishes for your next dinner party and create your own dream of an Arabian night. The recipes involved certainly require patience, but they are not difficult; nor are they expensive. On the menu, there is a classic stuffed aubergine starter followed by chicken in a refreshing lemon sauce and, to finish with, there are nut sweets including the famed rahat lokum and, of course, tiny cups of strong Turkish coffee.

The very suggestion of a Turkish dinner party should have your guests arriving in their harem pants and spangled tops and dreaming of sultans' feasts and belly dancers. It is an evening for bringing back memories of a spotlessly clean little café somewhere outside Istanbul or Diyarbakir, with an exuberant, smiling waiter, old men playing backgammon at the next table—and such amazingly good local food.

A persistent favourite all over Turkey is the stuffed vegetable starter—courgettes, peppers, aubergines or vine leaves with rich fillings of onions, tomatoes, herbs, spices and nuts. From the multitude of recipes which abound from this part of the world for these dishes, what better choice for your party than the classic imam bayildi?

There follows a less well-known main course—chicken (since chicken, apart from lamb, is the most popular meat in Turkey and the Middle East) in an egg and lemon sauce. This sauce owes its origins to the Byzantine influence on Turkish cuisine, but the bed of nutty and herby rice on which it is served is typical of Arab Turkey.

Nuts will appear yet again in the sweets that replace a Western dessert course. Serve nuts and a little dish of honey separately. Guests then dip the nuts into the honey before popping them into their mouths. Also serve home-made almond drops (nuts coated with icing sugar) and nuts chopped small and hidden inside delicious cubes of grape jelly. The last of these is, of course, the exquisite rahat lokum—known in English as 'Turkish delight'. The rose-coloured version sold in other countries bears little resemblance to the genuine article, but is, none the less, delicious. Such commercial Turkish delight rarely contains nuts but even the most avid nut eater could be relieved to find just one dish on the menu without them. In fact, you had better check with your guests that no one is averse to nuts before you choose this Turkish menu for them. Nuts so abound in Turkey that a meal totally without them would be almost unthinkable to the Turks.

The menu ends with Turkish coffee. It should be served in tiny cups called 'fincan'; so this is an occasion where your coffee cups really come into their own.

On a hot afternoon behind closed shutters, Turkish ladies make their coffee in a beautiful brass pot with a long handle known as a cezve. You can picture them seated on their rich carpeted cushions, sipping and talking as they wait for the cool of evening to come.

Few people outside Turkey are fortunate enough to own a cezve but, technically speaking at least, an ordinary saucepan will work just as well—in one respect better, since a cezve will hold only enough for two cups and for this party you will need to serve six. As for those cushions—if you have a suitable area perhaps the more outgoing of your guests might feel sufficiently in the mood to take coffee seated on cushions on the floor.

GETTING ORGANIZED
Your countdown timetable begins the day before your party, when you do your special shopping and make the imam bayildi.

On the morning of the day itself, make the almond drops.

After lunch, you can start cooking the chicken and, since the dining table will not be needed again before dinner, you can set the table. You can even put out your dishes of honey, walnuts, almond drops and rahat lokum; they will look decorative and help create the atmosphere.

The last 35 minutes are going to be pretty hectic; the chicken demands a lot of attention at this stage, and you must not forget to garnish the imam bayildi.

After the main course, you will have to disappear for a few minutes to make the coffee. Then while it is heating, bring glasses of iced water to the table for your guests to drink while eating the nuts and sweets. If you are going to serve the coffee and sweets away from the dining table, it might be a good idea to serve a new napkin, folded, under the coffee cup. This can then be used to wipe sticky fingers.

SHOPPING CHECKLIST
For a menu from such a far country, there is suprisingly little special shopping to be done. Nuts, of course, you will need in abundance. If you get 175 g [6 oz] shelled walnuts all at once, you can divide them half and half: the good ones for the sweets

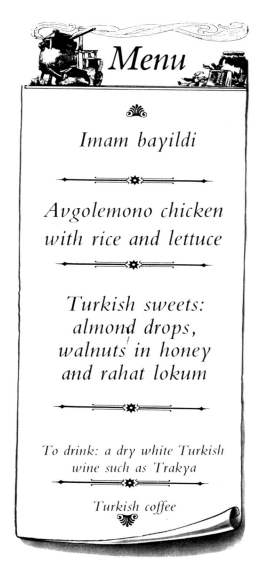

Menu

Imam bayildi

Avgolemono chicken with rice and lettuce

Turkish sweets: almond drops, walnuts in honey and rahat lokum

To drink: a dry white Turkish wine such as Trakya

Turkish coffee

and the broken ones for the rice. You also need almonds, or alternatively hazelnuts or pine nuts, for the first course, and pistachio nuts and ground almonds for the sweets.

The orange blossom water for the almonds could cause difficulty. Buy it from the chemist—if neccessary, rose-water could be substituted.

Buy ready-made Turkish delight. It is usually cheaper bought loose from a confectioner than in the made-up boxes generally sold in supermarkets. You can always make it look more attractive by putting it in paper cases. You need to buy paper cases anyway for the almond drops. These may be found in supermarkets or stationery shops.

Essential to the imam bayildi are the cumin seeds so favoured in Middle Eastern cookery. If you live in an area where specialist delicatessens do not abound, make a point of buying cumin seeds next time you pay a visit to town.

Countdown timetable

THE DAY BEFORE
Do any special shopping.
Imam bayildi: cook, cool and refrigerate—steps 1–12.

ON THE DAY
In the morning
Clean the house.
Almond drops: make and put in paper cases—steps 1–3.
Fill ice-cube trays with water and freeze.

3 hours before the meal
Set the table, including arranging the nut sweets on platters, preferably of brass. Pour honey into a dish.

2 hours before
Avgolemono chicken with rice and lettuce: boil chicken in its flavourings and prepare other ingredients—steps 1–4.
1 hour free to get yourself ready.

35 minutes before
Avgolemono chicken with rice and lettuce: put the cooked chicken in the oven to keep warm, make the sauce and put the rice to boil—steps 5–10.
Imam bayildi: remove from refrigerator and garnish—step 13.

20 minutes before
Avgolemono chicken with rice and lettuce: drain the rice, stir in the herbed nuts and place on a warm serving dish—step 11.

15 minutes before
Avgolemono chicken with rice and lettuce: divide into six joints, skin and arrange on top of rice—step 12.

10 minutes before
Avgolemono chicken with rice and lettuce: heat the sauce and pour over the chicken. Add the herb and nut garnish—steps 13–14.

3 minutes before
Avgolemono chicken with rice and lettuce: prepare and blanch the lettuce; arrange on a serving dish and add chives—step 15.
Imam bayildi—serve.

After main course
Serve the sweets.
Pour ice and water into a jug and serve.
Turkish coffee: make and pour out—steps 1–5.

You will want certain fresh herbs: chives for the chicken, and parsley for both courses. At the greengrocer's buy your lettuces, a beauty of a lemon, garlic if you need it, and three large aubergines. Look for firm ones with gleaming purple skins and no blemishes.

Finally, do note that although the chicken is to be boiled, you need a roasting chicken for this recipe, not a boiler. If you buy a frozen chicken, allow yourself sufficient time for it to thaw completely.

THE DRINKS
To sustain the Turkish feel, you will obviously want to serve a litre of white wine from the right country. Trakya is dry and good, but you may have trouble tracking down a bottle. There has been a deliberate policy to encourage the growing of vines in Turkey, but the Turks still prefer to eat their grapes rather than drink them! The national drink is, of course, coffee—and water.

A Turk is very proud of his local water, and will encourage the passing visitor to taste water from his well rather in the same way as a Frenchman might entreat you to try wine from his own vineyard. He will stand, waiting for your praise, jealous in his belief that his village's water is superior to that of the next. Although there is little you can do to improve your local water, do serve it ice cold in your most attractive tumblers. It should then be produced with the sweets in order to cleanse and freshen the palate for the coffee. In Turkey, the water is often sipped with the coffee as well, as a longer drink to quench thirst.

Turkish coffee does not denote that it is grown there; it describes the method of making it. You can buy any dark roast coffee for the purpose; be sure, though, to ask for a fine ground.

If you feel wildly extravagant, Club Raki is an exotic aniseed-flavoured liqueur from Turkey.

Imam bayildi

This cold stuffed vegetable dish is one of the most famous (and one of the most delicious) of all Turkish hors d'oeuvres. It is easy to make and can be cooked a day before eating. The name means 'the high priest swooned' and legends vary as to the reason why: some say it was because of the cost of the olive oil involved, while others say he swooned from sheer gastronomic delight. Pine nuts are a traditional ingredient and give special quality to the dish but blanched split almonds or hazelnuts make very acceptable substitutes. In order to avoid astronomical prices, which might make you swoon, this version of imam bayaldi uses only a modest amount of olive oil.

SERVES 6
3 large aubergines
coarse salt
350 g [¾ lb] onions
350 g [¾ lb] tomatoes
2 garlic cloves
a few parsley sprigs
2.5 ml [½ teaspoon] cumin seeds
1 large lemon
150 ml [¼ pt] olive oil
40 g [1½ oz] pine nuts or blanched split almonds or hazelnuts
50 g [2 oz] raisins
2.5 ml [½ teaspoon] ground cinnamon
freshly ground black pepper
5 ml [1 teaspoon] granulated sugar
lettuce 4–6 leaves

1 Cut each aubergine in half lengthways and wipe the skins clean. Carefully scoop out the pulp, using a small spoon and taking care not to pierce the skins.

2 Place the pulp in a colander, sprinkling generous quantities of coarse salt between the layers. Put a plate on top and weigh it down to encourage the slightly bitter aubergine juice to be drawn out. Sprinkle the inside of the empty aubergine shells with salt, too. Set aside—on a draining board is best—for half an hour.

3 Meanwhile prepare the other ingredients. Peel and chop the onions quite finely. Skin and chop the

tomatoes, peel and crush the garlic. Chop the parsley, and crush the cumin seeds with a pestle in a mortar or with the back of a spoon. Squeeze the lemon.

4 Heat the oven to 180°C [350°F] gas mark 4. Rinse aubergine shells and pulp under cold running water and dry on paper kitchen towels.

5 Warm half the olive oil in a saucepan. Add the cumin, the aubergine pulp (not the shells), the onions and garlic and fry gently for about 10 minutes or until the onions are slightly coloured. Stir the pan from time to time.

6 Increase the heat a little, add the tomatoes and continue cooking for another 10 minutes or so, stirring frequently, until the tomatoes have pulped down and most of their moisture has evaporated.

7 Remove the pan from the heat, stir in the nuts and dried fruit, the cinnamon, 30 ml [2 tablespoons] chopped parsley and salt and

pepper to taste. Add a little lemon juice to the mixture, if you wish.

8 Stuff the aubergine shells with the mixture and place them, side by side (just touching each other is best, as they will help to support each other that way) in a flameproof dish with a lid.

9 Carefully pour the lemon juice and remaining olive oil round the aubergine shells—but not actually into them. (It is safest to use a jug for this job.) Add the sugar and enough water to come at least half way up the sides of the aubergine shells.

10 Place the dish in the oven. Cover with a lid and leave to cook for 1 hour, by which time the vegetables should be quite tender.

11 Remove the dish from the oven but leave the aubergines in their cooking liquor until they are quite cold. Wash and dry lettuce.

12 Then lift out the aubergines carefully with a draining spoon and transfer to a serving dish. Cover with a dome of foil and refrigerate until required.

13 About 30 minutes before serving, remove the dish from the refrigerator and arrange the lettuce. Garnish each aubergine half with chopped parsley.

Avgolemono chicken with rice and lettuce

☒☒ *The name avgolemono shows that this dish includes eggs and lemon, a favourite combination in Greek and Turkish cooking. Tender chicken flesh and creamy lemon sauce are nicely offset by the nutty textured rice and an unusual lettuce garnish, producing a feast of a dish at relatively modest cost. This dish is an excellent example of just how good boiled chicken can be.*

SERVES 6
1 roasting chicken weighing about 1.8 kg [4 lb]
1 large lemon
1 large onion
1 large carrot
bouquet garni
2.5 ml [½ teaspoon] whole peppercorns
60 ml [4 tablespoons] fresh chives
30 ml [2 tablespoons] fresh parsley
75 g [3 oz] walnut pieces
1 large egg yolk
150 ml [¼ pt] thick cream
250 g [9 oz] long grain rice
30 ml [2 tablespoons] butter
30 ml [2 tablespoons] plain flour
salt and pepper
half a lettuce

1 Wipe the chicken inside and out. Grate the lemon zest, skin and slice the onion. Scrub and slice the carrot.

2 Place the chicken in a pan or flameproof casserole into which it fits snugly. Add the lemon zest, onion, carrot, bouquet garni and peppercorns and pour on enough warm water to cover the chicken thighs.

3 Place over medium heat and bring to simmering point. Immediately reduce heat to the lowest possible simmer, cover and leave to poach gently for 1½ hours or until the chicken is quite tender.

4 Meanwhile prepare the other ingredients. Chop 45 ml [3 tablespoons] chives and all the parsley and mix together with the nuts. Beat the egg yolk into a paste with the cream. Squeeze the lemon juice.

5 Strain the poaching stock, discarding vegetables and seasonings, and let the chicken rest in a low oven.

6 Reduce 575 ml [1 pt] of the chicken stock to 450 ml [¾ pt] by fast boiling.

7 Put the rice into a jug to measure volume. Using the remaining stock—plus a little water if necessary—measure out twice the volume of the rice in liquid.

8 Pour this liquid into a large pan, and add the rice and some salt. Place over a medium heat and bring to the boil, stirring once.

9 When boiling point is reached, lower the heat so that the water is just simmering and cover the pan. Cook for 15 minutes.

10 Meanwhile, make a roux with the butter and flour. Blend in the reduced stock and the lemon juice. Bring to the boil and simmer for 2 minutes, stirring all the time.

11 Drain the cooked rice, fluff it with a fork and stir in most of the nuts, chives and parsley. Arrange the rice mixture on a warm serving dish. Keep warm.

12 Joint the chicken into six pieces. Remove the skin, then arrange the pieces on the rice.

13 Blend a few tablespoons of the hot sauce into the egg and cream liaison, then carefully stir this mixture into the saucepan. Reheat very gently without boiling.

14 Season to taste with salt and pepper and pour the sauce over the chicken. Garnish with remaining herb and nut mixture, cover and keep warm.

15 Wash and shred the lettuce. Place in a colander and pour boiling water over it. Drain, salt and arrange the lettuce garnish in a ring round the dish. Chop the remaining chives over the sauce to decorate.

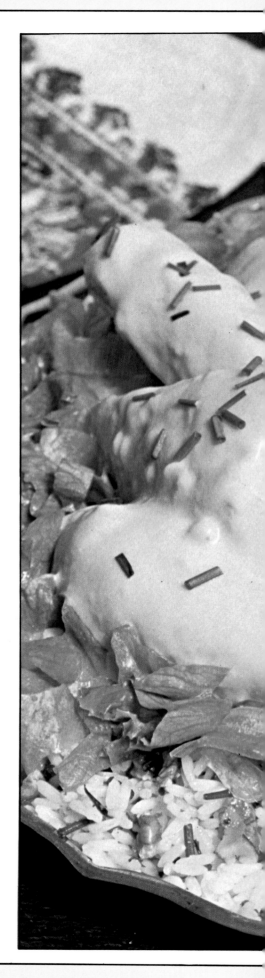

Almond drops

In middle Eastern fare, petits fours frequently replace a full dessert. They are always very sweet and are eaten with the traditional strong black coffee. This is a recipe for a nut-based sweet, exotically flavoured with orange blossom water.

MAKES ABOUT 20
100 g [¼ lb] ground almonds
100 g [¼ lb] icing sugar
75 g [5 tablespoons] orange blossom water

For the decoration:
additional icing sugar
halved and skinned pistachio nuts

1 Mix the ground almonds, icing sugar and enough orange blossom water to make a stiff paste. Knead by hand until smooth. Let the paste rest for a few minutes.

2 With clean dry hands, shape the paste into little balls the size of large marbles, then roll them in the extra icing sugar.

3 Press a halved pistachio nut into the top of each sweet to decorate. Serve in individual paper cases.

Turkish coffee

Turkish coffee, it is said, should be black as night, hot as hell and sweet as love. So use a dark roast coffee, pour out as soon as it is ready and—even if you do not normally take sugar in coffee—accept that for this Turkish brew it is essential. Turkish coffee is traditionally drunk black and, since the bottom half of the cup is sediment, is never stirred.

SERVES 6
45 ml [3 tablespoons] fine ground coffee
30–45 ml [2–3 tablespoons] sugar, according to taste

1 Pour 500 ml [18 fl oz] water into a saucepan.

2 Add the coffee and the sugar and stir well.

3 Place the pan over low heat and cook till coffee rises to the boil.

4 Spoon off the froth into each of the cups and return pan to the heat.

5 When the coffee returns to the boil, pour over the froth to fill the cups and serve. Allow grounds to settle before drinking.

An Italian dinner for six

Produce a little sunshine for your friends with this luscious and colourful menu from the land of Venice, vineyards and Vesuvius. The meal starts with a pasta dish that stands comparison with any from a smart restaurant in Rome. And no one present will ever again accuse veal of lacking flavour after tasting the vitello tonnato—cold and succulent in an exciting tuna fish marinade. To accompany it, there is a zucchini salad, followed by a Mediterranean dessert of figs and oranges. The whole meal is served with the best of Italian vino.

Menu

❧

Tagliatelle con prosciutto

❧

Vitello tonnato
Insalata di zucchini
Bread

❧

Insalata di fichi e arancia with orange cream Chantilly

To drink: Verdicchio with the pasta, Bardolino with the meat and Marsala Garibaldi with the dessert

Italians love life, music, food and romance—not necessarily in that order. Eating is not merely a matter of survival in that warm and hospitable country; it's an exuberant pleasure. As extroverts, Italians expect their efforts to be noticed and praised. They cook with a combination of love, instinct and skill—and they serve with style.

For your table setting use crisply starched linen tablecloths and napkins; in Italian restaurants they are very often in pastel pink or green instead of white. Sparkling cutlery and wine glasses create a mood of expectancy, while a romantic label on the wine bottle and the beautiful glow of candles suggest bella Italia in a flash. You may even have an empty straw-covered chianti flask from an earlier party to act as a candle holder.

The traditional Italian menu starts with an antipasta—meaning before the pasta. This is a small hors d'oeuvre of perhaps salad or salami or a cold seafood. If you want a small antipasta, a delicious salad combination is cubes of mozzarella cheese with quartered tomatoes in a garlicky oil and vinegar dressing.

The antipasta is often followed by a soup, such as classic minestrone, although this is so filling you're unlikely to have room for anything else in this menu.

The menu for this meal starts with the pasta course. Italy is world famous for its pasta, which is intended to provide the filling element of a meal. For a simple family dinner this will make the main course, with suitable accompaniments. For a more formal meal it precedes the main course.

Pasta varies according to the part of Italy you are in. The larger tubes like rigatoni are favoured in the south, the stuffed pastas like ravioli are specialities of the north, and ribbon noodles are more prevalent in central Italy. Spaghetti, of course, is found everywhere. For this particular menu, tagliatelle has been chosen, served in a rich butter, cream and cheese sauce.

Unlike the French, who are prudent with their use of ingredients, the Italians are generous to the point of extravagance. Cream, fine cheeses and eggs abound in their recipes, and you will find two such dairy products contained in this version of tagliatelle. There is also a garnishing of parsley and minced ham to give colour.

You will find plenty of colour in the main course, too—the zucchini and tomato salad makes a vivid combination of scarlet and green, with the occasional gleaming black olive for contrast. An alternative—also in green and red—would be green beans with tomatoes, using the same vinaigrette dressing. Chill the cooked beans and serve them cold.

Veal is the queen of Italian meat, here adorned with a tasty and attractive-looking tuna sauce, making the meat piquant, as a change from the rather bland dishes normally prepared with veal. Serve bread with it, plain without butter.

As great lovers of cheeses of all kinds, Italians often eat cheese and raw fruit to end a meal. Oranges and figs appear on this menu as the dessert. In Italy they would possibly be served in their natural state, on a plate with a knife and fork to eat them with; or the fruit might appear in a macedonia di frutta, a fruit salad, as given in the recipe here, when the oranges are steeped in the fig syrup. An orange-flavoured cream is offered as an optional extra.

THE DRINKS

When you give a dinner party Italian-style, the wine is almost as important as the food. It does not have to be expensive—although good wine from Italy is like good wine from any other country: usually worth the extra—but it does have to be there, and in generous quantities. Since you will probably have to buy at least a couple of bottles anyway for six, it might be fun to have two different wines: white for the pasta and red for the meat.

Bardolino is the choice of the Italian Institute for Foreign Trade to go with the veal. Though white wine is more usual for veal, they felt that this piquant sauce could take a red wine. They also suggested that Marsala Garibaldi would be delicious with the fruit salad. Marsala keeps well, providing it's stoppered, and as you would not expect to finish the bottle, this could be used for another Italian party on a different occasion to make Italy's most celebrated dessert, zabaglione, or a sabayon sauce for a pudding.

For aperitifs, you will probably want to serve one of the famous Italian vermouths like Martini, Cinzano or Punt e Mes.

Verdicchio, a white wine, is suggested for the pasta. This is a comparatively inexpensive wine, so a cheaper solution would be to buy two or three bottles of Verdicchio and to drink it both before and with the two courses of the meal.

ITALIAN WINES

Italy loves her wines and produces a staggering 9,000 million bottles a year, many of which find their way overseas. Italian wines are sometimes regarded as something to be drunk when you cannot afford French or German wines, but this is unfair to Italy's many excellent wines.

To help you make an informed choice, the Italian Government has introduced its own control system. 'DOC' on a bottle stands for 'Denominazione di Origine Controllata' and is the Italian equivalent of 'Appellation Controlée' in France, indicating wines of a particular worth, and guaranteeing the place of origin, type of grape used and alcoholic content.

1 Frascati is one of the strong and fragrant Castelli Romani white wines, grown on the hills near the capital. Both dry and abboccato (semi-sweet) are available.

2 Chianti is a classic ruby-red wine made from the grapes of two red and two white vines. The popular Chianti—to be drunk when young—is usually bottled in the famous straw-covered flasks. Vintage Chianti is always shipped, after ageing, in Bordeaux-type bottles.

3 Bardolino, a light red wine with a touch of sharpness from the beautiful Venetian shores of Lake Garda, is the menu choice.

4 Marsala is a fine rich dessert wine from Sicily. A dry Marsala, chilled, makes an unusual aperitif; drink a sweet one at room temperature after dinner in place of port.

5 Asti Spumante is the most famous sparkling wine after champagne. Made from the Moscato grape and produced in the vineyards around Asti in Piedmont, it is sweet and aromatic. If a champagne substitute is desired, buy a dry sparkling Asti instead.

6 Lacryma Christi means Tears of Christ—a sad name for a wine that reminds people of happy and unforgettable sightseeing holidays around Pompeii: for the grapes are grown on the volcanic slopes of Vesuvius. As well as the white, there is also a red and a rosé.

7 Soave is a pale white wine which has smoothness and a fresh flowery bouquet. A popular party wine, this is widely available in 1 and 2 litre-sized bottles.

8 Valpolicella is a cherry-red wine from the Romeo and Juliet country which is at its prime after two or three years ageing.

Countdown timetable

THE DAY BEFORE
In the morning
Vitello tonnato: cook the veal and leave to cool in its own liquid—steps 1–8.

In the afternoon
Vitello tonnato: make the tuna sauce and marinate the joint overnight—steps 9–16.

ON THE DAY
2 hours before the meal
Insalata di zucchini: prepare vegetables, cook and chill the zucchini—steps 1–2.
Put white wine to chill.
Set the table.

1 hour before the meal
Orange cream Chantilly: make and reserve in refrigerator—steps 1–3.
Insalata di fichi e arancia: prepare fruit salad and place on sideboard—steps 1–3.
Uncork the red wine.

45 minutes before the meal
Insalata di zucchini: make the vinaigrette and reserve. Combine the vegetables in the salad bowl—steps 3–5.
Vitello tonnato: add the lemon gar-nish and put on the sideboard—step 17.
Tagliatelle con proscuitto: boil the water—step 1.
Serve aperitifs.

15 minutes before the meal
Tagliatelle con proscuitto: cook the noodles, make the cheese sauce and mince the ham—steps 2–5.
Put pasta plates and serving dish to warm.

5 minutes before the meal
Insalata di zucchini: toss in the vinaigrette ready for serving—step 6.
Tagliatelle con proscuitto: toss the noodles in the cheese sauce, transfer to serving dish and garnish—steps 6–8.

GETTING ORGANIZED
This is a wonderful meal to organize because the only recipe which is at all complicated, vitello tonnato, is finished completely the day before. It has to be, in order to give the tuna sauce sufficiently long to permeate the meat. An egg white left over from the mayonnaise for the tuna can be used to make the Chantilly cream variation to serve with the dessert.

On the evening of the party, the salad served with the main course can be fitted in between other jobs—it is really very straightforward. The fruit dessert and accompanying cream will take you only 15 minutes or so to prepare.

That just leaves the pasta first course to be cooked at the last minute. It will tie you to the kitchen for the final quarter of an hour—hardly an eternity, considering the magnificent meal you have in store for your guests.

SHOPPING CHECKLIST
There is a fair amount of special shopping to be done for this menu, although only the veal itself should present any problem to find. Do order this from the butcher in advance to be sure of obtaining it. You will find that a long, thin sausage shape will look most impressive and carve most economically. Ask the butcher to tie the meat for you. Also ask for a veal bone. Do not, however, collect the veal until the day you intend to cook it, as veal quickly goes off if stored. The butchery may also be the place to buy the two or three slices of ham needed to top the tagliatelle.

You may also have a big order for the delicatessen: you will need to buy tagliatelle, two types of canned fish for the veal, and parmesan cheese. Check, and replenish where necessary, your supplies of capers, cloves, wine vinegar and French mustard, and buy 75 g [3 oz] black olives. You will want 425 ml [¾ pt] olive oil to have enough for the vinaigrette and the mayonnaise for the veal. If you buy these at a supermarket, also get two items from the dairy department: some unsalted butter and a pot of thick cream—the 275 ml [½ pt] size because, as well as cream to serve with the figs, you will need 150 ml [¼ pt] to blend into the tagliatelle sauce. Also buy a can of figs.

Wherever possible, buy fresh herbs as they are far superior to dried; sometimes you will find them boxed and covered with film in the greengrocery departments of supermarkets. Your list includes parsley, chives (which are excellent even in winter) and tarragon. Bay leaves and oregano are available dried.

As far as ordinary greengrocery is concerned, tomatoes, lettuce and zucchini (courgettes) are your main concern, and also, of course, 3 large luscious oranges for the dessert. In addition, there are extras that you may already have in stock anyway: a small onion, a celery stick, 2 carrots and a clove of garlic. You will also need two lemons for the marinade and for garnishing the veal—but, thinking about aperitifs in sunny Italian tradition, you had better buy 3 lemons to be on the safe side.

SPECIAL EQUIPMENT
Plenty of water is one of the secrets of producing non-sticky, melt-in-the-mouth pasta, so you will need a pan which holds 2.5 L [4½ pt] water comfortably.

For cooking the veal, choose a pan into which the joint fits snugly. This means that the amount of liquid used can be kept to a minimum.

The dish on which the veal is served is also the one in which it is marinated in the mayonnaise in the refrigerator. A gratin dish is suitable for taking to the table, and is better than a serving dish as the sauce cannot then overflow. The dish also needs to be covered in the refrigerator to prevent the smell of the mayonnaise permeating other food. If you own a large plastic storage box of the size that takes a roasting chicken, or a cake tin, this can be turned upside-down over the dish to prevent the mayonnaise top being touched and marked. Put this over the dish then cover the whole dish with foil and tuck this neatly round the edges and crimp it to seal.

Tagliatelle con prosciutto

This is a speciality of many restaurants in and around Rome, where it is usually eaten plain with butter and cheese. Because pasta of any description is served hot and is fairly filling, it makes a perfect first course to precede a cold main dish like the one on this menu. However, on other occasions, tagliatelle con prosciutto can stand as a light lunch all on its own—in which case the amounts specified here would serve only 3–4. Toss the pasta at the table just before serving.

SERVES 6
250 g [9 oz] ribbon noodles
15 ml [1 tablespoon] salt
15 ml [1 tablespoon] oil

For the sauce:
50 g [2 oz] ham
50 g [2 oz] unsalted butter
150 ml [¼ pt] thick cream
75 g [3 oz] grated parmesan cheese
freshly ground black pepper
45 ml [3 tablespoon] chopped fresh parsley

1 Choose a large pan and pour in 2.5 L [4½ pt] of water. Add the salt and bring to the boil. Then add the cooking oil to prevent the noodles sticking.

2 When the water is boiling steadily, add the noodles, cover and cook for 7–10 minutes. Stir occasionally to prevent noodles sticking to the bottom of the pan while they are cooking.

3 Mince or finely chop the ham. Leave on one side.

4 Put the noodles in a colander to drain.

5 Put the butter in the pan over a low heat and let it melt. Add the cream and half the cheese. Blend smoothly together.

6 Return the noodles to the pan. Toss in the cheese mixture and season with pepper.

7 Transfer to a hot serving dish. Put the minced or chopped ham on top in the centre.

8 Garnish by scattering parsley over the noodles. Serve remaining parmesan cheese separately, in a small bowl.

Vitello tonnato

This recipe combines two of Italy's favourite foods: veal and tuna fish. The veal is cooked, allowed to cool and is then served in a distinctive marinade made from classic mayonnaise and canned tuna. This is quite an expensive dish, but it is very special.

The classic version calls for an expensive cut of boneless leg or loin of veal, which cuts into neat, seamless slices. For a more economical version, try boned and rolled shoulder. Boned shoulder will need a slightly longer simmering time, of not less than 1½ hours. Ask the butcher to tie the meat into a neat shape and to give you the veal bone after boning. The simmering in broth leaves the meat soft and crustless, ideal for a coating of mayonnaise.

Also, as a bonus, you have all the ingredients for a first-rate white stock for another occasion. When you remove the veal from its liquid, save that liquid, the bone and the vegetables and boil them for a further 3 hours, watching of course that your precious stock doesn't boil away altogether, as can so easily happen!

SERVES 6
1.1 kg [2½ lb] fillet of loin
   or leg of veal (boned)
1 veal bone
1 small onion
1 celery stick
2 medium-sized carrots
2 cloves
4 black peppercorns
6 parsley stalks
2 bay leaves
salt

For the tuna sauce:
90 g [3½ oz] canned tuna fish
   in oil
5 ml [1 teaspoon] capers
5 anchovy fillets
2 egg yolks
25 ml [5 teaspoons] lemon
   juice
freshly ground black pepper
200 ml [7 fl oz] olive oil

For the garnish:
1 lemon
heart of a lettuce

1 Wipe the veal with a clean, damp cloth and, if necessary, tie it with string so that it keeps its shape during cooking.

2 Put the meat and bone in a large saucepan.

3 Prepare the vegetables: skin and slice the onion, scrub and slice the celery and carrots.

4 Put all the vegetables into the pan, add the cloves, peppercorns, parsley stalks, bay leaves, salt and cold water to reach half way up the meat.

5 Bring slowly to the boil and with a skimming spoon skim off any grey scum that rises to the surface. Cover the pan tightly and simmer gently for a little over 1 hour, calculating the time from the point at which the liquid reaches the boil.

6 Turn the meat over half way through cooking time.

7 At the end of cooking time, lift the veal out of the pan into a colander and put it under running cold water in order to reduce the temperature rapidly.

8 Transfer the meat to a clean, cold pan or other dish into which it fits neatly. Strain the cooking liquor over it and put aside until the meat is absolutely cold. Cooling in liquid keeps the meat moist and succulent and ensures that the meat will not be dry when cold.

9 Now start making the tuna sauce. In a liquidizer blend the tuna fish with its oil with the capers and anchovy fillets; or blend to a smooth paste in a mortar with a pestle; or press through a sieve.

10 If you are using a liquidizer, add the egg yolks and the lemon juice to the liquidizer goblet and season with black pepper. Blend.

11 If you are not using a liquidizer, whisk the egg yolks and the lemon juice into the fish. Add the pepper. Add the oil, drop by drop, to make mayonnaise until all the oil is incorporated and the sauce is

thick. Or use the bought mayonnaise.

12 If you are using a liquidizer, continue to add the oil to the paste in a thin stream until all is incorporated.

13 Check the consistency of the sauce: it should be of a coating consistency. Thin it with a little of

the cold veal stock if necessary.

14 When the veal is cold and firm, drain it well or lift it from the veal jelly. Remove strings. Take off any fat settling on the meat and pat dry with kitchen paper.

15 Cut the meat into thin even slices, bearing in mind the number of diners. Arrange on a suitable dish.

16 Pour the sauce over the meat. Cover and leave to marinate overnight in the refrigerator.

17 Next day, slice the lemon and garnish the top of the veal. Arrange the lettuce leaves round the dish and serve cold.

Insalata di zucchini

▨▨ *This is a colourful and typically Italian salad that makes use of the most popular natives of the Mediterranean: tomatoes, black olives, garlic and zucchini (courgettes). If you keep tomatoes in the refrigerator, remember to take them out in advance to give them time to come to room temperature—the cold numbs the taste. The herb vinaigrette gives this salad an irresistible aromatic scent. Do not dress the salad until the last minute, as the vinegar makes the tomatoes give off their juice.*

SERVES 6
700 g [1½ lb] tomatoes
350 g [¾ lb] zucchini
salt
75 g [3 oz] black olives

For the vinaigrette:
150 ml [¼ pt] olive oil
45 ml [3 tablespoons] white or red wine vinegar
15 ml [1 tablespoon] French mustard
1 garlic clove, crushed
salt
freshly ground black pepper
30 ml [2 tablespoons] mixed finely chopped herbs (choose from chives, parsley, oregano and tarragon)

1 Prepare the vegetables. Skin and quarter the tomatoes and reserve in the salad bowl in a cool place but not the refrigerator. Wash, trim and slice the zucchini into 4 cm [1½"] pieces.

2 Boil the zucchini for 4 minutes in salted water. Drain and allow to rest in the colander for 15 minutes, until cool. Transfer to a dish, cover and chill in the refrigerator.

3 Meanwhile, make the vinaigrette. Combine all the ingredients and beat well to emulsify.

4 Halve olives and remove stones.

5 Add the chilled zucchini and the olives to the tomatoes in the bowl.

6 When ready to serve, add the vinaigrette and toss the salad.

Orange cream Chantilly

◩ *This is not a true Chantilly cream, which is classically flavoured with vanilla essence and caster sugar—but is a delicious topping for fruit. Grate the orange first then use it for the orange salad. The orange in the cream sets off the fruit well, while the volume of the whisked egg white makes the cream lighter (and therefore less rich) and at the same time makes the cream go further.*

If the same whisk is used for the cream and for the egg white, make sure that it is washed and dried efficiently before use.

SERVES 6
1 orange
150 ml [¼ pt] thick cream
15 g [½ oz] icing sugar
1 egg white

1 Grate zest from orange. Reserve.

2 Whip the cream until stiff. Sift the icing sugar into the cream and stir to incorporate. Add the orange zest and stir in.

3 With a clean and thoroughly dry whisk, whisk the egg white until it will stand in stiff peaks. Fold gently into the cream. Decorate with a few julienne strips of orange rind. Reserve in the refrigerator until needed.

Insalata di fichi e arancia

◩ *This fig and orange dessert may sound very luxurious to us, but in the Mediterranean figs grow wild everywhere and are taken very much* for granted. Canned green figs are used in this recipe, but fresh ones could be substituted if available. Oranges combine deliciously with figs and also help to stretch the more expensive fruit.

SERVES 6
825 g [1 lb 13 oz] canned green figs
3 large oranges

1 Drain the can of figs and arrange the fruit in the centre of an attractive fruit plate or in individual bowls.

2 Peel and segment the oranges, taking care to remove all pith and membrane. Arrange round the outside of the figs.

3 Pour over a little of the fig syrup to give the fruit a glaze. Serve remaining syrup separately in a jug.

Chinese supper for four

Just to prove that Chinese cooking isn't as inscrutably oriental as it is made out to be, here is a Chinese supper for four that any western cook will be able to accomplish with ease. There is only one course but it is made up of four very substantial dishes so there is no need for a first course or dessert. Follow these simple instructions and the culinary mysteries of the Orient will be made clear.

Menu

Quick-fried beansprouts

Sliced sweet and sour chicken

Special fried rice with foo yung

Chinese spare ribs

❖

To drink: China tea, Riesling or lager

CREATING THE ATMOSPHERE

If you are having a Chinese meal, it is well worth going the whole hog and creating a really oriental atmosphere.

In the summer, a nice place to eat is in the garden or on a patio. For a Far-Eastern feeling, hang Chinese lanterns and burn joss sticks which also repel insects. Whether you eat indoors or out, choose a selection of oriental-looking bowls in which to serve the food. If possible, provide Chinese soup spoons to serve the rice, beansprouts and chicken. For the spare ribs, provide a fork and spoon.

In Chinese restaurants, food is always kept warm at the table on a small warmer. If you don't have one of these available, you can improvise by placing two night-lights in a shallow dish and standing a wire cake rack on the top to support dishes of food.

No Chinese meal would be quite right without chopsticks, so provide these but be sure to put out knives, forks and spoons as well, for hungry guests who can't quite master the technique of handling them.

As spare ribs are finger food, provide little Chinese bowls filled with tepid water to rinse fingers and guest towels to dry them on. A nice touch is to float a flower on each bowl. Provide napkins.

GETTING ORGANIZED

One of the problems of serving four dishes at once is how to have everything ready at the same time. Here are three tasty dishes that can be wholly, or in part, prepared in advance, so the only last minute cooking is the beansprouts and the foo yung for the fried rice.

The spare ribs can be made as far as step 10 the day before and reheated and dried in the oven just before the meal. Preparing the ribs in advance does, in fact, improve the flavour, as the spices soak into the meat.

The chicken can be prepared the day before, kept in the refrigerator in a covered container and reheated for 10 minutes over moderate heat just before serving. The rice can be boiled the day before too, but must not be fried too far in advance, or it will turn greasy. Fry it about 10 minutes in advance and keep warm in a low oven or warming drawer.

If you follow the timetable, all will be ready at the same time and will taste just as good as any offering from a Chinese restaurant.

Just some of the equipment you will need to make the authentic Chinese dishes featured in this menu. The teapot and cups are only needed if you are serving tea.

Countdown timetable

TWO DAYS BEFORE

Order meat and buy 'dry goods' from supermarket and oriental grocers.

THE DAY BEFORE

Chinese spare ribs: prepare as far as step 10. Turn into a bowl, allow to cool, cover and leave in the refrigerator.

Sliced sweet and sour chicken: prepare—steps 1-11. Turn into a bowl, cool, cover and leave in the refrigerator until needed.

Special fried rice with foo yung: boil the rice—steps 1-3. Drain, leave until cold, cover and place in the refrigerator until needed—step 4.

If serving Riesling or lager, put it in the refrigerator to chill.

ON THE DAY

An hour before

Prepare the décor, putting up lan-

DRINKS

The traditional drink to serve with a Chinese meal is China tea with slices of lemon. Oolong, lapsang, souchong and jasmine are all delicious and aromatic teas. Follow packet instructions carefully when preparing. Tea is served at the beginning of the meal, instead of an aperitif, and continues to be drunk with all the dishes.

Alternatively, serve a light white wine, such as Riesling, or lager.

SPECIAL EQUIPMENT

To stir-fry food, you should traditionally have a Chinese wok and a pair of chopsticks. If however, you don't own either of these, a heavy-based frying-pan with sloping sides and two forks will do just as well. Ideally, you should have two such frying-pans for this menu; one for the rice and ribs and one for the chicken and beansprouts. Cook the ribs and rice in the pans first and keep them warm; then wash pans to cook the beansprouts in one and the chicken in the other and serve immediately.

For the foo yung, you will need an omelette pan, or small sloping-sided frying-pan. To cut up the foo yung, you will need a pair of kitchen scissors.

SHOPPING CHECKLIST

As there are quite a large number of ingredients in this menu, shopping will need to be well organized. Two days before (if you are cooking in advance) call at the butcher's and order the spare ribs (only city butchers have these readily available). You must buy the American or Chinese type of spare ribs, which consist largely of bone, and not spare-rib chops. While you are at the butchers, also order the chicken breasts.

Go to the supermarket and buy any necessary 'dry goods'—rice, soy sauce, cooking sherry, tea, wine, lager, corn oil, eggs, frozen peas, sugar, stock cubes (if you have no home-made stock available), red wine vinegar and tomato purée.

If you have an oriental grocer's near you, this is the place where you will find canned bamboo shoots, beansprouts and ginger root. If there is no such shop in your area, the bamboo shoots may be omitted from sweet and sour sliced chicken. Drained, chopped, preserved ginger may be substituted for ginger root. It is best to leave the purchase of the beansprouts until the day you need them, then they will be fresh.

Beansprouts are easy to grow at home, as you will see from the instructions. So if you know they are unavailable in your area, buy seeds and start growing 3-5 days in advance of the meal.

On the day you plan to cook it, collect the meat from the butcher's. On the day of the meal visit the fishmonger's for the shrimps. It is best to buy these ready peeled then you are only paying for the weight of the fish and you will save yourself a fiddly job. Also visit the green-grocers for mushrooms and Chinese cabbage or cos lettuce.

Equipment such as chopsticks and joss sticks can often be bought from take-away Chinese restaurants or at department stores.

---

terns, if used, and placing joss sticks, finger-bowls, napkins and chop-sticks on the table.

30 minutes before
Place plates in warmer.

Chinese spare ribs: heat the oven to 190°C[375°F] gas mark 5—step 11.

Special fried rice with foo yung: prepare mushrooms and onions —step 5.

10 minutes before
Chinese spare ribs: turn into a shallow dish and place in the oven—step 12.

Sliced sweet and sour chicken: turn into a pan, cover and place over moderate heat.

Special fried rice with foo yung: fry the vegetables, ham and shrimps Add rice, cook and turn into dish—steps 6-9. Place in a warmer or the bottom of the oven to keep warm. Make the foo yung—steps 10-13. Remove the rice from the oven, cut up the foo yung and decorate rice—step 14. Cover and return to the oven.

5 minutes before the meal
Make the tea.

Quick-fried beansprouts: prepare and cook—steps 1-6.

Place all food in serving dishes and take to the table.

How to use chopsticks

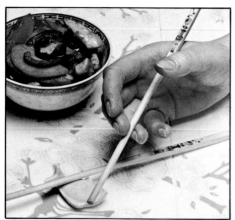

1 Hold one chopstick between thumb and index finger, against middle and ring fingers.

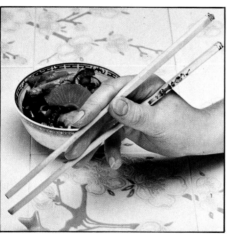

2 Place the second chopstick under the thumb against the index finger like a pencil.

3 To pick food up, move the second chopstick and support the food with the first.

GROWING YOUR OWN BEANSPROUTS

Beansprouts are an important ingredient in Chinese cookery and are excellent in salads too. Unfortunately, they can be hard to obtain. Beansprout seeds are obtained from garden shops and by post from most seedsmen. They are very easy to grow at home and are ready to harvest within a week of planting.

All you will need is a packet of Mung bean seeds (sometimes sold as sprouting seeds), a jam jar, a piece of muslin, which will cover the top of the jar and an elastic band. Take about 10 ml [2 teaspoons] of the seed and rinse it thoroughly. This is most easily done by placing the seed in the jam jar, filling it with tepid water and shaking vigorously. Drain and repeat the operation two or three times.

After the final draining, cover the top of the jar with the piece of muslin and secure with the elastic band. Lay the jar on its side to allow remaining water to drain off.

Place the jar anywhere out of direct light—in a corner, on a shelf or in a cupboard. The temperature should be between 15-18°C [55-65°F] for growing. Repeat the rinsing and draining process twice a day, in the morning and the evening.

The beans are ready to eat when the sprouts have reached 4 cm [1½"] in height. Normally this takes about 3-5 days. To harvest, simply pull the sprouts out of the jar, and nip the sprouts away from the bean husk. The crop from one jar will serve four.

Special fried rice with foo yung

Before rice can be fried, it must first be boiled, as the frying process only heats the rice and amalgamates it with other flavours. Good fried rice should be dry and aromatic, never sloppy or greasy. Use long grain, pre-fluffed rice and resist the temptation to remove the lid or stir during boiling. This will spoil the rice and make it sticky. Cooked properly, pre-fluffed rice will separate of its own accord and there is no need to rinse it after cooking.

The boiled rice should be allowed to become cold before being fried so this part of the dish can be prepared in advance.

Foo yung is a Chinese omelette. It is drier and firmer than the classic French omelette and is often used in Chinese cookery, as here, to garnish a dish of rice or meat. If you wish to make a foo yung on its own, without the rice, it may be filled with beansprouts, chopped ham or mushrooms. Cook the filling in the pan before adding the eggs.

SERVES 4
225 g [½ lb] pre-fluffed long grain rice
5 ml [1 teaspoon] salt
2 medium onions
50 g [2 oz] button mushrooms
75 ml [5 tablespoons] oil
60 ml [4 tablespoons] cooked peas
100 g [4 oz] peeled shrimps
50 g [2 oz] cooked ham

For the foo yung:
2 large eggs
15 ml [1 tablespoon] soy sauce
salt
freshly ground black pepper
15 g [½ oz] unsalted butter

1 Put rice, salt and 550 ml [1 pt] cold water into a large saucepan. Place over medium heat, bring to the boil and stir once. Cover.

2 Reduce the heat to as low as possible. Simmer for 15 minutes without removing the lid or stirring.

3 Test the rice by biting a grain. If it

is not quite tender, or if the liquid is not quite absorbed, cook for a few minutes longer.

4 Remove the pan from the heat and turn the rice into a dish. Leave until cold. If cooking in advance, cover and leave in the refrigerator until needed.

5 Peel and finely chop the onions. Wipe and thinly slice the mushrooms.

6 Heat the oil in a heavy-based frying pan over medium heat. Add the onions, mushrooms, peas and shrimps and stir-fry for a minute.

7 Cut the ham into small strips and add to the pan. Stir-fry for a

minute to mix ingredients

8 Add the rice to the pan. Stir-fry for 2 minutes, mixing well with the vegetables.

9 Mound the rice in a serving dish and place in a low oven to keep warm.

10 Break the eggs into a bowl. Add the soy sauce and seasonings. Beat with a fork until frothy.

11 Heat the butter in a 25 cm [10"] omelette pan over fierce heat. When it has stopped foaming, add the eggs.

12 Stir the eggs twice and then leave to set. Heat the grill to medium.

13 When the bottom of the foo yung has set (after about 2 minutes), remove from the heat and place under the grill for a minute to set the top.

14 Tip the foo yung out on to a warmed plate. Cut into strips and use to decorate the rice with a lattice pattern.

Sliced sweet and sour chicken

☒ *Many people think that a sweet and sour dish automatically includes food in batter. In traditional Chinese cooking, however, the meat is simply thinly sliced and has no coating of batter. This dish is extremely quick to make and can be kept warm in a low oven for up to an hour without harm.*

SERVES 4
225 g [½ lb] chicken breasts
2.5 ml [½ teaspoon] salt
2.5 ml [½ teaspoon] cornflour
45 ml [3 tablespoons] corn oil
25 g [1 oz] bamboo shoots
1 green pepper
1 small onion
1 ginger root
1 garlic clove

For the sweet and sour sauce:
15 ml [1 tablespoon] soy sauce
15 ml [1 tablespoon] red wine vinegar
15 ml [1 tablespoon] soft brown sugar
15 ml [1 tablespoon] tomato purée
60 ml [4 tablespoons] chicken stock

1 Remove the skin and any small rib bones from the chicken breasts.

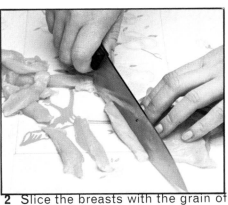

2 Slice the breasts with the grain of

chop the slice finely. Skin the garlic clove and chop finely.

9 Mix together all the sauce ingredients in a small bowl.

10 Return the frying pan to the heat. Add the bamboo shoots, pepper, onion, garlic and ginger and stir-fry over moderate heat for 1 minute.

11 Return the chicken to the pan and mix well with the sauce so that each piece is coated. Cook for 1 minute then serve.

Quick-fried beansprouts

All too often beansprouts served in Chinese restaurants are limp and tasteless because they have been cooked for too long. The secret of preparing beansprouts, and indeed any vegetable, the Chinese way is to cook quickly so that the vegetables retain their crispness.

SERVES 4
450 g [1 lb] plump beansprouts
45 ml [3 tablespoons] sesame seed oil
1 spring onion
45 ml [3 tablespoons] finely chopped Chinese cabbage or cos lettuce
5 ml [1 teaspoon] salt
30 ml [2 tablespoons] chicken stock

1 Heat the oil in a large heavy-based frying pan or wok over fierce heat.

2 Cut the root end off the spring onion. Remove any transparent skin. Chop the onion, stem and bulb, finely and add to the pan.

3 Stir-fry the onion for half a minute.

4 Add the beansprouts and chopped cabbage or lettuce. Turn and stir-fry briskly until all the sprouts are coated with oil. This will take about 2 minutes.

5 Sprinkle the sprouts with salt. Stir-fry for a further 1½ minutes.

6 Add the chicken stock. Stir-fry for a further minute and serve.

the meat, into oblique slices, about 12 mm [½"] thick.

3 Mix together the salt and the cornflour and rub into the sliced chicken.

4 Heat the oil in a heavy-based frying pan over moderate heat.

5 Place the sliced chicken in the pan, spreading it out in a single layer. Stir-fry for 4 minutes to cook the chicken.

6 Remove the chicken from the pan, drain on kitchen paper and set aside in a warm place.

7 Slice the bamboo shoots. De-seed and thinly slice the green pepper. Peel and chop the onion.

8 Cut 1 slice from the ginger and

Chinese spare ribs

For this dish, you need American cut or Chinese pork spare ribs. These are long thin rib bones, usually sold joined together. Although there does not appear to be much meat on these bones, they are very succulent when cooked in the Chinese manner.

SERVES 4
1 kg [2 lb] American cut pork spare ribs
5 ml [1 teaspoon] salt
2 garlic cloves
half a small onion
1 ginger root
60 ml [4 tablespoons] corn oil
15 ml [1 tablespoon] caster sugar
60 ml [4 tablespoons] soy sauce
45 ml [3 tablespoons] sherry
freshly ground black pepper
150 ml [¼ pt] chicken stock

1 Cut the spare ribs into individual ribs by cutting between each bone with a sharp knife.

2 Rub the ribs with salt. This will help the skin to crisp.

3 Skin and crush the garlic cloves. Peel and finely chop the onion. Cut two thin slices off the ginger root and chop finely.

4 Heat the oil in a heavy-based frying-pan or wok over fierce heat.

5 Place garlic, onion and ginger in the pan. Stir-fry for a minute.

6 Add the ribs, lower the heat slightly and stir-fry for a further 5 minutes. Remove ribs.

7 Add the sugar, soy sauce, cooking sherry and pepper. Stir-fry for 2 minutes. Return ribs to pan.

8 Now pour in the chicken stock. Turn the ribs in the sauce until all sides are coated. Lower the heat

so the liquid is just simmering. Turn into a heavy-based saucepan. Place over low heat.

9 Cover the pan with a lid or a plate and leave to cook gently for 20 minutes.

10 Remove the lid. Turn the ribs. Cover and cook for a further 10 minutes.

11 Heat the oven to 190°C [375°F] gas mark 5.

12 Arrange the ribs in a roasting tin and spoon over any remaining sauce. Leave in the oven for 5-10 minutes until the surface of the ribs is dry. If you have prepared the ribs in advance, cook for 15 minutes so they are well heated through. Serve immediately.

A dinner from Paris for six

Paris: city of sophisticates, lovers and gourmets. Honour this beautiful capital with a meal derived from the best of French cuisine: chicken mousselines in a tangy sauce, fillets of white fish sautéed in butter and served with courgettes, and to finish a sensational French pastry gâteau. As a menu—c'est magnifique.

Outside, the weather may be cold and wet, the newspaper headlines full of economic gloom, the trains late or cancelled—but just mention Paris and none of it seems to matter any more. People sigh and smile, and in an instant all the memories come flooding back: Montmartre and that little open-air café where you drank wine till 3 am, that elegant tea on the Champs Elysées while you watched the world stroll by, the market stall with its unforgettable onion soup.

It is a funny thing about Paris but almost everything you remember

about it has food or drink in it somewhere. For this reason it makes a perfect theme for a dinner you wish to serve at home. The food—providing it is authentic and, of course, well cooked—is bound to revive in every one of your guests some idyllic dream of a spring afternoon in the Tuileries Gardens or of an evening on the Seine. The only additional mood-setters you need to supply are a generous dab of best French perfume on your wrist and Piaf on the record player. The rest comes out of the kitchen.

Parisienne food is, like the food of most of the world's capitals, not peculiar to itself but rather a mixture of the best from all over the country. Thus this menu brings you an assortment of superb dishes that might be in the repertoire of any Paris restaurant.

You start with mousselines, the richness of the famous chicken and cream liaison set off by a cunning gold-coloured sauce with a hint of anchovy. Put French bread—a long baguette—on the table with this.

To follow are parcels of sole—of all fish the firm French favourite. Sole à la meunière, sole Colbert and sole Véronique are national classics for very good reason—the versatile sole lends itself beautifully to so many treatments. Now it is the turn of the lesser-known paupiettes of sole—sole wrapped in lettuce leaves and sautéed. Cooked lettuce may sound weird to a die-hard who firmly believes that lettuce is a salad vegetable to be eaten raw with ham or hard boiled egg. The French think differently, and this delicate treatment in which the fish is poached and served in a white wine or vermouth sauce may convert such doubters. It is accompanied by a vegetable that grows readily all over France: courgettes.

For sweet, there is a gâteau. Every district in France has its own traditional gâteau, and the St-Honoré gâteau featured in this menu is said to have originated near Amiens. It combines several very French culinary skills: pâte sucrée in the base, French choux for the pastry ring and buns on top, and crème frangipane for the confectioners' custard which goes in the centre.

To conclude your French evening, serve fresh coffee and, if funds permit, brandy. For the coffee, why not try a continental roast?

THE DRINKS

Both mousselines and fish have very subtle flavours, and an aperitif of powerful spirits could easily kill the palate for what is to follow. Instead, hand round French vermouth with lots of crushed ice and twists of lemon. Dubonnet, which can be blonde (white) or rouge (red), is always popular. Chambéry vermouth is mildly sweet and is a safe bet if you are unsure of your guests' preferences. Noilly Prat is another well-liked vermouth. If you are serving dry white vermouth, a little could be used to make an excellent sauce for the sole in the main course.

With the meal itself, nothing beats the incisive character of a chablis: dry, golden in colour and so French it almost makes you bilingual just to look at it. But be careful: chablis is a generic term for a lot of white wines from Burgundy. If it is sold at a plonk price it will almost certainly be plonk inside the bottle. Be prepared to pay a medium price for 2 bottles—or buy something different. Many a Frenchman has a grudging respect for German white wines and might very well choose a Moselle for this menu. For the same money you could certainly buy a larger quantity of an acceptable wine.

EQUIPMENT

Small moulds are essential for the mousselines. Castle pudding (dariole) moulds look pretty when unmoulded because they have more height than ramekins (which would make acceptable substitutes).

You will probably not own two sizeable sauté pans, needed for the main course, so use a wide-based casserole for the fish.

To show off the gâteau, a cake platter is very desirable. Alternatively, if you own a round bread board of traditional design, you could cover this with wide kitchen foil, tucking the ends neatly underneath. This would give you something resembling a silver cake board, with a clear border round the pastry to help with cutting. Otherwise, use a large dinner plate.

GETTING ORGANIZED

This is a menu that keeps you very busy on the dinner day itself and which cannot, in the main, be cooked ahead of time. (The exceptions here are the pâte sucrée base for the

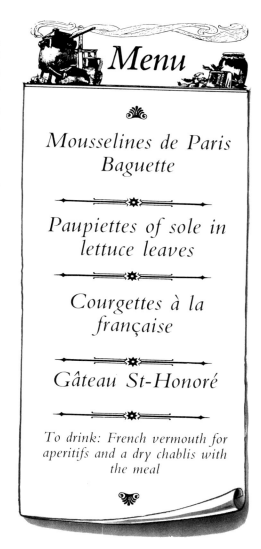

Menu

Mousselines de Paris
Baguette

◆━━❈━━◆

Paupiettes of sole in
lettuce leaves

◆━━❈━━◆

Courgettes à la
française

◆━━❈━━◆

Gâteau St-Honoré

◆━━❈━━◆

To drink: French vermouth for
aperitifs and a dry chablis with
the meal

gâteau, the crème frangipane filling, the mousseline mixture and the sauce for the mousselines.) For this reason, if you are out at work all week, it is a meal beat suited to a Saturday night dinner-party.

During the morning of your big day, shop for the sole and prawns, which should never be purchased in advance and also buy the bread. You will have to buy cream the day before in order to make the mousselines. The cream will stretch sufficiently to fill the choux buns on top of the gâteau as well, so you will not have to buy extra.

During the dinner party afternoon, finish baking the pastry for the gâteau. You may find there is more choux paste than is needed for the gâteau. Pipe extra buns for the children. Filled with a commercial ice-cream, with a spoonful of honey on top, these will make a bed-time bribe for a child who is not allowed to attend the party.

Set the table and chill the wine.

Countdown timetable

THE DAY BEFORE
Do the shopping, except for fish.
Gâteau St-Honoré: make the pâte sucrée base—steps 1–4.
Crème frangipane: make, transfer to a bowl, cover with cling film and store in the refrigerator—steps 1–6.
Mousselines de Paris: mix the mousselines and chill in the refrigerator in their moulds or ramekins. Make the sauce—steps 1–8.

ON THE DAY
In the morning
Buy the sole and prawns.
Gâteau St-Honoré: make the choux ring and buns and leave to cool—steps 5–12.

In the afternoon
Gâteau St-Honoré: fill the choux buns with cream and coat with caramel. Coat sides of choux ring with caramel. Assemble—steps 13–18.

2 hours before the meal
Set the table.
Chill the wine.
Take 45 minutes off to get ready.

1 hour before the meal
Paupiettes of sole in lettuce leaves: prepare the parcels—steps 1–7.
Courgettes à la française: dégorgé—step 1.

45 minutes before the meal
Greet guests with aperitifs and take 15 minutes off to be with them.

30 minutes before the meal
Mousselines de Paris: heat the oven—step 9.
Paupiettes of sole in lettuce leaves: sauté the fish and then cover and leave to cook—steps 8–10. Prepare the tomatoes and put in oven 20 minutes before the meal.
Gâteau St-Honoré: fill the gâteau with the crème frangipane—step 19. Warm the plates for the mousselines and the main course, and serving plates for the fish and the courgettes.

15 minutes before the meal
Courgettes à la française: pat dry the courgettes and sauté—steps 2–4.
Mousselines de Paris: poach in the bain-marie and warm the sauce—steps 10–12.

2 minutes before the meal
Courgettes à la française: transfer to warm vegetable dish—step 5.
Paupiettes of sole in lettuce leaves: transfer paupiettes to serving plate and make the sauce. Pour over the paupiettes ready for serving—step 11–14.
Mousselines de Paris: unmould, pour sauce over, garnish and serve—step 13.

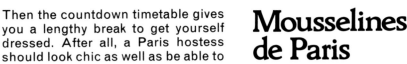

Then the countdown timetable gives you a lengthy break to get yourself dressed. After all, a Paris hostess should look chic as well as be able to cook!

Just before your guests' arrival, prepare the fish parcels and dégorgé the courgettes. Then open the door, pour the aperitifs and enjoy the delectable French art of conversation. The timetable allows you a free 15 minutes at this point, but nothing will spoil if you do not return to your kitchen for an hour. However, once you do decide your guests are beginning to look hungry and that it is time for you to slip out, accept that you will not get away from the kitchen stove again for a solid half hour. The countdown takes you step-by-step through your jobs to stop any last-minute panics. But in the final 5 minutes always accept any assistance that is offered.

Mousselines de Paris

⊠⊠⊠ *The term 'mousseline' describes a fish or meat forcemeat which is stiffened with egg whites and enriched with cream. These delicious and tender chicken ones are poached in castle pudding (dariole) moulds or ramekins in a bain-marie, rather than being poached directly in the liquid. Afterwards they are unmoulded and served in an attractive golden, tangy sauce garnished with sprigs of parsley.*

The amounts given here are sufficient for a starter course; when serving for a main course, double the quantities. Make sure that the chicken used is completely free of any skin or bone, but is nevertheless raw.

In this recipe both the mousselines

and the sauce are prepared ahead, so you can serve them within half an hour of when you start cooking. The sauce could equally well be prepared while the mousselines are cooking.

SERVES 6
225 g [½ lb] boned chicken meat
2 egg whites
275 ml [½ pt] thick cream
salt
freshly ground white pepper
15 g [½ oz] butter
sprigs of parsley for garnish

For the sauce:
275 ml [½ pt] béchamel sauce
15 g [½ oz] anchovy fillets in oil
15 ml [1 tablespoon] tomato purée
few drops of Tabasco sauce

1 Cut up the chicken in sufficiently small pieces to mince.

2 Either put the chicken through a fine mincer (twice if necessary) and then stir in the egg whites, or put the chicken into a liquidizer with the egg whites and blend both together.

3 Whip the cream until thick but not stiff.

4 Fold the cream into the chicken mixture either by using an electric pastry blender or preferably by hand, over a bowl of ice cubes. (The bowl with the chicken is stood inside a larger bowl containing ice cubes in order to help the mixture solidify.) Add the cream, a spoonful at a time.

5 Season the mixture generously.

6 Grease 6 castle pudding moulds or ramekin dishes with butter. Share the mousseline mixture equally between the moulds, spooning it in gently. Smooth the top. Cover the dishes with cling film and chill in the coldest part of the refrigerator for several hours.

7 For the sauce, use a pestle and morter to pound the anchovies in their oil to a smooth paste.

8 Add the anchovy paste, tomato purée and Tabasco to the béchamel sauce.

9 Heat the oven to 160°C [325°F] gas mark 3.

10 Take the covering off the castle pudding moulds and place them in a roasting tin. Add boiling water until it comes halfway up the sides of the dishes.

11 Place in the oven and bake until the mixture is firm—about 15 minutes. Warm 6 small plates.

12 Reheat the sauce gently.

13 Unmould the mousselines on to warm plates and put a couple of spoonfuls of the hot sauce over each one. Garnish with sprigs of parsley and serve.

Paupiettes of sole in lettuce leaves

These rolls of delicate white fish stuffed with prawns are wrapped in lettuce leaves, which are then—in the French style—gently sautéed. It is important to use the inside leaves—not the heart, which would be too small—rather than the coarse outside leaves of the lettuce. It may even be necessary to buy 2 small lettuces in order to have sufficient leaves of the right size to serve 6. In this case, serve the hearts with a plain French dressing as a side salad.

SERVES 6
6 fillets of sole
225 g [1 pt] fresh prawns
12 good lettuce leaves
salt
freshly ground black pepper
15 ml [1 tablespoon] lemon juice
nutmeg
50 g [2 oz] butter
150 ml [¼ pt] fish stock

For the sauce
75 ml [5 tablespoons] dry white wine or vermouth
1 large-sized egg yolk.
10 ml [2 teaspoons] cornflour

1 Peel the prawns.

2 Blanch the lettuce leaves by putting them in a large pan and pouring boiling water over them. Leave for 1 minute. Drain.

3 Lay out the lettuce leaves on a work surface, overlapping them in pairs.

4 Season the fish with salt, pepper and lemon juice. Place a fillet on top of each pair of lettuce leaves.

5 Share the peeled prawns equally between the fillets of fish. Roll them up firmly with the prawns inside.

6 Wrap the leaves round the fish and squeeze each gently in the hand to form a tight parcel, which need not be tied.

7 Grate a little nutmeg on to each paupiette.

8 Melt the butter in a wide heavy-based pan with a lid.

9 Add the paupiettes and cook them in the butter for a minute or so, turning them over.

10 Add the fish stock, cover and cook very gently for 30 minutes, until tender but not dry.

11 Beat the egg yolk and corn flour thoroughly and add to the wine or vermouth.

12 Transfer the cooked paupiettes to a warm serving dish, using a fish slice. Avoid damaging or disturbing the lettuce leaves.

13 Add the egg and wine or vermouth to the juices remaining in the pan. Stir over a low heat until the sauce has thickened.

14 Arrange the paupiettes at each end of the serving dish, pour the sauce over them and then arrange the baked tomatoes in the centre.

SERVING SUGGESTION

Serve the paupiettes with baked tomatoes for extra colour. Heat the oven to 160°C [325°F] gas mark 4. Cut a cross in the top of the tomatoes with a sharp knife, to prevent the skins from bursting unevenly. Brush them with oil, stand on baking tray and bake for 15–20 minutes.

Crème frangipane

Frangipane is said to have been invented by an Italian perfumer named Frangipani who lived in Paris during the reign of Louis XIII.

It is based on crème pâtissière—made rather differently—with ground almonds or crushed macaroons. Use the crème to fill the gâteau St-Honoré given overleaf.

MAKES 575 ML [1 PT]
1 medium-sized egg
1 medium-sized egg yolk
125 g [¼ lb] granulated sugar
25 g [1 oz] plain flour
275 ml [½ pt] milk
40 g [1½ oz] butter
5 ml [1 teaspoon] vanilla extract
1.25 ml [¼ teaspoon] almond extract
75 g [3 oz] crushed macaroons or freshly ground almonds

1 Place egg and egg yolk in a bowl over a saucepan of hot but not boiling water. Beat the eggs together lightly.

2 Add the sugar and whisk until the mixture is thick and foamy.

3 Whisk in the flour, sprinkling it into the mixture a little at a time.

4 Bring the milk to the boil then pour the milk into the egg mixture in a stream, beating continuously.

5 Return mixture to a clean saucepan and put over a gentle heat. Stir until mixture forms a stiff paste.

6 Remove from heat and add remaining ingredients. Beat until butter has melted. Allow to cool.

Courgettes à la française

Shallow frying courgettes on their own with just seasoning and lemon juice is possibly the most basic way of cooking them, but this typically French method shows off the vegetable's subtle taste. If desired, the courgettes may be cooked in a low oven instead but, if so, use only melted butter and no oil, and cook for 30 minutes rather than 15. The salting of courgettes before cooking is called dégorger.

SERVES 6
700 g [1½ lb] small courgettes
salt
half a lemon
freshly ground black pepper
40 g [1½ oz] butter
30 ml [2 tablespoons] cooking oil
5 ml [1 teaspoon] freshly chopped chives
10 ml [2 teaspoons] freshly chopped parsley

1 Top and tail the courgettes and slice across into rings. Layer in a colander, sprinkle a little salt betweem each layer. Cover and leave for at least 30 minutes to drain.

2 Rinse the courgettes and pat dry.

3 Heat the butter and oil in a wide, heavy-based pan, taking care not to overheat.

4 Add the courgettes and sauté gently for 15 minutes without the lid. Cover only when you shake the pan in order to stop the vegetables sticking.

5 Squeeze the juice from the lemon over the courgettes. Sprinkle on herbs and season to taste. Transfer to a warm vegetable dish and serve.

Gâteau St-Honoré

XXX *This classic French sweet which combines pastry, cream and almonds, is said to have been named after Bishop Honorus, patron saint of bakers. It has a circular base of pâté sucrée (a sweet French short-crust, made by the fingertip method —see glossary) with a ring of choux pastry on top and is crowned with small choux buns. The centre is traditionally filled with crème frangipane, an almond-flavoured confectioner's custard. (For the recipe for this, see previous page.)*

SERVES 6–8
For the base:
pâte sucrée made with 100 g [¼ lb] plain flour

For the choux ring and the choux buns:
65 g [2½ oz] plain flour
2 medium-sized eggs
50 g [2 oz] butter or margarine
a pinch of salt
few drops vanilla extract

For the decoration:
200 ml [⅓ pt] thick cream
225 g [½ lb] white sugar
50 g [2 oz] flaked almonds
575 ml [1 pt] crème frangipane (see page 193)

1 Heat the oven to 190°C [375°F] gas mark 5.

2 Flatten the chilled pâte sucrée with the palm of your hand. Roll out until you have a 20 cm [8"] round. Pinch the edge decoratively and afterwards prick the base all over with a fork.

3 Bake on a lightly greased baking sheet for 15–20 minutes, until firm and golden.

4 Using a fish slice, transter the cooked pastry to a wire rack and leave to cool.

5 Set the oven to 200°C [400°F] gas mark 6. Put one oven shelf at the top of the oven and one immediately below. Prepare two baking sheets by first greasing and then flouring. Draw out a ring 20

cm [8"] in diameter on one baking sheet.

6 Make the choux pastry and put into a piping bag with an 18 mm [¾"] nozzle. Pipe the ring, following your mark.

7 Use the remainder to pipe 12 buns on the second baking tray, but be very careful to leave 4–5 cm [1½–2"] between each bun. Each one should be larger than a teaspoonful, but not quite a full tablespoon size.

8 Put the tray containing the ring on the top shelf and one with the buns on the shelf beneath. Bake for 20 minutes.

9 Reduce the oven temperature to 190°C [375°F] gas mark 5 and continue baking for a further 15 minutes.

10 Remove the ring from the baking tray to a wire rack, sticking a knife point into each side to make a small hole to let any steam escape.

11 Slit the base of each of the buns with a knife-point. Insert the handle of a small spoon into each one and scrape out any uncooked pastry, if necessary.

12 Leave the pastry to cool completely on a wire rack.

13 Whip the cream and use to fill a piping bag with a 12 mm [½"] nozzle. Carefully fill each bun from the base and then fill the ring.

14 Make caramel by placing the sugar in a small heavy-based saucepan with 90 ml [6 tablespoons] of water. Put over a low heat until the sugar has dissolved. Increase the heat to high and boil for about 4 minutes—until the sugar has turned to a deep golden caramel.

15 Put the buns in turn on a skewer and dip the tops of the buns into the caramel to coat them.

16 Using a little cream to stick it, place the choux ring on top of the pâte sucrée base.

17 Place a tray under the base and spoon caramel over the top and sides of the ring.

18 Stick the buns round the top of the caramelled ring.

19 Just before serving, fill the centre of the choux ring with crème frangipane. Sprinkle the surface with flaked almonds.

Party Menus

A two-year old's birthday party

Here is one lovely way to celebrate your child's second birthday—with both his or her friends and your own coming round for tea. And what a tea—with novelty sandwiches and home-made biscuits, cake and starry custard in individual dishes—not to mention the toys and the balloons and the fun. Turn to the countdown timetable to learn the secrets of organizing a party for the little ones the easy way.

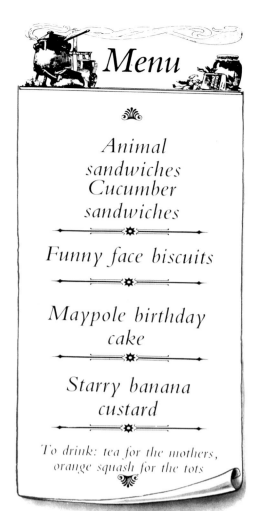

Menu

Animal sandwiches Cucumber sandwiches

Funny face biscuits

Maypole birthday cake

Starry banana custard

To drink: tea for the mothers, orange squash for the tots

The second birthday is a big event in a little life, because it is the first party to which you invite the toddler's own contemporaries. (The first birthday is usually a family affair, with the baby host or hostess rather bewildered by all the sudden fuss he or she is receiving.) By two, though, when he is only 'nearly new', he can understand the importance of his day, if not its full significance.

Pick out five or six other children around the same age, asking their mothers to accompany them. At feeding-time and for separating the inevitable quarrellers, you need far more than one pair of hands. Mothers of young children are notoriously housebound and appreciate nothing better in the afternoons than a cup of tea and a natter with other mums.

The menu is aimed at the children, but since the mothers more often than not wind up finishing off their own child's rejects, the food has to be special enough to please an adult palate too.

There are animal-shaped Marmite or egg sandwiches to start with, then little dishes of starry banana custard, followed by home-made funny face biscuits. As a grand finale, there is the maypole birthday cake, complete with its two candles for the mini host(ess) to blow out.

If you think you have some hearty eaters among your toddlers, it would be nice to include a fruit jelly, perhaps set in small animal-shaped moulds and then turned out.

For the mothers, you will be serving tea, of course, and because they deserve one thing of their very own that the children haven't picked at first: a few sandwiches. Cucumber sandwiches are on the menu because, ever since the Edwardian era, they have been highly popular.

THE TABLE

Lay the table for your six little guests and the mothers can then stand around behind them. High stools lift tots to the right height but if you do use them, warn the mothers to watch that their children do not fall off backwards! For the remainder, on dining chairs, you will probably need cushions to make them taller. Piles of old magazines, if you have them, are less likely to slip off the chair.

Veteran party-giving mums lay newspaper out of sight under the table, where crumbs and blobs of custard tend to collect. It will save your carpet and your nerves—and will cut clearing up time afterwards.

With all the inevitable bits and pieces of a children's tea party, it is always difficult to achieve a colour harmony on the table. Perhaps the easiest way is by picking a colour theme and sticking to it as far as possible. Here the choice is pink, blue and yellow.

There are bound to be spills and upsets with so many young visitors all eating together, so it's a sensible idea to buy a paper cloth for the occasion. Admittedly, this is an extra outlay, but you will find there will be plenty of clean areas left over afterwards which you can use for packing up the odd slice of cake for mothers to take with them and for wrapping presents for months to come. Buy a blue paper cloth and napkins for the mothers while you are about it.

The food has deliberately been chosen with tiny hands in mind—even a one-year-old can happily feed himself with the animal sandwiches and the funny face biscuits. The banana custard is served in small, individual dishes and can be eaten with teaspoons. Children not yet able to manipulate a spoon can easily be fed by their mothers. The cake, too, can be sliced up for them beforehand by a prudent mother.

Although paper plates and beakers are both labour-saving and extremely attractive for most children's parties, for this very young age-group, it is better to use your ordinary crockery—unbreakable mugs if you have them. Under-threes would never cope with chasing custard around a paper jelly case and some of them could still be drinking out of trainer mugs and would certainly not be able to manage a beaker without handles on their own. If you have only enough tea-plates for the mothers' sandwiches, however, by all means buy a small pack of paper ones for the children's cakes and biscuits.

THE ENTERTAINMENT

The tea itself is undoubtedly the star spot of the afternoon. Decorative little faces iced on these biscuits will amuse the children—even quite a small baby can recognize a face. It is only older children who appreciate their personal initials in icing. In the same way, the animal-shaped sandwiches are popular with this age-group.

Banana custard may sound modest for a party; but it's pretty, it's easy to eat and—most important—most young children love it. The maypole cake is pretty, too, even if the children do eat only the sweets and the frosting off the top and leave the cake part for Mummy!

The tea will probably take place at 3.45 p.m. and last for about half an hour. Presumably you will be inviting your guests for about 3 o'clock and they won't be leaving you again until 5 p.m. so what do you do during the hours before and afterwards?

The mothers want to sit down and talk. But what about the children? Do not try organized games; two-year-olds cannot understand even the simplest 'rules' and quickly become bored and frustrated. Apart, perhaps, from a couple of bouts of ring a-roses, you would do better to set out your own child's more salubrious toys in play areas (rather like a play-group does) and let the children simply wander from one activity to another.

Here are a few suggestions to start you off—simple construction toys,

Countdown timetable

THE WEEK BEFORE
Issue invitations.
Shop for party items.

TWO DAYS BEFORE
Do the shopping.
Funny face biscuits: make and ice and store in an airtight tin—steps 1–14.

THE DAY BEFORE
Starry banana custard: make the banana custards, cool and cover and store overnight in the refrigerator: steps 1–3.
Buy the bread.
Sort out toys, blow up balloons and pack up take-home sweets.
Starry banana custard: make the meringue stars and store overnight in a tin—steps 4–8.
Maypole birthday cake: make and bake and, when cold, cover and store overnight—steps 1–10.

ON THE DAY
In the morning
Maypole birthday cake: ice and start to decorate—steps 11–16.
Starry banana custard: arrange meringue stars on the custards—step 9.
Clear bedroom, if necessary, for visiting babies.
Maypole birthday cake: decorate with ribbon and candles—steps 17–18.

1½ hours before the guests' arrival
Prepare the bathroom.
Set the table.
Set out toys.
Get yourself ready.

30 minutes before the guests' arrival
Animal sandwiches: make and cover with cling-film—steps 1–8.
Make cucumber sandwiches.
Dress mini host or hostess.

10 minutes before tea
Make tea for the mothers.
Funny face biscuits: put on serving plates.
Arrange food on table.

---

bricks and bits of wood for building, and huge sheets of drawing paper (possibly backs of old wallpaper) with crayons. A big tub of sand, on newspaper with (if your home circumstances permit) a supply of spades, buckets, empty yoghurt cartons, plastic cars and a toy rake, are always fun.

Another popular choice, which could be restricted by where you live, is a huge bowl of water (or the bath if you can guarantee to have a grown-up on constant duty there) with plastic mugs, a colander, toy boats, wooden pegs an empty squeezy bottle and perhaps the odd length of hose. Soft toys and even dolls are popular with both sexes at this age, as are cars and trains.

In the summer, transport half these activities out into the garden, if you have one, and spare the wear and tear on your home.

Don't be too distressed if war suddenly breaks out—and, worse, if the host himself (or herself, as the case may be) actually starts it. Two-year-olds are more than capable of sudden tempers—just be ready with something to comfort the loser: a special sweet, perhaps, and a toy to play with that you have kept hidden as a diversionary tactic. A tambourine, for example, is grasped at with glee.

At going-home time, each child will appreciate a tiny bag of sweets to take with him, and a balloon. Have balloons in reserve for the ones that burst before their new owners get them off the premises!

GETTING ORGANIZED
Mothers of young children seldom have long free periods—perhaps an hour at a stretch here and there. So try to space your preparations for this party over three days, having issued your invitations and bought the party frippery some time before that.

On the first day, do the shopping, which is fiddly rather than problematic, and make the biscuits. Then the day before the party, make the starry banana custard and the maypole cake but do not decorate them yet. Other items to attend to a day in advance are the blowing up of all those balloons—a job for the man of the house—and packing up some take-home sweets.

In the afternoon, while your child is having a nap, you could sort out some toys for playing with: a little judicious cleaning or mending may be a good idea for some of them. Do not set them up at this stage; your own child may demolish them. Sometime during the day you will have to pop out and buy the bread—unless you have a baker who calls or you can shanghai a kindly neighbour to shop for you.

On the party morning itself, decorate the maypole cake and arrange the meringue stars on their banana custards. Also, if you're expecting any tiny babies in carry-cots, tidy a spare bedroom for them where they can sleep in peace—out of the way of exuberant big brothers and sisters but still within earshot.

During the hour and a half or so between finishing your lunch and the arrival of your guests, put your toddler in a restricted area and get busy setting the tea-table, arranging play corners and seeing to the bathroom. Obviously you will need a potty in there, and also standard toilet articles like tissues, Vaseline and cotton wool on prominent display. A packet of disposable nappies and some spare pants might be very welcome too.

Your last kitchen job before your guests descend on you is to make the sandwiches and cover them with cling-film. Next, get yourself ready and the final preparation of all, before guest number one rings the bell, is to get your tiny host dressed in party best and smiling.

SHOPPING CHECK-LIST
Party extras: balloons, paper cloth, napkins and plates. Drinking straw and metre-length ribbons for the maypole cake. Toiletries.
Dairy produce: 1 doz eggs, 450 g [1 lb] butter, a little Cheddar cheese, and an extra bottle of milk.
Groceries: flour (plain and self raising; also maybe cornflour for the custard), sugar (icing and caster), drinking chocolate, Marmite, raspberry jam, pink edible food colouring. Cake decorations for biscuits, sweets for maypole cake. Squash.
Greengrocery: cucumber, 3 bananas, cress (or parsley) for garnish.
Baker: 2 thin-sliced loaves (1 brown, 1 white).

Animal sandwiches

Young children love these—as much for their shape as their savoury fillings. You make sandwiches in the ordinary way using large slices of a cut loaf and then cut out shapes with a metal pastry cutter. So you can offer a choice, it might be worth buying four or five different animal-shaped cutters. Any smooth firm filling will be suitable: the choice here is Marmite and cheese or cold scrambled egg. One-day-old thin sliced bread is ideal, and making the bases in brown bread and the tops in white adds extra fascination. Unused slices from both loaves will make cucumber sandwiches.

SERVES 6
10 thin slices of white bread
10 thin slices of brown bread
50 g [2 oz] soft butter
about 5 ml [1 teaspoon]
    Marmite
45 ml [3 tablespoons] grated
    cheese
cold scrambled egg, based on
    2 eggs, 1 yolk
cress for garnish

1 Cut the crusts off the white and brown bread, and spread with the butter.

2 Spread a thin layer of Marmite on 5 of the buttered brown slices.

3 Divide the grated cheese into 5 and top Marmite-spread slices with cheese.

4 Complete sandwiches by topping with a slice of buttered white bread.

5 Divide the scrambled egg into 5 and make egg sandwiches in the same way with the remaining slices of bread.

6 Take one sandwich at a time and place on a wooden board. Select an animal cutter. Position it so there is the minimum of waste bread, then press firmly through all layers until the shape is cut out.

7 Cut a second and third animal from the slice if the cutter is a small one. If you work economically, you should be able to get between 2 and 4 (according to cutter size) animals out of each sandwich. Repeat with remaining sandwiches.

8 Arrange sandwiches on a serving plate. Garnish with cress. Cover with cling-film until ready to serve.

Cucumber sandwiches

Peel a cucumber and slice it very thinly. Make cucumber sandwiches with the bread left over from making the Animal sandwiches. Season each layer of cucumber before you top it with bread. Offer a choice of brown sandwiches or white ones. For a dainty touch, trim off the crusts and cut sandwiches into tiny triangles.

Funny face biscuits

Here are biscuits which will amuse even the youngest of guests. They are chocolate flavoured for taste and the faces are iced on top, using glacé icing in different colours and any other suitable cake decorations from the store cupboard. You will need two greaseproof piping bags which you can either make yourself or buy commercially.

MAKES ABOUT 24 7.5 CM [3"]
BISCUITS
175 g [6 oz] plain flour
a pinch of salt
**30 ml [2 tablespoons] drinking
    chocolate**
100 g [$\frac{1}{4}$ lb] butter or margarine
50 g [2 oz] caster sugar
1 large egg

For the decoration:
125 g [$\frac{1}{4}$ lb] icing sugar
**few drops of edible pink food
    colouring**
**selection of Smarties or
    chocolate buttons, dried
    fruit such as currants, glacé
    cherries, nuts etc. for
    features**

1 Heat the oven to 160°C [325°F] gas mark 3. Brush a large baking tray with melted fat or oil and set aside.

2 Sift the flour, salt and drinking chocolate into a mixing bowl. Cut butter into the flour with a round-bladed knife until the pieces are pea sized and coated in flour.

3 Rub the butter into the flour until the mixture resembles even-sized breadcrumbs. Stir in the sugar. Make a well in the centre of the ingredients.

4 Lightly whisk the egg until just frothy. Pour into the well and draw in the dry ingredients using a round-bladed knife. Gently form the mixture into a ball with your hands.

5 Knead gently until the mixture is smooth and free from cracks, turn on to a lightly floured board.

6 Using a lightly floured rolling pin, roll out to a round, 6 mm [$\frac{1}{4}$"] thick.

7 Dip a 7.5 cm [3"] biscuit cutter into flour, shake cutter so that it is lightly coated in flour and use to cut out biscuits. Transfer each biscuit on to the tray as cut.

8 Roll scraps into a ball, re-roll and use to cut more biscuits. Place on the prepared tray as before.

9 Prick the surface of each biscuit lightly with a fork. Place on a shelf near the top of the oven.

10 Cook for 10–12 minutes until lightly browned. Transfer to a wire rack with a fish slice or palette knife and leave to cool.

11 Sift the icing sugar into a bowl. Stir in 15 ml [1 tablespoon] of warm water and beat vigorously until smooth.

12 Place half of the icing into another bowl and colour with a few drops of pink food colouring.

13 Prepare two greaseproof piping bags or use commercial piping bags and fit them with small plain tubes. Put the pink icing into one, and the white icing into the other.

14 Pipe faces on to the biscuits; they look more fun if they are not all the same. Use Smarties, chocolate buttons and dried fruit to make eyes and mouths. Store biscuits in an airtight tin until required.

Maypole birthday cake

This is an exceptionally pretty birthday cake which can be adapted to suit an older age-group by using crystallized rose petals in place of the sweets and perhaps by using longer ribbons with tiny presents on the ends. Alternatively, use straws which have the advantage of being cheap and are light enough not to upset the centre pole. Buy them in varied colours and unravel them, so that they twizzle. Glue or tape them to the central straw.

The cake mixture itself has more egg yolks than a basic Victoria sandwich which uses only 3 eggs and is therefore considerably richer—a real treat of a cake for a special occasion.

MAKES 20 CM [8"] CAKE
225 g [½ lb] self-raising flour
225 g [½ lb] butter or margarine
225 g [½ lb] caster sugar
3 medium-sized eggs
2 egg yolks
edible pink food colouring
45 ml [3 tablespoons]
   raspberry jam

For the decoration:
450 g [1 lb] icing sugar
pink edible food colouring
1 drinking straw
yellow, pink and blue ribbons
jelly babies
Jelly Tots

1 Position the shelf above centre and heat oven to 180°C [350°F] gas mark 4. Grease two 20 cm [8"] sandwich tins with melted fat or oil. Line the base of each tin with greaseproof paper and re-grease.

2 Sift flour into a bowl and reserve.

3 Put softened butter or margarine in a mixing bowl and beat until soft and light. Add sugar and cream it with a wooden spoon until light in colour and fluffy in texture.

4 Whisk the eggs and egg yolks lightly. Add them to the mixture a little at a time, beating well after each addition. Take care to scrape off any mixture adhering to bowl sides or spoon and beat in.

5 Gently fold in the flour, one-third at a time, until incorporated.

6 Place half the mixture in a separate bowl and colour with a few drips of pink food colouring. Put pink mixture into one tin and plain mixture into other tin. Level the tops with a palette knife.

7 Bake for about 30 minutes until risen and golden brown.

8 When cooking time is up, test by pressing lightly with fingertips. The cake should be springy but firm. If ready, remove from oven. Leave in the tin for 5 minutes to cool.

9 Turn out cake on to a tea-towel. Remove paper and then turn right way up on to wire rack to cool.

10 When cold, place pink cake on serving plate or cake board and spread surface with jam. Sandwich other cake on top. Keep moist by covering with an up-turned cake tin or foil until ready to ice.

11 Make icing by mixing the sugar to a spreadable paste with water. Add the colouring.

12 Pour the icing over the cake and use a palette knife to ensure the sides are covered.

13 After about an hour, when the icing is beginning to set, press a straw into the centre of the top, just penetrating the cake beneath, to form the centre maypole.

14 Press jelly babies on to the side of the cake to form a border as though holding hands.

15 Place the Jelly Tots in a circle around the top of the cake and in another ring around the base of the maypole. Leave for a further one hour to set.

16 Meanwhile cut the ribbons to make 6 equal lengths.

17 When the icing is completely set, poke each ribbon in to the top of the maypole. If necessary secure with glue. Arrange ribbons at even intervals around the cake.

18 Arrange two candle-holders containing birthday candles safely out of range of ribbons.

Starry banana custard

☒☒☒ *This is a traditional nursery favourite which small children find easy to spoon up as well as to digest. For a thick custard, normally only egg yolks are used and the egg whites left over are here made into meringue and piped into stars to make a pretty decoration for the banana custard. If you do not own a suitable bag and nozzles, make tiny round meringues.*

SERVES 6
3 bananas
575 ml [1 pt] made thick custard
2 egg whites

pinch of salt
100 g [¼ lb] caster sugar
pink food colouring

1 Slice the bananas into rings and divide equally between 6 individual glass (or plastic) fruit bowls.

2 Pour on the custard while still warm and make sure it covers all the fruit.

3 Leave to cool and then chill in the refrigerator.

4 Meanwhile use the spare egg whites, salt and sugar to make the meringue mixture for decorating the custard.

5 Heat the oven to 110°C [225°F] gas mark ¼.

6 Divide meringue into two. Put the first lot into a nylon piping bag with a star nozzle and pipe rosettes on to a baking tray.

7 Colour the remaining meringue pink, refill the piping bag with this coloured meringue and pipe pink rosettes on to the baking tray.

8 Dry out on the lowest shelf in the oven for 2–3 hours.

9 Arrange pink and white meringue stars on each banana custard.

Teenage party for fourteen

Too old for party games and birthday teas, too young for dinner dates and cocktails—the best answer for teenagers is to give them a supper party. You can prepare and cook for this one in advance, and then tactfully disappear for the evening, leaving your young proxy hosts to reheat and serve the food. That way, it will indeed become their own party—but with guaranteed culinary success, because you've done the work beforehand. There are snacks to bite at between dances, and then there's a vast mock cannelloni and a refreshingly rich cold sweet—all inexpensive food that is satisfying and undeniably popular. Combine these eats with the kids' own music, a little room rearrangement and nothing stronger to drink than home-made ginger beer shandy. Those 13-15 year-olds will have themselves a night to remember!

Menu

Cocktail snacks

---

*Mock cannelloni
special
Fresh tomatoes*

Orange chiffon fiesta

---

*To drink: home-made
ginger beer with lime
and/or ginger
beer shandy
Coffee*

GETTING ORGANIZED

Once you and your teenager(s) have agreed that a supper party is what you want, discuss the menu between you. Today's kids are pretty sophisticated, and any suggestion of ham sandwiches or strawberry jelly would bring howls of derision; on the other hand, anything too unusual will be admired but not eaten. Many of the easy alternatives are too expensive. This menu seems, therefore, to fit the bill: unusual, good-looking, enjoyable, and not too costly.

Invitations

Next, issue the invitations. Keep the age-span tight and the sexes even—but not necessarily paired. The number catered for here is 14—enough to have a noisy good time but not so many to get out of hand or, indeed, for you to cater for in an ordinary domestic kitchen.

It's a wise idea to send proper invitation cards, rather than asking guests by word of mouth. Invitations don't have to be formal; most stationers have fun ones. Sending invitations will spare you from an influx of friends of friends on the night who just thought they'd drop by. Invitations also inform parents where their youngsters are going to be on that night—and what time to expect them home. From 7.30 until 11 p.m. might be a sensible time; starting late enough not to be confused with a children's party, but finishing in time for last buses and weary dads in waiting cars.

Mum's evening out

The time from 7.30 to 11 o'clock is a neat period for you to fill in at the cinema, or to visit a friend or to dine out at a restaurant, if you are leaving your teenagers to give their own party. You don't want to be killing time walking the streets, or trying to break into your own bedroom without the party hearing you!

Of course, the ideal place to go for the evening would be to visit your neighbour, so that you would be within reach if needed. In any event, do warn your neighbours that your kids are having a party and there is likely to be some noise. If their children are the right sort of age, it might be tactful to include them in the invitation list.

Music

Organizing any successful party requires giving a lot of thought to atmosphere. Music is undoubtedly a must, but the kids will provide their own—warn them to mark record sleeves with the owner's name, otherwise you will end up with a whole heap of new discs and not a clue as to the owners. Fortunately for parents, most kids' love of music encompasses the machine that plays it so, on the whole, you need not fear for the fate of your hi-fi in their hands. They are probably more experienced at operating one than you are! Even so, when the time comes, it might be a good idea to appoint just one operator (perhaps your son's or daughter's best friend) and leave him in charge of sound. It will save a jostling crowd all having a go at playing disc jockey, with perhaps disastrous results.

Organizing the rooms

Once the music has been taken care of, concentrate on the room itself. Take out unnecessary furniture and clear a space for dancing. Cushions piled on the floor will give a more relaxed, welcoming 'feel' than chairs. Joss sticks—those aromatic-smelling tapers—provide an exotic, almost sinful air without, of course, being in the least harmful.

It's a sensible precaution to remove any ornaments or treasures to safer shores. Even if accidental damage is covered by your insurance, you don't want to ask for trouble. Also, lock up your drinks cupboard. Your own son or daughter may have more sense and honesty than to touch your whisky, but it takes only one of his or her friends in high spirits to start an orgy. Put your bedroom firmly off limits and utilize children's rooms as cloakrooms.

Lighting always adds mood—table lamps are more romantic than a centre light. Do not let the kids burn candles—however attractive—they are too much of a fire risk. To make the room belong more to their generation, suggest they hang a few posters about. Purpose-made sticky putty should spare your paint and wallpaper.

Consult your teenager about whether any older friends smoke and if you should get out ashtrays. The chances are that you will not have to bother, but if you feel that any of the guests might not only smoke but also stub out cigarettes on your carpet, then roll it back or cover it.

Cutlery and crockery

Now, how about glass and china? Fortunately, 14 isn't an impossible number to cater for. You probably already own enough glasses—they don't have to match—but if you do not, then buy some cheap ones. Picnic beakers will do and are nearly unbreakable and they will be a good investment for parties to come. For a teenage party half-pint beer mugs will prove especially popular. You might be able to borrow these from the wine merchant from whom you buy the beer.

Buy disposable plates both for the main course and the dessert—far more trendy and far less precious than using your own china. Put out forks only for both courses.

Make the kids help

Over all, remember that this is the kids' party and half the fun comes in the preparation. Let them share in it, cooking and all.

THE CATERING

If there is one cliché that is true about 'growing lads and lasses', it's that they're always hungry. This menu has been planned, therefore, with a two-course supper to be eaten around nine o'clock, but with lots of filling snacks to be nibbled at before that. Have large bowls or crisps, cheese straws and cocktail bits available.

Recipes for cheese straws and party nibbles are easily made from savoury pastry. Young people also like the seeming sophistication of appetizers on sticks.

Make these yourself and use wooden cocktail sticks; the plastic ones have an annoying habit of snapping and their bright colours often clash with the food you put on them. Cubes of Cheddar cheese— cut 12 mm [½"] square—are unbeatable for being substantial yet inexpensive. Get the kids to team them with pieces of celery, apple (dipped in lemon juice to stop it turning brown), slices of tomato, quartered tinned peaches, tiny rolls of ham—anything, in fact, that you have in stock which needs using up—provided the combinations remain appetizing. Other cheeses can be used instead of Cheddar if you prefer.

Cut grapefruit and melon in half and cover the rounded side in foil (or leave it plain) and stab in your finished kebabs. This displays them attractively rather than heaping things higgledy-piggledy on a plate.

You can get all this ready a couple of hours before the guests arrive, and both the mock cannelloni special and the orange chiffon fiesta can be prepared several hours in advance, too. The chiffon, of course, is cold and can wait its entry in the refrigerator. The mock cannelloni, however, will need to be baked by the kids themselves half an hour before they are ready to eat.

Leave a written instruction about the time and temperature at which it should be cooked, tape this on the oven door where it will not get lost, and remind them they will have to heat the oven first.

Set up the 'bar' in the kitchen, with glasses and bottles of your ginger beer, and lime or ale according to the age of the guests. It will be up to them to replenish stocks and ice from the refrigerator during the course of the evening.

Finally, just before home-time, a mug of coffee would probably be appreciated. 'Instant' coffee is the thing for teenagers; it will undoubtedly be your teenager's tipple, and a beverage with which they all feel at ease. A home-going drink will also tactfully make the point that the party's over and it's time to go. When you return, turn off the music and say goodbye to any stragglers. Then all that remains is for the home team to stay up and help clear away the debris and any leftovers.

Countdown timetable

3 WEEKS BEFORE
Send out invitations.
Start saving bottles for ginger beer.
Begin shopping for items needed.

2 WEEKS BEFORE
Home-made ginger beer; grow a ginger beer 'plant'—steps 1-3.

1 WEEK BEFORE
Home-made ginger beer: strain the ginger beer liquid and mix with other ingredients, then bottle—steps 4-8.

THE DAY BEFORE
Do the remainder of the shopping.
Orange chiffon fiesta: make the biscuit base and chill—steps 1-9.

ON THE DAY

In the morning
Clear the room for dancing, do any necessary cleaning, decorate with posters etc.
Orange chiffon fiesta: make the chiffon and pour into prepared bases. Leave in refrigerator to set—steps 10-21.

During the afternoon
Fill the ice-cube trays for the ginger lime. If serving it, put ale in the refrigerator to chill.
Set the buffet table with disposable plates, paper napkins, forks and cruet.
Cocktail snacks: make and arrange on covered grapefruit halves.
Mock cannelloni special: prepare for baking—1-13 and 15-17. Allow an hour for making 50 pancakes.

One hour before the party
Set up the bar.
Tomatoes: wash and polish and place in bowl on buffet table, preferably garnished with watercress.
Orange chiffon fiesta: decorate and put it on table—step 22.
Teenager to dress; parents to depart.

45 minutes before the meal
Mock cannelloni special: heat the oven—step 14.

30 minutes before the meal.
Mock cannelloni special: bake $\frac{1}{2}$ hour—step 18.

15 minutes before home-time
Make nightcap coffee and close down disco.

SHOPPING CHECKLIST
About a month beforehand, accompany your teenager to your best local stationer and buy invitation cards, disposable plates and paper napkins. Then a good fortnight ahead of the big event, buy yeast, sugar and ground ginger for making your ginger beer.

Any other shopping could be done as late as the day before the party, but it would make your shopping basket less heavy if you spread the load and bought a few things for the supper each time you went to the shops.

Most of the ingredients in this menu are basic store-cupbaord items anyway, so it is unlikely you will need to buy everything. You will definitely want cans of tomatoes for the cannelloni and canned orange juice for the chiffon. Then buy onions, garlic, lemon, oranges, nutmeg, Parmesan, gelatine, herbs, tomato purée, digestive biscuits and chocolate vermicelli as necessary. Make a special point of checking your supplies of flavourless oil because you are going to require practically half a litre [pint].

The day before, shop for lean beef with which to make the mince. Go for the best quality you can possibly afford. The difference will be apparent in your finished dish. Be fussy about the tomatoes to accompany the cannelloni and insist on small firm red ones. They are intended to be a decoration as much as a vegetable, and they must be good enough to be enjoyed raw. To give 14 people one each with one or two left over, 900 g [2 lb] should be enough.

Remember to order extra from your milkman or dairy. With the chiffon, cheese sauce, pancakes and some home-going coffee, you will want about 4.5 L [8 pints] of extra milk, 14 eggs and $\frac{1}{2}$ kg [1 lb] butter. Don't forget Cheddar for the cheese sauce and the snacks, and a small carton of whipping cream for the chiffon.

DRINKS
One batch of ginger beer makes five 1 L [1¾ pt] bottles of the stuff— so taken neat or with lime, that's enough to serve one generous round to your 14 guests. If the teenagers are older and you are serving a shandy, then mixed half-and-half with 5 L [9 pt] of ale, one batch of ginger beer will make more than two rounds. Estimate that teenagers will want about four drinks per head throughout the whole evening, and double up accordingly.

SPECIAL EQUIPMENT
For the ginger beer, collect one empty jam jar and six big empty bottles per batch.

As for the mock cannelloni, use a frying-pan about 17.5 cm [7"] diameter which is heavy enough to disperse the heat; but note dish(es) on which you then bake your pancakes must also be the one(s) on which you will serve them. You will need large baking dishes to cook and serve as many as 50 pancakes rolls. A baking tray therefore will not do because the cheese sauce will drip out. Three or more gratin dishes are ideal, according to size. The simplest answer is to try to borrow them. The bottom of a covered roaster can be used, if not too deep. If you are desperate, fixed-bottomed rectangular cake tins or roasting tins can be used. Cover with foil and arrange this over the edges of the tin to hide it for serving.

Mock cannelloni special

⧅⧅ *This mock cannelloni is not difficult to make and is an excellent substitute for the genuine Italian pasta. Mince is the basis of the filling, so it makes a reasonably priced dish even for a large number. This dish can be prepared and assembled several hours in advance and then baked half an hour before the meal. Allow up to an hour for making the pancakes. This recipe makes about three stuffed pancakes per person with a few spare. It's a filling meal richly flavoured with tomato and cheese.*

SERVES 14

For the filling:
1.1 kg [2½ lb] lean chuck steak
5 medium-sized onions
5 garlic cloves
150 ml [¼ pt] cooking oil
25 ml [5 teaspoons] dried basil
6 ml [1¼ teaspoons] dried thyme
45 ml [3 tablespoons] tomato purée
1.2 kg [2 lb 10 oz] canned tomatoes
salt
freshly ground black pepper

For the cheese sauce:
100 g [¼ lb] margarine
100 g [¼ lb] plain flour
1.15 L [2 pt] milk
225 g [½ lb] Cheddar cheese
salt and pepper
10 ml [2 teaspoons] dry English mustard

For the pancakes:
550 g [1¼ lb] strong plain flour
2.5 ml [½ teaspoon] salt
5 large eggs
5 egg yolks
1.4 L [2½ pt] milk
75 ml [5 tablespoons] melted butter or flavourless oil
275 ml [½ pt] flavourless oil

For the garnish:
freshly grated nutmeg
90 ml [6 tablespoons] grated Parmesan cheese

1 First make the filling. Mince the meat. Peel the onions and garlic cloves and finely chop them both.

2 Heat the oil in a large heavy-based saucepan or casserole, or divide it (and the subsequent cooking) between 2 large heavy-based frying-pans. Add the onions and garlic and fry gently for about 10 minutes.

3 Add the minced beef and brown it, carefully stirring all the time.

4 Add the herbs, tomato purée and the canned tomatoes and their liquid. Stir thoroughly to amalgamate.

5 Season and leave to cook over a very gentle heat for about 30 minutes or until there is no 'free' liquid. Remove from the heat.

6 Meanwhile, make the cheese sauce. Melt the margarine slowly in a small, heavy-based pan.

7 Remove pan from heat and stir in the flour. Return to low heat and cook gently, stirring for 1-2 minutes to cook the roux.

8 Meanwhile pour the milk into a separate pan and scald.

9 Remove the roux pan from heat. Add a little hot milk, stirring vigorously. Add the remaining milk gradually, still stirring.

10 When the mixture is smoothly blended, return the pan to the heat and bring the sauce to the boil, stirring continuously.

11 Turn the heat to low, cover the pan and simmer for 5 minutes to complete cooking of the starch.

12 Grate the cheese and add it, with the seasoning and mustard to the pan. Stir until the cheese has completely melted. Remove the pan from the heat.

13 Now make the batter and, using as little fat as you possibly can, cook the pancakes. As each is ready, pile it up on top of the previous one, interleaving them with kitchen paper. If you are not eating them immediately, there is no need to keep them warm. If eating immediately, stack them on a plate over a pan of simmering water and cover the pile with foil. Transfer to the warmer as each pile is ready.

14 If planning to eat immediately, heat the oven to 220°C [425°F] gas mark 7.

15 Grease 3-4 ovenproof dishes to take about 50 stuffed pancakes.

16 Place a little of the filling on each pancake, roll up and arrange side by side in the greased dishes.

17 Cover the pancakes with the cheese sauce, and over it sprinkle some freshly grated nutmeg and Parmesan.

18 Bake for 30 minutes or until the tops are golden.

Orange chiffon fiesta

◪◪◪ *A tangy, glamorous dessert, Orange chiffon fiesta is made with an orange-flavoured cold soufflé filling, set with gelatine, which is paired with a biscuit-crumb base. Cream is added for a richer taste. The orange juice is used undiluted for the strongest possible flavour and the finished dessert is decorated with fresh orange segments in party style. The quantities here make three separate chiffons, so that there's enough for the whole crowd to have a helping. Alternatively, use this basic recipe for the chiffons, but choose different flavourings for the second and third—perhaps chocolate and mocha.*

SERVES 14
2 oranges
4 medium-sized eggs
125 g [¼ lb] caster sugar
850 ml [1½ pt] milk
120 ml [8 tablespoons] concentrated frozen canned orange juice
25g [1 oz] gelatine
150 ml [¼ pt] thick or whipping cream
pinch of salt
chocolate vermicelli

For the biscuit base:
700 g [1½ lb] digestive biscuits
350 g [¾ lb] butter or margarine
125 g [¼ lb] caster sugar

1 First make the biscuit base. Butter the sides and base of three 20 cm [8"] plain-sided flan tins with removable bases.

2 Break the biscuits into pieces and put in a polythene bag. Push air out of the bag and seal the top. Then, with a rolling pin, crush the biscuits into crumbs.

3 Tip the crushed biscuits into a coarse sieve over a mixing bowl. Sieve, rubbing large pieces through the mesh with the back of a spoon.

4 Melt the butter or margarine over a low heat. Remove from heat and stir in the sugar.

5 Pour the sugared butter over the crumbs and mix until the crumbs cling together.

6 Scatter a 6 mm [¼"] layer of crumbs evenly over the base of each of the tins. Press evenly in place with the back of a spoon.

7 Coat the sides of the first tin by tilting the tin towards you and then placing two spoonfuls of crumbs on the side of the tin nearest to you. Press into place with the back of a spoon. Work all the way round the tin, building up the sides.

8 Stand the tin level again and, using a clean jam jar, work across the biscuit base and around the sides to achieve a smooth finish. Repeat this process for the second and third tins.

9 Refrigerate for at least 5 hours or preferably overnight.

10 Separate the eggs then cream the egg yolks in a bowl with the caster sugar.

11 Pare the zest from one orange with a swivel-bladed potato peeler and put the zest into a small pan with the milk.

12 Heat the milk until bubbles begin to show around the edge of the pan, then remove from heat. Cover and leave the orange zest to infuse for 30 minutes.

13 Peel the oranges, removing all pith. Segment the oranges reserving the segments, covered, in the refrigerator for decoration. Squeeze the membranes of all juice and reserve this.

14 Strain the orange-flavoured milk into a bowl to remove the zest. Pour the milk on to the egg yolks and sugar, stirring all the time.

15 Cook the mixture in the top of a double boiler, stirring all the time, until it is just thick enough to coat the back of a wooden spoon. Remove from the heat.

16 Wash the milk pan and put the concentrated orange juice in it and add the reserved orange juice. Sprinkle the gelatine over the juice. Put over a low heat and simmer for 3 minutes without stirring, until the gelatine has dissolved. Allow to cool a little.

17 Pour the gelatine while still warm into the custard. Stir well and leave to half set in a cool place.

18 When the custard is on the point of setting, whip the cream and fold into the custard.

19 Whisk the egg whites with a pinch of salt until they are stiff. Fold the half-set custard into the egg whites, using light movements.

20 Transfer the biscuit bases from the tins to serving dishes.

21 Pour one third of the chiffon into each base and leave to set.

22 Decorate chiffons with the segments from the 2 oranges and the chocolate vermicelli.

Home-made ginger beer

⊠⊠⊠ *This is a refresher for hot summer days and long party nights that the kids will enjoy making as much as drinking. The process takes a fortnight, however, so start 'brewing' a good two weeks before any special date when ginger beer might be in demand—either on its own, with lime or as a base for shandy.*

The ginger beer 'plant' is grown in a jam jar, and even quite young children can be made responsible for the job of 'feeding' it each day. When you come to the straining stage, do not discard the sediment; half is enough to start off your next ginger beer. And the other half? Give it away to a neighbour.

Never use screw-top bottles as the ginger beer ferments and could cause the bottles to explode.

MAKES 5 L [9 PT]
**25 g [1 oz] fresh yeast or
  15 g [½ oz] dried yeast
45 ml [9 teaspoons] sugar
45 ml [9 teaspoons] ground
  ginger
1 kg [2 lb] sugar
2 lemons**

1 Put the yeast in a clean jam jar and pour over 275 ml [½pt] water.

2 Stir in 10 ml [2 teaspoons] of the sugar and the same amount of ground ginger. Cover the jar with a piece of polythene and leave for 24 hours.

3 The next day, add another 5 ml [1 teaspoon] each of sugar and ginger. 'Feed' the ginger beer 'plant' in this way for 7 days in all.

4 At the end of the week, strain the liquid through a piece of muslin, inside a sieve, into a bowl. Retain both the sediment and the liquid.

5 Put 1 kg [2 lb] sugar into a large pan of at least 5.6 L [10 pt] capacity. Add 550 ml [1 pt] water. Bring to the boil, stirring with a wooden spoon and boil rapidly for 2 minutes until all the sugar has dissolved.

6 Squeeze the lemons and add the lemon juice and the strained ginger beer liquid to the dissolved sugar. Then add 3.4 L [6 pt] cold water to the dissolved sugar and stir well.

7 Dip a jug into the pan of liquid and pour the ginger beer into bottles. As the pan becomes emptier, pour the ginger beer into the jug and then into bottles.

8 Cork the bottles while still warm and store in a cool place for a week before drinking.

Ginger lime

Mix three parts ginger beer to one part lime cordial. Decorate the glasses with a slice of lemon and a sprig of mint, and serve with ice.

Ginger beer shandy

Serve ginger beer mixed half and half with light ale.

Drinks party for forty

If the people are fun and the drink is plentiful, your party's more than halfway to being a success. Tip the scales further in your favour by making the food special, too. This menu gets away from infamous sausage rolls and bits of Cheddar on soggy biscuits by suggesting some really inspired nibbles—both hot and cold—which will keep festivities going happily into the early hours.

Menu

❧

Cheese sablés
Party garlic pâté on biscuits
Smoky fish barquettes
Asparagus rolls
Hot mushroom vol-au-vents
Goblins on horseback
Tomato waterlilies
Celery boats

━━━━━━ ❊ ━━━━━━

Grapes and dates

━━━━━━ ❊ ━━━━━━

To drink: wine, beer and fruit juice.

Every woman wants to treat herself to a party occasionally—a big full-scale evening party with lots of drinking and dancing and making merry. Once you have set the date, the next thing to do is to invite your guests. This menu has settled for 40—about as many as can be coped with in an average house. However, ideas on this subject vary. Young people may fit 80 into one room and reckon that's just about right, others feel that 20 is the maximum.

So write down your chosen number and then decide who is to come. The old adage about inviting your next-door neighbour still holds good: nobody complains about noise if he or she is part of it.

Kick-off time will vary with the age-group you are catering for. Older people tend to favour an 8–8.30 start. Younger guests prefer a later arrival time—and a much, much later departure time. At any event, this is not a dinner party or even a supper party. It presumes your guests have all eaten before they come. The food you supply will be of the nibbles variety—something to eat throughout the occasion, with hot pick-me-ups appearing at intervals.

THE FOOD

When catering for large numbers, the general rule is not to choose anything based on expensive ingredients. Dishes based on cheese, chicken, rice, and large salads and bread are good party staples.

The hot savouries are mushroom vol-au-vents and chicken livers and water chestnuts in bacon rolls. The cold ones to precede them include a pâté on biscuits, triangular cheese pastries and barquettes with a delicious filling of smoked cod in a cream sauce.

You can also put out celery sticks or better still make celery boats: cut celery stalks into 2.5 cm [1"] pieces and fill them with a cream cheese mixture (225 g [½ lb] cream cheese and 225 g [½ lb] blue cheese mashed together).

Tomato waterlilies are simple to make. Cut the tomatoes into halves, using a sharp knife to make a zigzag pattern, then pull the halves apart. Scoop the seeds and pulp out of each half and sprinkle with salt. Turn the tomato halves upside down and leave to drain for 30 minutes, then rinse with cold water and pat dry. Season and sprinkle with freshly chopped basil if available or parsley. Alternatively add a few drops of olive oil. These will contrast well with all the other foods you are serving, and help the appearance of your table, adding colour. Watercress and sprigs of parsley are used liberally elsewhere for garnishing but you can use your imagination to add to these: radish roses, twists of orange or lemon etc.

The asparagus rolls are made with thin brown bread and canned or frozen seasoned asparagus. Two 298 g [10½ oz] cans of asparagus will be enough for about 40 rolls if you use two spears to a slice of bread. To make the rolls, remove the crusts from the bread and spread each slice with softened butter. Place two asparagus spears at one end of each slice and roll up tightly. Cut each roll in half or into three on a slant. Chill for 30 minutes before serving.

As a concession to the odd sweet tooth, grapes and dates are on the menu—only a small amount of each, because they are both expensive.

Countdown

3 WEEKS BEFORE THE PARTY
Send out invitations.

2 WEEKS BEFORE
Order drinks and arrange loan of glasses.

4 DAYS BEFORE
Do the shopping, with the exception of perishables.
Party garlic pâté: marinate the meat—steps 1–2.

3 DAYS BEFORE
Party garlic pâté: cook the pâté in the oven and then weigh down and leave somewhere cool—steps 3–8.
Tape party music or select suitable records.

2 DAYS BEFORE
Smoky fish barquettes: make the pastry and store in the refrigerator—step 1.
Party garlic pâté: remove weights, scrape off fat and re-cover. Refrigerate—step 9.
Collect the drinks order and glasses. Polish glasses if necessary.

THE DAY BEFORE
Smoky fish barquettes: mould and bake the pastry—steps 2–7.
Party garlic pâté: make 40 gherkin fans. Cover them with cling film and keep cool.
Clear the party room of excess furniture and vulnerable ornaments. Organize ashtrays. Clean and tidy all rooms where guests are likely to go.
Cheese sablés: make, bake and leave on baking sheet to cool—steps 1–8.

ON THE DAY
In the morning
Shop for cod and brown bread. Arrange a room for guests coats.

Finally, for a party where you want lighter refreshments altogether, serve bowls of nuts, crisps, black olives and seedless raisins. Or, if you prefer, put out a platter of crudités, comprising raw vegetables.

timetable

Celery boats: trim, scrub and cut into short lengths. Cover and leave in refrigerator to crisp. If stuffing, mix cream cheese and blue cheese. Season and chill.

Smoky fish barquettes: poach the fish and make the sauce—steps 8–10.

Hot mushroom vol-au-vents: make the filling and cool—steps 1–9.

In the afternoon
Chill the white wine.

Goblins on horseback: make the bacon rolls ready for the oven—steps 1–8.

Asparagus rolls: make with canned asparagus and brown bread. Wrap in cling-film and chill.

Smoky fish barquettes: fill cases and garnish—step 11.

Cheese sablés: arrange on serving plates and garnish with parsley—step 9.

Arrange the bar. Set the buffet table in the party room. Put out the dates and grapes (rinse and provide small scissors to encourage tidy eating).

Tomato waterlilies: cut the tomatoes, scoop out insides, sprinkle with salt and drain. Garnish.

Hot mushroom vol-au-vents: fill the cases and transfer to baking sheet—step 10.

1½ hours before the party
Get yourself dressed.

30 minutes before the party
Smoky fish barquettes: spoon filling into cases, garnish each one with a caper and arrange on a serving plate—step 11.

Party garlic pâté: spoon on to biscuits, garnish with gherkin fans and arrange on serving plates—steps 10–11. Add to buffet table.

During the party
Heat the oven.

Goblins on horseback: heat in the oven and serve hot—steps 9–11.

Hot mushroom vol-au-vents: heat in the oven and serve garnished with watercress—steps 11–13.

THE DRINKS
Unless you make it a bottle party—and this is quite acceptable these days—very few people can afford to set up a complete bar: serving spirits and shorts and the whole range of mixers. As well as being expensive, this is not suitable for a large group because of the problems of serving. If you feel your lot is to pay for everything and chivalrously do not expect any contributions from your friends, then the only practical answer is to stick to beer and wine.

Everyone lives in fear that their party will fizzle out because guests are standing about with empty glasses; yet on the other hand, no one wants to pay for drink that will be wasted. If you can persuade your wine merchant to take your drinks order on a sale-or-return basis, you have a tremendous advantage. You can risk over-ordering in the knowledge that you won't have to pay for any unopened bottles or cans. But if you cannot get him to agree to this, you will just have to estimate your requirements.

How much are people likely to drink is almost as difficult a question as asking how long is a piece of string. It depends—on their age and gender, on their alcoholic capacity, on their mood on that particular evening and, very simply, on how much you offer them. And even if you can answer all those things accurately about your friends, you still have to decide which of them are beer drinkers and which are wine, and buy more of one or the other accordingly.

At a very rough calculation, for beer you guess that 15 of your 40 guests will drink beer exclusively, so you will want about 27 L [6 gallons]. If you fancy a touch of the old British pub, you can hire a 5 gallon keg complete with tap. They are usually made of metal these days, unfortunately, rather than being wooden barrels, but they still add atmosphere. Appoint experienced pint-pullers as operators—a half-hour shift per man. The keg will run out after a couple of hours or so, freeing all your amateur barmen for the dance-floor. At this stage, you would be wiser to move on to cans of beer rather than opening up a second keg as beer does not keep. Once opened, you would have to finish an entire second keg, and your guests might not want that much. Pipkins contain 4 L [7 pt] each and so, with them, the absolute maximum you could have left over would be 4 L [7 pt]—far less extravagant.

As for the wine, bear in mind that at a party most people find white wine lighter than red, and many women prefer it to red wine, so order more of the former. The large 2-litre bottles are definitely the most economical buy, but do spare some consideration for what is actually in those party-sized bottles. Some contain rough wine, and it is worth paying just a little more to avoid them. Soave (white) and Valpolicella (red) are usually reliable and reasonably inexpensive buys.

Your minimum wine requirements would be five 2-litre bottles of Soave and three 2-litre bottles of Valpolicella. In addition, buy cans of tomato juice and cartons of orange juice for teetotallers and drivers.

GETTING ORGANIZED
Invitations for your big event should be issued about three weeks in advance, especially if happening at a weekend. People's Fridays and Saturdays tend to get filled up and, when there are young couples on the guest list, you must give them time to find a baby-sitter too! For a week night party, you might very well get a 90% acceptance rate at only a couple of days' notice, but it is less disappointing for hosts as well as guests if everyone receives fair warning.

Next on your list of priorities comes ordering the drinks and arranging for the loan of glasses. It is worth knowing that most wine merchants will lend you the necessary 9 dozen or so (a mixture of beer mugs and wine glasses) free, charging only for breakages. This is a neater solution than using all your odd ones of different shapes and sizes and scrounging from neighbours.

Then there is the music to choose—either on record or, if you have a music centre with a tape attachment—on tape. It saves all that record changing and choosing in semi-darkness if you can tape the party music from start to finish in advance.

All the shopping, with the exception of the few perishables (see shopping checklist), can be done 4 days ahead of time. You can also start the garlic pâté that early, because it needs time to marinate and mature. The rest of the cooking is spaced out over the following two days and on the party day itself.

Inevitably, some jobs do have to be done within hours of guests' arrival. For instance, there would be no point in cleaning and clearing the party room days in advance; it would only get littered up again in the intervening period. Most important, don't forget to clear a room for guests' coats.

The buffet table has to be set during the party afternoon; so does the bar—but that last item is left to your man. On the whole, he gets off pretty lightly with catering for 'our' party, and this is one worthwhile contribution he can make—he will probably offer to do it.

The timetable gives you all the time you need to get dressed and leaves only the final touches to be seen to when you reappear in your finery.

At the height of the party, serve your hot savouries. This will involve thinking about them half an hour before you want them, because the oven needs heating. Baking the goblins on horseback will take up to quarter of an hour then reduce your oven temperature and pop in the vol-au-vents.

SPECIAL EQUIPMENT

One of the great advantages of this stand-up buffet is that there is no crockery or cutlery to worry about. Everything is hand-held, bite-into food. However, you will need up to a dozen serving plates on which to arrange the canapés. If you haven't enough, use your dinner plates—with this menu, they are not in demand for anything else.

You need a dish in which to cook the pâté. It doesn't have to be special, for it won't be on show. Anything ovenproof of the right capacity will be fine.

Lastly, you cannot bake barquettes without proper barquette moulds, known rather irreverently by some ironmongers as 'oval tartlet tins'. The menu recommends you make 24 barquettes, which means, of course, you need 2 dozen moulds. You could get away with a dozen if you were prepared to bake one lot, cool, unmould, and then bake the rest.

Shown here is part of the party spread. From left to right are cheese sablés, delicious triangles of cheesy pastry topped with chopped nuts, party garlic pâté on biscuits topped with gherkin fans. For quick nibbles, serve salted nuts, black olives and potato crisps. As a change from so much savoury food, put a bunch of grapes on the table.

SHOPPING CHECKLIST

Shopping for a big party is always a momentous task, so get it over and done with several days in advance. The only exception is a flying visit, first thing on your party morning, to the fishmonger to buy your smoked cod and on to the baker for a thin-sliced loaf of brown bread for the asparagus rolls.

The only item which may prove difficult to find is the can of water chestnuts. Try the delicatessen or make a note to search for one when you next go into town. The can will keep. So, incidentally, will the jar of capers and bottle of gherkins, which are also on your shopping list. These things, too, are delicatessen fare. You will need the 70 ml [2½ fl oz] size to provide you with 40 capers and the 100 ml [3½ fl oz] size of cocktail gherkins to give you 40 of them.

The rest of the shopping list divides itself into categories.

Dairy: 700 g [1½ lb] butter (for the sablés, vol-au-vents and goblins on horseback), 700 g [1½ lb] of cheese for grating (this time for the sablés and the barquettes), eggs, an extra pint of milk, a small carton of thick cream for the barquette sauce, and 225 g [½ lb] cream cheese for the celery boats.

Butcher: 450 g [1 lb] of lean pork and 350 g [¾ lb] of pie veal for the pâté. You also require 575 g [1¼ lb] of chicken livers for the goblins. If you buy three 225 g [½ lb] cartons of frozen livers, it will save you having to make a special shopping trip for fresh ones later on. Admittedly, this will leave 125 g [¼ lb] left over, but you can always use them up in your favourite pâté recipe, or lightly fried in butter and served with scrambled eggs.

Greengrocer: buy a beautiful bunch of grapes, lots of watercress and parsley for garnishing (and flavouring in the case of the latter), 450 g [1 lb] of small tomatoes for making into waterlilies and a whole celery for cutting into boats or sticks (also one stick to go into the vol-au-vents). Then you need about 450 g [1 lb] onions for the pâté and the vol-au-vents (also a couple of shallots for which you may have to substitute another onion), 225 g [½ lb] of carrots, 450 g [1 lb] of mushrooms for the vol-au-vents and a garlic bulb for the pâté. Finally the barquette sauce takes a large cucumber.

Grocer: top of the list comes 40 vol-au-vent cases (about 5 cm [2"] in diameter). As for the water biscuits, it doesn't matter what they weigh, but

you do need 40 of them, a 450 g [1 lb] pack will probably do. For the sablés, barquettes, the goblins and the vol-au-vent sauce, you need a total of 1.4 kg [3 lb] of plain flour, and 500 g [1 lb 2 oz] of margarine. As always, buy fresh herbs whenever possible—this menu requires basil, oregano and tarragon or chives. Then there is 225 g [¼ lb] of walnuts—broken ones if you like—for the sablés, and chicken stock (stock-cube if you absolutely have to!) for the vol-au-vent sauce. Buy 225 g [½ lb] blue cheese, such as Roquefort, for the celery boats. The ingredients state 26 rashers of streaky bacon (for the pâté and goblins), which in terms of weight probably means about 450 g [1 lb]. Cocktail gherkins are needed to garnish the pâté. Two 298 g [10½ oz] cans of asparagus are needed for the rolls. Finally you want a box of dessert dates. Apart from this you may want some nuts and potato crisps.

Supplies: check the storecupboard for the following—olive oil, paprika, cayenne pepper, nutmeg, lard, mustard powder and white wine vinegar. If you don't have any sweet wine that needs finishing up, you will have to buy a half-bottle specially for the pâté.

Party garlic pâté on biscuits

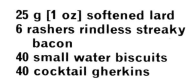

This is a smooth meaty pâté which contains no liver. The meat is marinated with a little carrot as well as onions, shallots, herbs and a generous amount of garlic are included for added flavour. Serve it on medium-sized round water biscuits, garnished with gherkin fans.

Remember to begin the pâté at least two days before you need it to allow for marinating and maturing. The flavour does improve given time.

MAKES ABOUT 40 CANAPES
450 g [1 lb] pork without skin or bone
350 g [¾ lb] pie veal
1 onion
2 shallots
1 carrot
2 garlic cloves
15 ml [1 tablespoon] chopped parsley
salt
freshly ground black pepper
30 ml [2 tablespoons] salad oil
175 ml [6 fl oz] sweet white wine
25 g [1 oz] softened lard
6 rashers rindless streaky bacon
40 small water biscuits
40 cocktail gherkins

1 Mince the pork and veal coarsely. Peel and finely chop the onion, carrot, shallots and garlic.

2 Mix all these ingredients in a bowl. Mix in the parsley and seasoning. Pour the oil and wine over the mixture. Leave in a cool place for 24 hours. Stir the mixture twice during this time.

3 Heat the oven to 180°C [350°F] gas mark 4. Grease a 1.3 L [2¼ pt] capacity dish with lard.

4 The meat mixture will have absorbed almost all the marinade. Stir it well into a soft, moist mixture and check the seasoning.

5 Turn the mixture into the prepared dish. Press down with a spoon.

6 Cover the dish with bacon rashers. Cover tightly with foil, and with a lid too, if possible.

7 Stand the dish in a large roasting tin of hot water which comes halfway up the sides. Bake for 1¾ hours or until the pâté has shrunk from the sides of the dish.

8 Remove from the oven and from the pan of water. Cover with foil-wrapped cardboard cut to fit just inside the rim. Press down with weights such as cans of fruit etc. Stand the dish in a pan of cold water in a cool place until quite cold—overnight if desired.

9 Remove the weights and cardboard. Scrape off any excess fat round the edges of the dishes. Re-cover with cling film and refrigerate for at least 24 hours.

10 To serve, take off the top bacon and use for a soup topping etc. Use a dessert spoon to scoop up the right amount of pâté to cover one biscuit. Do this in one neat sweep. Transfer to each of the 40 biscuits in turn.

11 Make fans with the gherkins and place one on top of each canapé. Arrange on serving plates.

Cheese sablés

⊠ *These rich, melt-in-the-mouth little savouries are always highly praised—and are in fact amazingly quick and easy to make—necessary when you are making them in quantity. The cayenne pepper makes them spicily hot, and the coating of nuts gives them the element of a treat. They are served cold, which means you can cook them the day before if desired.*

MAKES ABOUT 60
350 g [¾ lb] plain flour
5 ml [1 teaspoon] salt
generous pinch of cayenne
** pepper**
350 g [¾ lb] butter
350 g [¾ lb] grated cheese
milk and beaten egg for
** glazing**
225 g [½ lb] walnuts
sprigs of parsley for garnish

1 Heat the oven to 190°C [375°F] gas mark 5.

2 Sift the flour with the salt and the cayenne pepper into a mixing bowl.

3 Add the butter and cut into small pieces with a round-bladed knife. Rub into the flour.

4 Add the cheese to the flour and press the dough together with your fingertips.

5 Roll out fairly thinly on a floured board and cut into 5 cm [2"] strips. Brush with beaten egg glaze.

6 Cut each strip into triangles and transfer them to 2 baking trays. Chop the walnuts and press lightly on to pastry.

7 Bake in the oven for about 10 minutes until golden brown.

8 When baked, remove from the oven but leave on the baking sheet to cool—about 30 minutes. (Sablés are very crumbly when hot and should not be handled as they may break.)

9 When cold, arrange on serving plates and add sprigs of parsley for garnish.

Smoky fish barquettes

⊠⊠⊠ *When eaten cold, these unusual and superb savouries are less crumbly and far easier to hold in the hand—which, of course, makes them an excellent choice for a running buffet. The pastry for the barquettes is a rich cheese shortcrust, using a hard cheese (such as Cheddar, Caerphilly or Emmenthal) and it is fitted into the special little oval moulds called barquettes or tartlet moulds.*

The filling on this occasion is smoked cod mixed into cold cucumber sauce.

MAKES 24 BARQUETTES
For the shortcrust pastry:
675 g [1½ lb] plain flour
4 ml [¾ teaspoon] mustard
** powder**
4 ml [¾ teaspoon] black
** pepper**
4 ml [¾ teaspoon] salt
500 g [1 lb 2 oz] margarine
350 g [¾ lb] Cheddar cheese
2 large-sized egg yolks

For the filling:
675 g [1½ lb] filleted smoked
** cod**
1 large cucumber
150 ml [¼ pt] thick cream
30 ml [2 tablespoons] white
** wine vinegar**
15 ml [1 tablespoon] freshly
** chopped tarragon or chives**

1 Make the rich cheese shortcrust pastry and, unless required immediately, wrap in cling film—making sure all air is expelled. This will store in the refrigerator for up to 5 days.

2 No earlier than the day before required, roll out the dough and use to line 12 (or 24) oval barquette moulds.

3 Position oven shelf to just above centre. Heat the oven to 200°C [400°F] gas mark 6.

4 Transfer the barquettes to a baking tray, line with beans, and bake blind for 7–10 minutes.

5 Remove the beans and bake for a further 5–10 minutes to set the pastry.

6 Remove from the oven and leave to cool completely before unmoulding.

7 Repeat steps 2–6 for a second batch. When cold reserve in an airtight tin until required.

8 On the day the barquettes are to be served, poach the cod very gently for 10 minutes in just enough water to cover the fish. Remove from water and leave to cool.

9 For cucumber sauce, peel and chop 1 cucumber and mix with 150 ml [¼ pt] thick cream.

10 Flake the cooled fish, discard any bones and mix into the sauce.

11 Spoon the filling into the barquettes and garnish with a caper. Arrange on a serving plate.

Hot mushroom vol-au-vents

⊠ *For a party treat, these vol-au-vents are served hot. But to save the hostess labouring in the kitchen while her guests are present, preparation to step 10 can be done in advance.*

To eat cold, omit steps 11–13. The cases are already baked—either shop ones or your own. Allow the filling to cool before filling the vol-au-vents.

MAKES 40 VOL-AU-VENTS
40 made vol-au-vent cases
watercress for garnish

For the sauce:
1 medium-sized onion
1 medium-sized carrot
1 celery stick
350 ml [12 fl oz] milk
350 ml [12 fl oz] chicken stock
2.5 ml [½ teaspoon] nutmeg or
** mace**
salt and pepper
90 g [3½ oz] butter
90 g [3½ oz] flour
15 ml [1 tablespoon] lemon
** juice**

For the solid filling:
2 small onions
450 g [1 lb] mushrooms
50 g [2 oz] butter
45 ml [3 tablespoons] freshly
** chopped parsley**

1 Peel and dice the onion and scrub and dice the carrot and celery for the sauce. Put them into a pan with the milk, chicken stock and seasonings.

2 Slowly bring the milk to scalding point. Remove from the heat, cover and leave to infuse for at least 30 minutes.

3 Peel and finely chop the other 2 onions for the solid filling. Wipe clean and roughly chop the mushrooms.

4 Melt the 50 g [2 oz] butter in a saucepan, add the onions and sweat over a low heat until soft.

5 Add the mushrooms and parsley and cook, stirring occasionally, until the mushrooms are just tender.

6 Meanwhile make a roux for the sauce with the equal quantities of butter and flour. Remove from the heat.

7 Strain the infused milk, then gradually stir into the roux.

8 Cover and simmer for 5 minutes.

9 Stir in the mushroom, onion and parsley mixture. Stir in the lemon juice. Taste and add more lemon juice and seasoning as necessary.

Cover and leave to cool.

10 Remove the tops from the vol-au-vent cases and spoon in enough mixture to fill. Use the spoon to press the filling well into the case. Transfer to baking sheet.

11 If serving hot, heat the oven to 150°C [300°F] gas mark 2.

12 Bake for 20 minutes.

13 When hot, arrange on a serving plate and garnish with watercress.

Shown below are waterlily tomatoes, celery boats and mushroom vol-au-vents.

Goblins on horseback

For a change, this is a hot party savoury and is actually another variation on the classic devils on horseback (prunes stuffed with spicy fried almonds, wrapped in bacon rashers and then grilled). The stuffing this time consists of canned water chestnuts with chicken livers, a delightful mixture of textures.

Because no one wants to start cooking in the middle of a party, it is recommended that the livers and chestnuts are sautéed in advance and the bacon rolls completely prepared; then 15 minutes before the devils are required, they can be popped in the oven and heated.

MAKES ABOUT 40
575 g [1¼ lb] chicken livers
75 g [3 oz] flour
salt
freshly ground black pepper
15 ml [1 tablespoon] butter
15 ml [1 tablespoon] cooking oil
450 g [15½ oz] canned water chestnuts
20 streaky bacon rashers

1 Wash the livers under cold running water and pat dry with kitchen paper. Carefully trim away any tough skin and greenish parts. Keep the livers whole.

2 Season the flour and place in a clean polythene bag. Shake lightly. Add the livers, a few at a time and coat them. Turn the floured livers on to a plate. Shake off excess flour and transfer to a clean plate.

3 Put the butter and oil in a frying pan. Heat over a moderate heat until hot and sizzling.

4 Lay livers flat in the pan and cook for 2–3 minutes; turn and cook for a further 2 minutes. Remove from the pan and keep warm while any remaining livers are fried.

5 Drain the can of water chestnuts and add them to the butter and oil remaining in the pan. Sauté for 2 minutes until butter-coated. Transfer to a plate, using a draining spoon.

6 Stretch the bacon with the back of a knife and cut the bacon rashers in half.

7 Cut the chicken livers in half.

8 Place one piece of liver and one water chestnut at the end of a halved bacon rasher. Roll up and, for a cocktail savoury, secure with a cocktail stick. Arrange in a dry ovenproof dish or a roasting tin.

9 Heat oven to 200°C [400°F] gas mark 6.

10 Cook the devils for 10–15 minutes until bacon is golden brown.

11 Transfer to a warm serving plate; serve hot with the cocktail sticks.

An engagement party for twenty

An engagement party is the ideal opportunity for prospective relatives to meet their counterparts and for the engaged couple to meet members of each other's families. The meal chosen here will both break the ice and impress the in-laws to be!

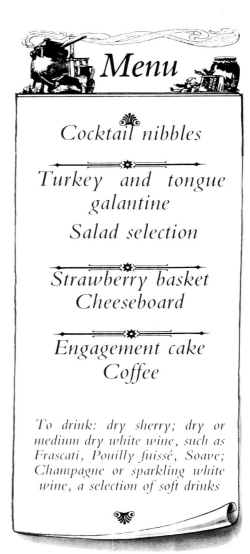

Menu

Cocktail nibbles

Turkey and tongue galantine
Salad selection

Strawberry basket
Cheeseboard

Engagement cake
Coffee

To drink: dry sherry; dry or medium dry white wine, such as Frascati, Pouilly fuissé, Soave; Champagne or sparkling white wine, a selection of soft drinks

Catering for twenty people is a big job, but there are times when a celebration is called for and the time, effort and money spent is an investment in the pleasure of a very special event. Whether it is an engagement, coming-of-age or wedding anniversary party, you may feel the occasion requires a gathering of family and friends. This means planning food and drink, and to be successful, you should start as long in advance as possible. Of course, you could get caterers and hire a hall but if there is a wedding at a later date the chances are that the engagement party will be a more modest occasion. However, by catering yourself you get good value for money and a free hand in the quantity and quality of the food. The drink is much cheaper too—a hired bar is usually a very expensive business.

This menu is for an engagement party for 20 people; however, it is equally suitable for an anniversary or a coming-of-age party provided the cake is a different shape to the heart used here. Twenty is a large number to cope with in the average home and a buffet-style meal therefore makes sense. If you wish to have a more formal dinner, then halve the quantities given here and have a sit-down meal for ten.

An engagement party is the perfect opportunity for prospective bride and groom to make an official announcement of what someone once described as a 'purely private intention', and for them to meet relatives from both sides on neutral ground.

As the family of the bride traditionally provide the engagement party, it is important that Mum and bride-to-be agree well in advance who is to come so that invitations can be issued, extra supplies ordered and crockery borrowed where necessary. Invitations are best kept to close relations and best friends on both sides. Be prepared therefore, for a mixed age-group party, where not all the guests know one another.

This is very much a mother and daughter affair, so arrange to help each other in order to have some precious time off on the day to do the essential beauty bits.

GETTING ORGANIZED

Invitations must be arranged as soon as you have fixed a date, so that you can cater with an exact number in mind. Hire glasses from a wine merchant and borrow any extra crockery you need from a neighbour or relative.

Order drinks in advance, preferably on a sale or return basis, so that if you have any unused supplies they can go back to the shop and you will get a refund.

This party is buffet style, so where you eat what is an important consideration. If you have two rooms that guests can use, the cocktail nibbles and engagement cake could go in one part while the main part of the feast remains in the other. If possible, arrange the cocktail nibbles in the vicinity of the bar. This way people won't stray and start the main course until you are ready and all the guests have arrived. Using two rooms also gives you a chance to do some furtive tidying up while the guests eat the main part of the food and also means you do not have to toast the bride- and groom-to-be in a room littered with dirty plates.

Organizing the food is fairly easy as much of it can be prepared in advance. Depending on what you serve, the cocktail nibbles can be made on the morning of the party (dips can be made the day before).

The galantine can be boned, stuffed and cooked two days before the party and coated with aspic and decorated the day before. Cover it with a 'dome' of foil to keep the aspic clear and sparkling. Don't let the foil touch the aspic or it will stick.

The strawberry basket can be as-sembled the day before the party but should not be filled. The basic puff pastry and the shortbread base can be made as far in advance as wished if you have a freezer.

The engagement cake can be made as much as three months in advance (in fact it will improve with keeping) and iced up to two weeks in advance. Stored in an airtight tin, it will keep fresh and beautiful until the day it is cut.

The cheeseboard should not be arranged until just before the party as cheese quickly cracks and goes stale.

DRINKS

However dearly you may wish to arrange a complete bar, restrain yourself and compromise between what you would like to serve, what people actually drink and what you can reasonably afford. Beer is not included on the menu card, but if you know several of your guests are beer drinkers, decrease your wine order

Countdown timetable

ONE MONTH BEFORE THE PARTY

Issue invitations.
Arrange to borrow necessary equipment.
Start buying non-perishable groceries.
Engagement cake: bake the cake—steps 1-6. Wrap in foil and store in an airtight tin.

TWO WEEKS BEFORE THE PARTY

Order drinks and arrange hire of glasses.
Engagement cake: ice—steps 7-17. Store in airtight tin.

TWO DAYS BEFORE THE PARTY

Turkey and tongue galantine: bone stuff and cook—steps 1-14. Cover with greaseproof paper and leave.
Strawberry basket: make base and puff pastry, bake—steps 1-9.

THE DAY BEFORE

Turkey and tongue galantine: coat in aspic and decorate—steps 15-18. Cover with a dome of foil and leave in the refrigerator.
Start making ice and store in polythene bags in the freezer compartment.
Cocktail nibbles: mix dips and chill.
Buy flowers, make sure table linen, cutlery, crockery and glasses are clean.

ON THE DAY
In the morning
Organize the rooms.
Wash the vegetables for the crudités and the salads. Make salad dressings. Cook the potatoes, drain, dress and allow to cool.

In the afternoon
Strawberry basket: assemble the basket—steps 10-12.
Turkey and tongue galantine: remove from refrigerator.
Lay the table.
Set up the bar.
Put the wine in buckets to chill.
Salad selection: assemble chosen salads but do not dress them yet.

1 hour before the meal
Strawberry basket: fill the basket. Lightly whip cream—steps 13-15.
Arrange the cheeseboard
Push cocktail sticks into sausages and arrange on a serving plate.

15 minutes before the meal
Take all the food to the tables. Dress the salads.

and allow them this indulgence.

With the cocktail nibbles, you can serve dry sherry. Many people will only want one glass of this, so two standard-sized bottles will be sufficient. If you have a 'sale or return' order and have nothing to lose, order three or four bottles just in case.

With the meal itself, a white wine is called for. Good choices would be Frascati, white Valpolicella, Soave, or a Pouilly Fuissé, depending on the state of your pocket. Allow one standard-sized bottle between two people. Don't open all the bottles at once so that if there are any left over, they can go back to the supplier and you will get a refund. The wine will, of course, need to be chilled. The best way to do this, when the refrigerator is fully booked, is in buckets of iced water.

To toast the happy couple and accompany the cake, something bubbly is required. Real champagne is undoubtedly the nicest, but it is also the most expensive—you would need about 5 bottles to cater for 20 people. Take heart though, there are plenty of cheap, sparkly alternatives which still make a satisfying pop when the cork comes out. Excellent suggestions are Veuve du Vernay, Asti Spumante or any sparkling hock. Alternatively, you could hand round glasses of sweet sherry, Marsala or Madeira with the cake.

If you want to simplify things and stick to one wine from start to finish, then go for a sparkling white wine; but try to find a dryish one—look for 'sec' or 'brut' on the label—because too much sweet wine becomes sickly after an entire evening.

For non-drinkers, provide a selection of fruit squashes and 'mixers' such as tonic, soda, ginger ale and bitter lemon. This will also cater for any children present although they might like a little taste of the bubbly!

After the meal and after the happy couple have been toasted, most people would welcome a cup of coffee. To cope with 20 people, you would need to make about 2.3 L [4 pt] coffee. This may seem rather a lot but some people may want two cups.

The strawberry basket requires 30 ml [2 tablespoons] brandy. If you don't have this in stock, buy a miniature bottle. You also need a small quantity of sherry for the cake—use brandy instead, if this is more convenient.

SHOPPING CHECKLIST

The shopping list is a long one. Start with the groceries as most of these can be bought as soon as you have decided to have the party. You will need quite a lot of the items to make the cake (this can be done as much as three months in advance but do not ice and decorate it until a fortnight before required).

Groceries
For the cocktail nibbles you will need small salted biscuits. These are better than crisps for holding dips. Buy a selection of assorted biscuits for your cheeseboard. Digestive biscuits are also popular with cheese. If making pineapple dip buy a can of crushed pineapple. Canned cocktail sausages are a useful addition—serve them on cocktail sticks. You can, of course, add any other of the usual bits and pieces such as nuts and crisps to the list. However, as a full meal is being served these fillers are really an unnecessary extravagance.

For the galantine you will need pistachio nuts, 25 g [1 oz] nuts should be sufficient to give you 15 g [½ oz] when shelled. The galantine is garnished with black olives or olives stuffed with pimento. Only a few are needed so you can use some of the 225 g [½ lb] olives required for the tomato salad.

For the salad dressings you will need 1.4 L [2½ pt] oil—275 ml [½ pt] of which must be olive oil for the tomato salad. The salad dressings will also require about 575 ml [1 pt] vinegar. You may need tarragon vinegar if you are making tarragon cream dressing.

The strawberry basket needs redcurrant jelly to assemble the basket

and it is again used to glaze the strawberries.

The engagement cake requires dried fruit: 150 g [5 oz] glacé cherries, 450 g [1 lb] raisins, 175 g [6 oz] currants, 30 ml [2 tablespoons] mixed peel, 15 ml [1 tablespoon] angelica, 100 g [¼ lb] walnuts. Brown sugar is used in the cake—225 g [8 oz] is sufficient but you may wish to buy more to serve with coffee. To decorate the cake, 700 g [1½ lb] almond paste is used (or marzipan). This is covered with 900 g [2 lb] icing sugar. Buy 1.5 kg [3½ lb], as you will need more for the decorations. The icing sugar is mixed with liquid glucose.

You will also need 100g [¼ lb] caster sugar, 900 g [2 lb] plain flour and 100 g [¼ lb] rice flour for the strawberry baskets. Plus 450 g [1 lb] self-raising flour for the cake.

The butcher

The main course is a turkey galantine. The meat can be bought 2 or 3 days ahead but it must be the day on which you start to make the galantine. A 5 kg [11 lb] turkey is the main ingredient of the galantine. Buy 450 g [1 lb] cooked tongue and the same quantity of ham in one piece. The pie veal—450 g [1 lb]—can be bought in one piece or chopped, whichever way your butcher sells it. The stuffing also uses 225 g [½ lb] lean belly of pork. Ask the butcher to remove rind and bones.

The dairy

The dairy produce is perishable so plan your shopping to coincide with the food preparation.

You will need 6 large eggs for making the cake (this could be well in advance of when other dairy produce is required). Nearer the time buy another 6 large eggs and 6 medium eggs; 2 large ones for the galantine; one medium one to glaze the pastry; 2 whites for the icing—leaving 7 should you need eggs for a mayonnaise or hard boiled eggs for garnishing.

Cream features in the dips and again with the strawberry dessert. For the dips 150 ml [5 fl oz] thin cream will be sufficient to spare you the quantity required for the galantine. You will need an extra 575 ml [1 pt] if you are serving tarragon cream dressing. Cream cheese and soured cream are needed for dips, 450 g [1 lb] cottage cheese and at least 900 g [2 lb] butter for the dessert and the cake—buy another 450 g [1 lb] if you wish to serve French bread and also for the cheeseboard. For the cheeseboard buy a choice of 3 or 4 cheeses, vary them to contrast in texture and flavour.

The strawberry dessert is served with thick cream: 575 ml [1 pt] is the absolute minimum, buy more and with a little bit of luck you will have some left over to offer around when serving coffee.

The greengrocer

This needs to be arranged so that you have vegetables for the stock and an onion for the stuffing a day or two before the party. There will probably not be enough room for all the saladstuff in the refrigerator so some items might be better left until the day. If you order in advance you will probably be able to collect what is required without having to wait.

For the dips and crudités, buy carrots, celery, cucumber and cauliflower. Cucumber crops up again; a small piece is used to garnish the turkey and another 3-4 cucumbers are required for a cucumber salad. There is always room somewhere for onions and garlic. Radishes are used for the galantine garnish and a lemon or two will also be useful. For the salads: 2.7 kg [6 lb] new potatoes; 2.2kg [5 lb] tomatoes; 4 lettuces and 2 bunches of watercress for the green salad and spring onions for garnishing. Fruit adds colour and interest to the cheeseboard; apples, pears and grapes are suitable. The strawberry dessert requires 1.4 kg [3 lb] fresh strawberries and 2 large oranges.

Unless you grow your own herbs buy a selection of fresh herbs: tarragon, chives, parsley and basil are good choices. If fresh herbs are not available, you may need some lettuce hearts or a few delicate fennel fronds for garnish.

The store cupboard
Check that you have chilli powder, mustard, curry powder, liquid glucose, white fat, tarragon vinegar, dried thyme, allspice, apricot jam for a glaze, gelatine and red food colouring, as well as the usual seasonings.

Cocktail nibbles

Nibbles to serve with drinks before people get down to serious eating are great ice-breakers. They are easy to eat while talking and circulating—the ideal fare for prospective relatives who are strangers to one another.

Make dips and serve these with small salted biscuits. These are more useful than potato crisps as they do not break as readily. Also serve crudités with the dips—they are refreshing and also add colour to the table. Try to use vegetables which will not duplicate the salads.

● For a pineapple dip, sieve 450 g [1 lb] cottage cheese and mix with 60 ml [4 tablespoons] thin cream. Stir in drained, crushed pineapple. Season with salt and a touch of chilli powder.

● For a soft cheese dip mix Philadelphia cream cheese with soured cream. Thin with milk if necessary. Add freshly chopped chives, mustard, salt and pepper.

● Cocktail sausages on sticks make a useful addition. Canned ones can be used for convenience.

● For a curry dip, flavour mayonnaise with curry and add grated cucumber.

Turkey and tongue galantine

⊠⊠⊠ *This galantine has an attractive, chequerboard effect when cut. It is achieved by distributing the tongue carefully when stuffing the galantine. A medium turkey is needed. The bones are removed and the turkey is stuffed with a substantial filling so the meat will be easy to slice and will go quite a long way. Use the turkey bones and carcass to make stock, poach the turkey in this and use this liquid for the aspic finish. Aspic lends itself well to garnishing and decorating dishes. This dish must be started at least one day before it is required. When carving the galantine make sure you cut it across the lengths of ham and tongue otherwise the chequerboard effect will be lost.*

SERVES 20
5 kg [11 lb] turkey
450 g [1 lb] cooked tongue
450 [1 lb] cooked ham
15 g [½ oz] pistachio nuts, shelled weight
1 small onion
25 g [1 oz] butter
450 g [1 lb] pie veal
225 g [½ lb] lean pork belly, rindless and boned
2 large eggs
50 ml [2 fl oz] thin cream
5 ml [1 teaspoon] dried thyme
5 ml [1 teaspoon] allspice
salt
freshly ground black pepper

For the glaze:
550 ml [1 pt] aspic

For the decoration:
6 well-shaped radishes
7.5 cm [3"] piece cucumber
4 stuffed olives or black stoned olives
fresh tarragon leaves

1 Bone the turkey yourself or have your butcher prepare it for you (this is much easier!). Be careful not to pierce the skin.

2 Cut the tongue and ham into long fingers 1.25 cm [½"] wide. Reserve.

3 Blanch the pistachio nuts by plunging into boiling water for 2 minutes. Pull away the skins.

4 To prepare the stuffing, skin and finely chop the onion. Put the butter in a small heavy-based pan and sauté the onion for 2 minutes to soften without colouring. Cool.

5 Cut the veal and the belly of pork into chunks and mince using the fine blade of your mincer. Place in a bowl with the onion, eggs, cream, herbs and seasoning. Add the pistachios and, keeping them whole, mix well.

6 Shape a teaspoonful of the stuffing into a ball and sauté in a little butter. Taste this and correct seasoning, bearing in mind that the tongue and ham are salty.

7 Spread the turkey out flat, skin down. Season. Spread a third of the stuffing in an even layer over the centre of the turkey.

8 Lay half the tongue and ham fingers lengthwise over the stuffing. Layer with stuffing, tongue, ham and a final layer of stuffing.

as tightly as possible. Put the galantine between two plates and put a weight on top. Leave to become quite cold.

15 Undo the muslin. Cut through the stitches and pull away. Place the galatine on a wire tray. Pour about half of the aspic over to give a thin coating. Pour the aspic along the centre first and then down the sides.

16 Wash and trim the radishes. Cut into circles to form flower petals. Using a potato peeler, pare long thin strips of skin from the cucumber to make a stalk. Slice the olives to form the centre of the flowers.

17 Decorate the top of the roll with a bouquet of flowers, using olives for the centres, radish circles for the petals, cucumber for the stalk and tarragon leaves for the leaves. Impale solid pieces on a skewer and dip in aspic before positioning.

18 Coat with a second application of aspic. Leave until set (for about 2 hours or overnight if wished). Transfer to a serving plate. You can use the excess aspic, chopped, as a garnish for the galantine.

Salad selection

Salads are the best accompaniment to galantine as they can be prepared well in advance, and you will not have to struggle with pans of boiling vegetables as guests arrive. Do not serve too many salads. Three or four should be sufficient. Increase the quantities of your favourite salads or use the ones given here. If you wish to adapt recipes for four to serve twenty, make about six times as much as this will allow for the odd person who eats more than you bargained for, as well as the unexpected guest.

Choose one starchy salad such as potato, rice, pasta or pulse. Contrast this with one or two green salads, a tomato salad and one colourful interesting salad. Try to vary textures and flavours as much as possible.

Use fresh herbs as far as possible—dried ones are unsuitable. If fresh herbs are not available use other items, such as olives, radishes, nuts, lettuce, fennel and slices of hard-boiled egg for the garnishing.

9 Fold the neck and tail ends inwards. Bring the two other sides together to form the turkey into a neat roll.

10 Thread a trussing needle with fine string. Stitch along one end, along the sides and the remaining end.

11 Wrap the roll in a double thickness of muslin. Tie the ends to make a secure parcel.

12 To cook the turkey use a saucepan just large enough to hold the roll. Cover with hot stock and bring to the boil. Simmer for 3 hours.

13 Drain the galantine over the pan then set aside. (Reserve the stock for the aspic.)

14 When cool enough to handle, undo the muslin and re-tie again

- For a potato salad allow 2.7 kg [6 lb] of potatoes. Cook new potatoes in their jackets. Drain, and while still hot roughly chop and dress with 700 ml [1¼ pt] vinaigrette. Leave to cool. Garnish generously with freshly chopped chives or parsley.
- For a tomato salad allow 2.2 kg [5 lbs] tomatoes. Slice tomatoes. Dress with salt, black pepper and 275 ml [½ pt] olive oil. Garnish with 225 g [½ lb] black olives or a generous sprinkling of freshly chopped basil.
- For a green salad allow 4 lettuces, depending on size, plus 2 bunches of watercress. Dress with 700 ml [1¼ pt] vinaigrette. Garnish with spring onions.
- For a cucumber salad, allow 3 large or 4 small cucumbers. Slice and dégorgé the cucumbers. Dress with 575 ml [1 pt] tarragon cream (see page 30) and garnish with fresh tarragon leaves.

Cheeseboard

For those who are not sweet eaters it is a nice idea to provide a cheeseboard. This might include a soft cream cheese, Camembert; Cheddar and a blue cheese. Serve a selection of crackers and biscuits and fruit such as apples, pears and grapes.

Engagement cake

⊠⊠⊠ *Despite the professional finish, this is a very simple cake. Make your own almond paste or use bought marzipan. The icing is a quick fondant which is moulded over the cake. A different icing is used to make the roses.*

SERVES 20
150 g [5 oz] glacé cherries
450 g [1 lb] raisins
175 g [6 oz] currants
30 ml [2 tablespoons] mixed peel
15 ml [1 tablespoon] angelica, chopped
100 g [4 oz] walnuts, chopped
225 g plus 30 ml [8 oz plus 2 tablespoons] self-raising flour
225 g plus 30 ml [8 oz plus 2 tablespoons] butter
225 g [8 oz] brown sugar
6 large eggs
7.5 ml [1½ teaspoons] ground allspice

5 ml [1 teaspoon] salt
30 ml [2 tablespoons] sherry

For the almond paste:
700 g [1½ lb] almond paste, made weight
apricot glaze

For the roses:
5 ml [1 teaspoon] gelatine
5 ml [1 teaspoon] white fat
22.5 ml [1½ tablespoons] water
175 g [6 oz] icing sugar
few drops of red edible food colouring

For the icing:
900 g [2 lb] icing sugar
2 egg whites
60 ml [4 tablespoons] liquid glucose

1 Pre-heat the oven to 150°C [300°F] gas mark 2. Line a heart-shaped cake tin (about 3.4 L [6 pt] capacity, width at widest point 20 cm [8"], length 18 cm [7"]) with a double thickness of greaseproof paper and use 30 ml [2 tablespoons] butter to grease the tin.

2 Roughly chop the cherries, combine all the fruit and nuts and toss them lightly in 30 ml [2 tablespoons] flour.

3 Cream the butter and sugar in a bowl until light and fluffy. Lightly beat the eggs, then add to the creamed mixture a little at a time.

4 Sift the flour, spice and salt then fold into the mixture with the fruit. Stir in the sherry.

9 Sift the icing sugar into a basin, make a well in the centre and pour in the liquid, with a few drops of colouring. Work together to form a smooth paste. If necessary, add a little more icing sugar.

10 Form the paste into small balls of varying sizes. Press most of them between sheets of greaseproof paper to flatten, making the edges very smooth. Make the remainder into small cone shapes with a point at one end.

11 Take one of the pointed shapes and fold a flattened shape around it to form a petal. Repeat to make rosebuds or larger roses.

12 Continue until all the shapes are used up. Leave on· greaseproof paper to dry.

5 Turn the mixture into the prepared cake tin. Make a dip in the centre. Bake in the centre of the oven for 2½-3 hours until a skewer inserted into the centre of the cake comes out clean.

6 Allow the cake to go cold in the tin before turning out.

7 Before applying the almond paste, glaze the cake with a small amount of melted apricot jam to make it stick. Because of its shape, press the paste on to the sides of the cake rather than rolling it on the paste. Leave to dry out on a cake board for two to three days.

8 To make the roses, dissolve gelatine, white fat and water in a basin over hot water.

13 To make the fondant icing, sift 800 g [1¾ lb] icing sugar into a basin. Make a well in the centre.

14 Pour egg whites and liquid glucose into the centre and work together to form a firm but manageable paste. If necessary, work in a little more icing sugar.

15 Dredge a little icing sugar on to a working surface. Roll out icing so it is 5 cm [2"] larger all round than the top of the cake.

16 Place icing on top of cake and roll and shape it over the heart to evenly cover.

17 Press dried roses into the soft fondant in an attractive design. Tie round with a pink ribbon.

Variation
●For an anniversary cake bake the mixture in a 23 cm [9"] round cake tin. Cover the cake with almond paste and icing. Decorate appropriately.

Strawberry baskets

This very special shell is made in three layers to give extra height and interior capacity for the delicious filling. The base of the basket is made from a shortbread mixture or 2 bought shortbread rounds. To serve 20, you will need two baskets which, although quite small, are rich and only small portions are needed.

SERVES 20
For the base:
700 g [1½ lb] shortbread mixture or 2 bought shortbread rounds, 18 cm [7"] diameter

For the sides:
700 g [1½ lb] puff pastry, made weight
1 medium-sized egg
90 ml [6 tablespoons] redcurrant jelly

For the filling:
1.4 kg [3 lb] fresh strawberries
30 ml [2 tablespoons] redcurrant jelly
grated zest of 1 orange
30 ml [2 tablespoons] brandy

To serve:
575 ml [1 pt] whipped cream

6 Transfer the circles to dampened baking trays. Use the puff pastry trimmings to cut out 20 crescent shapes, using either a knife or petits fours cutters. Put these on the baking trays.

7 Chill for 30 minutes. While chilling, heat the oven to 200°C [400°F] gas mark 6.

8 Beat the egg and use to brush the pastry. Bake in the centre of the oven, baking two trays at a time until golden and puffy.

9 Cool the pastry rings and crescents on a cooling rack.

10 Prepare the glaze. Place redcurrant jelly in a saucepan and heat gently until melted. Place the shortbread circles on two flat serving plates. Brush around the edges with redcurrant glaze.

11 Place one pastry ring on each base. Brush liberally with glaze. Place another ring on top. Continue in this way until all the rings have been used.

12 Decorate the top of each basket with the crescents and glaze.

13 Wash and hull the strawberries. Put the redcurrant jelly for the filling in a pan. Warm gently and then add orange zest and brandy. Mix well. Remove from heat.

14 Slice large strawberries but leave small ones whole. Add to the pan and stir until well glazed.

15 Just before serving, pile into the pastry cases. Serve with lightly whipped cream.

1 Heat the oven to 160°C [325°F] gas mark 3. Divide the shortbread mixture into two equal sized pieces.

2 Roll out each piece into 18 cm [7"] diameter round. Place each round on a greased baking sheet.

3 Prick lightly with a fork. Bake the rounds for 45 minutes until pale golden and firm. Leave to cool.

4 Meanwhile, divide the puff pastry into two equal pieces. Roll out to 3 mm [⅛"] thick.

5 Cut a circle 20 cm [8"] in diameter from one piece of the pastry. Using a saucer as a guide, cut a ring about 10 cm [4"] in diameter from the centre. Cut out another 2 circles in the same way, re-rolling pastry if necessary. Repeat with second piece of pastry.

Buffet supper for eighteen

With the rising costs of outside caterers, more and more cooks are choosing to prepare the food for small, semi-formal gatherings themselves. Catering on a very large scale is, of course, impossible in the home but there is no reason why a well-organized cook should not be able to cope with this buffet-style meal for 18 with ease—and still have enough time to get ready and look glamorous for the party.

Menu

Kipper and fennel salad
Brown bread

Coronation chicken
Salad selection

Raspberry and almond tart

To drink, Soave, Frascati or a white Bordeaux.

Choosing a meal which will suit the varied tastes of 18 people is never easy, but here is a menu which should find favour with all.

One of the most important things about a buffet is that the food should be easy to eat with a fork. The food chosen here certainly fits the bill and is a practical choice because it is all cold, giving you plenty of time to enjoy the party.

To begin with, there is a tangy marinated kipper salad, accompanied by thin slices of brown bread. Most people like kippers and the marinade prevents the dish from being too 'fishy'. After marinating, the kipper fillets become beautifully tender—almost like smoked salmon in fact, giving this relatively inexpensive dish a taste usually associated with more expensive and luxurious gourmet dishes.

The main course is a version of coronation chicken—cold boiled chicken in a light curry sauce. This original dish was created for the coronation of Queen Elizabeth II by the famous cook Constance Spry She was faced with the problem of finding a dish that would suit 300 people of various nationalities, yet could be prepared well in advance, and was not too taxing to make. The result was coronation chicken, which has been a popular buffet dish ever since that great occasion.

To accompany the chicken, there is a range of salads. Providing several

different salads is a good idea as it gives plenty of choice and adds colour and attraction to the table.

To end the meal, there is a raspberry and almond meringue tart which is deliciously light, easy to eat and just the thing after the rich main course.

GETTING ORGANIZED
A party on this scale requires long term planning to be a worry-free success. How you can organize the food shopping is detailed in the shopping checklist.

Ordering and hiring
One month before the planned date, send out invitations marked R.S.V.P. at the bottom—this is the abbreviation for the French 'répondez, s'il vous plaît'—and is the international code for 'please reply'. You should then hear quickly how many people are coming. As soon as you know this, make a list of the crockery, cutlery and glasses you will need.

Very few households are the proud owners of 18 sets of matching cutlery or crockery. Many people own 18 glasses that match but it is quite likely that they won't want to damage the set by risking breakages.

It is well worth hiring matching cutlery and crockery—not only for the sake of saving on washing-up but also to make the table look good. A mixture of plates looks messy and paper plates, though cheap, are not really suitable for buffets as they tend to deposit their contents on the floor if not placed on a firm surface.

The answer is to hire. Most hire companies have matching crockery, serving dishes and cutlery for hire and will give you terms inclusive of washing-up. You simply return the goods dirty and this is certainly worth the slight extra expense after you have cooked a meal for 18. Get several estimates and ask the companies for names of former customers so that you can check on the service and quality of the equipment. Be sure to arrange the hire a month in advance (confirm numbers after acceptances have been received) and ask for delivery the day before the party.

Glasses can usually be hired from

the place where the wine is purchased. The usual terms are a deposit which is returnable and you pay for any breakages.

At the same time, order the wine and flowers. Make sure that crockery and cutlery is to be delivered the day before, and wine and flowers on the day in good time.

The table
At a buffet, all the food usually appears on the table at once, along with the plates etc, which are usually in piles, and the cutlery. Quite a lot of space is needed for this. The best thing to do is to push two tables of the same height and width together to form one long table. Should this be impossible, you can hire trestle tables for quite a modest cost from caterers and hire shops.

To cover the table, you will need several cloths. A well-ironed sheet will cover the legs of trestle or joining tables and other tablecloths can be placed on top. To save washing afterwards, use paper cloths, arranging them diagonally so that the points make a pretty pattern at the bottom of the table. Paper tablecloths come in various sizes and are inexpensive.

Few people own enough easy chairs or sofas to seat 18. Leave those you have in the room and make up the numbers with hired stacking or folding chairs. Ordinary dining chairs will take up too much room. A few small tables well back from the centre of the floor with chairs grouped around them is a good idea. Coffee or even small bedside tables are ideal and these can usually be borrowed. A trolley to wheel away plates etc, is helpful too.

To serve the wine, a smaller table which has enough space for bottles and glasses is best. Cover with a paper tablecloth to match the one on the larger table.

Organizing the rooms
Make sure that you are free the day before the party so that the rooms to be used can be made ready. Remove all but necessary furniture from the room where the food will be, push your own or the hired table against the longest wall. Also place a trolley or small table near the large table for dirty plates. A trolley is best as it can be quickly wheeled away when full. (It might be worth detailing a member of the family to cope with this during the party.) Leave a few easy chairs in the

room but make sure the centre of the floor is clear.

It is well worth having the food in one room and the wine in another to encourage people to circulate and prevent traffic jams. The wine room need really only have a table for the wine and glasses and perhaps a few chairs.

On the day, set a bedroom aside for coats and see that there is plenty of soap and clean towels in the bathroom. Make sure there are plenty of ashtrays in all rooms to be used by the guests; ramekins or small saucers will serve the purpose. Finally, when the rooms are all clear, have a good clean and then ban the family until it is time for table setting.

Setting the table
On the morning of the day, you can part-set the table. Put out small plates for the kipper salad, large plates for the main course and dessert plates for the tarts in piles. Wrap your forks for the kipper salad in napkins and place on the table. Also wrap up forks for the main course and forks and spoons for the dessert.

Glasses can be arranged on the wine table. The food and wine should not be brought into the room until just before the party.

Organizing the food
The countdown timetable shows how the food can be organized so that there is no last minute rush. The kipper salad should be served in two large, shallow dishes and the brown bread which accompanies it on three large plates. Do not use just one plate or there will be a queue for food.

Likewise, divide the coronation chicken between three dishes and the salads between two bowls each. The tarts can be removed from the tins and placed on 3 plates. Slice each tart into 6 portions. Serve thin cream with the tarts in 3 jugs.

The best way to organize the table is to place the two plates containing the first course at each end, plus bread, salt and pepper. Arrange the chicken and salad in a similar way and place the tarts and cream in the centre.

Organizing the wine
White wine should be well chilled before serving. As most refrigerators won't accommodate the number of bottles required, fill the bath with

cold water about 4 hours before the party and submerge the bottles. Take them out and dry them just before the party and make sure they are in a cool place so that the wine does not warm up again.

Cooking equipment
No really special equipment is needed for cooking but you will need more and slightly larger equipment than usual. To marinate the kipper salad you will need one large glass or glazed earthenware dish (or two small ones, but these take up more space). The dish(es) should be fairly shallow. Do not use plastic containers as the marinade will taint the plastic permanently.

To cook the chickens, you will need two really large saucepans. The pan should have enough room to allow the chicken to be covered with liquid. If you have only one pan which fits the bill, neighbours may be able to help in supplying a second.

To mix the chicken and sauce together before transferring to serving dishes, you will need a large bowl. A large, new plastic washing-up bowl is perfect as the curry flavour is not strong enough to permeate the plastic.

For the tarts, you will need three 20 cm [8"] fluted flan tins. You could use the same tin three times of course, but this would increase the preparation time and use of the oven considerably. Neighbours may be able to lend you suitable tins. If not, they are quite cheap to buy.

SHOPPING CHECKLIST
When there is so much shopping to be done, it is wise to plan and order well in advance and to organize deliveries or at least a car to save wear and tear on your arms and nerves.

Fish
The kipper fillets for the salad can be bought frozen from most supermarkets. Kipper fillets are not as good in flavour as kippers on the bone, but as the salad is marinated, this makes very little difference. Also kipper fillets are ready prepared and this saves time and waste. The fillets may be bought up to 3 months in advance and can be stored until required in the frozen food compartment of a refrigerator, depending on the star rating, or in a freezer.

Meat

You will need to cook the chickens the day before your party. As the birds are so large, order in advance. Capons are best as they come in large sizes and are usually very tender. Larger boiling fowl are apt to be stringy. Buying two large chickens rather than several smaller ones makes sense for various reasons. Firstly, if you only have two birds, then you'll only need two rings on your cooker, so saving fuel. Also, the larger the chicken, the higher the proportion of meat to bone so you will get more portions per chicken. Professional caterers estimate that 100 g [¼ lb] of boneless meat makes a portion. This may sound a little on the mean side, but remember that there are salads and a rich sauce. Two 2.2 kg [5 lb] chickens will give you approximately 2.2 kg [5 lb] of usable meat after cooking, boning and skinning. This means at 4 portions per 450 g [1 lb] meat, you will get 20 portions—just enough leeway for guests who may take a little more than anticipated.

Fruit and vegetables

Fruit and vegetables occur in all three courses so first of all make a list. This is easier than shopping piecemeal. Root vegetables, onions and apples may be bought up to two days before. Salad ingredients should not be bought until the day to ensure absolute freshness, but order in advance anyway. If your greengrocer delivers, ask him to bring the salad items early on the day of your party or send a member of your family out to collect them—you will be too busy to go yourself. The raspberries for the tart should not be bought until the day if fresh. If you are using frozen raspberries, they may be bought up to 6 months in advance of the party and stored in the frozen food compartment of a refrigerator or freezer.

Bread

Brown bread is served with the kipper salad. You will need two large loaves and for the sake of freshness, these should not be bought until the day of the party. Once again, arrange delivery if you can. Ready-sliced bread makes life easier.

Cream

Thick cream is needed for the coronation chicken sauce and thin cream for the dessert. The amount of thick cream required is given in the recipe. You will need about 850 ml [1½ pt] thin cream. Do not get this until early on the day.

Other ingredients

The ingredients for the kipper marinade, salad dressings, coronation chicken (except chicken and vegetables) and for the pastry and topping of the tart can be divided in perishable and non-perishable. The non perishables—oil, vinegar, spices etc—can be bought as far in advance as you wish. You could, for instance, include one or two of the items in your weekly shopping for several weeks before the party. The perishables, in this case only eggs, can be bought a week before the party. You will need a dozen large ones (allowing for breakages): 9 whites for the meringues and 8 of the yolks for the mayonnaise.

Drinks

The drinks should be ordered about a month in advance of the party to be sure of getting the right kind and, if you can, order on a sale or return of whole bottle basis. Caterers allow half a standard bottle of wine per person so you would need 9 bottles for 18 people but if you know your friends and family are likely to drink more than this, allow more. When you are ordering wine in such large quantities, most shops will deliver.

Countdown timetable

ONE MONTH BEFORE
Send out invitations. Hire chairs, crockery, cutlery and tables.
Order wine and glasses.
Start shopping for non-perishables; spacing this out over the next four weeks is convenient.
Order flowers.

ONE WEEK BEFORE
Order chickens.

TWO DAYS BEFORE
Buy root vegetables, apples and fennel.

THE DAY BEFORE
Collect chickens from butcher.
Kipper and fennel salad: prepare kippers and marinade: steps 1–3.
Coronation chicken: boil the chickens and cool. Wrap in foil and store in the refrigerator. Make the sauce—cover and leave in the refrigerator: steps 1–11.
Raspberry and almond tart: make the pastry and then bake tarts blind: steps 1–2. Cool and cover.
Salad selection: make up vinaigrettes. Store in jars in cool place.

ON THE DAY

6 hours before
Collect salad items and raspberries. Collect bread and cream if not being delivered.

4 hours before
Raspberry and almond tart: add fruit and meringue: steps 3–7. Remove from tins, place on serving plates and leave in a cool place until required.
Chill the wine in a bath of cold water.
Part set the table and arrange the flowers.

3 hours before
Fresh potato salad: boil potatoes, peel and dress. Set aside in a cool place.
Kipper and fennel salad: drain and add rest of ingredients—steps 4–5. Place on serving dishes, cover and leave in a cool place.
Butter brown bread to accompany kipper salad, arrange on serving plates, cover with a damp tea-cloth and leave in a cool place.

2 hours before
Coronation chicken: add whipped cream to the sauce—step 12. Joint the chickens and pull away flesh. Mix with curry mayonnaise—steps 13–14. Place in serving dishes, cover and leave in a cool place.

30 minutes before
Salad selection: make other 3 salads and set aside in a cool place.

5 minutes before
Take all food to the table.
Remove wine bottles from water and take to table.

Kipper and fennel salad

⬛⬛⬛ *The sharp flavour of this salad is excellent when the main course is rich and creamy. This is a dish which must be part prepared in advance if the kippers are to be properly marinated. Ready-prepared kipper fillets reduce preparation time and are not so wasteful as kippers on the bone. Buying ready-prepared kipper fillets will cost a little more than buying whole kippers, however, the time saved will be useful for other things.*

SERVES 18
1.4 kg [3 lb] kipper fillets
200 ml [7 fl oz] olive oil
**75 ml [3 tablespoons]
  white wine vinegar**
**25 ml [5 teaspoons] German
  mustard**
**15 ml [1 tablespoon] caster
  sugar**
salt
freshly ground black pepper
**small bulb of Florentine
  fennel**
6 red eating apples
2 medium-sized onions
juice of 1 lemon

1 Cut the kipper fillets into long, thin strips. You will get about 4 strips from each fillet. Then cut each strip in half.

2 Place the kipper fillets in a large, shallow glass or glazed earthenware dish. Mix together the oil, vinegar, seasonings and 60 ml [4 tablespoons] of finely chopped fennel. Pour over the kipper fillets and turn so that all sides are coated. Cover.

3 Marinate the kipper fillets for at least 8 hours, turning from time to time.

4 Up to 2½ hours before the salad is required, core and slice the apples, skin and chop the onions, scrub and chop remaining fennel.

5 Drain the kipper fillets. Add chopped vegetables to marinade and toss with lemon juice (this prevents the apple from colouring). Cover and set aside in a cool place. Drain and add to kippers.

Coronation chicken

⬛⬛⬛ *This dish may look very complicated but is really a very simple and economical way to serve chicken. Make the mayonnaise for the sauce (or use bought if no time). It may be made a day in advance and stored covered in the refrigerator.*

SERVES 18
**2 chickens, each 2.2 kg [5 lb]
  dressed weight**
3 carrots
2 bouquets garnis
10 ml [2 teaspoons] salt
12 peppercorns

For the sauce:
**45 ml [3 tablespoons] olive
  oil**
1 large onion
**45 ml [3 tablespoons] curry
  powder**
**15 ml [1 tablespoon] tomato
  purée**
500 ml [18 fl oz] red wine
3 bay leaves
5 ml [1 teaspoon] salt
**15 ml [1 tablespoon] caster
  sugar**
freshly ground black pepper
3 slices lemon
**15 ml [1 tablespoon] lemon
  juice**
1.15 L [2 pt] mayonnaise
**45 ml [3 tablespoons] apricot
  jam**
**150 ml [¼ pt] lightly whipped
  cream**
2 small bunches watercress

1 Place the chickens in 2 large pans and cover with cold water. Bring to the boil very slowly.

2 Meanwhile, scrub the carrots and halve. When the chickens have reached boiling point, skim off any scum and lower the heat.

3 Divide the carrots between the pans. Add a bouquet garni to each pan. Divide the salt and peppercorns between the pans and bring back to the boil.

4 Cover the chickens and cook for 2 hours, checking from time to time to see that there is still enough water in the pan and replenishing as necessary.

5 When the chickens are cooked, remove from the pans. Place one at a time in a colander and place under running water for 2 minutes.

6 Allow the chickens to become cold. This will take about 1 hour in all.

7 Place the oil in a frying-pan. Skin and finely chop the onion. Heat the oil gently and add the onion. Fry over low heat for 3 minutes, stirring from time to time.

8 Stir the curry powder into the pan. Cook again for a further 2 minutes.

9 Add the tomato purée, wine and bay leaves. Bring to the boil. Add salt, sugar, pepper, the lemon slices and juice. Reduce heat and simmer, uncovered, for 10 minutes, stirring from time to time.

10 Remove the bay leaves and lemon slices from the pan. The sauce should now be thick. If it is very liquid, return pan to heat and reduce further. Remove from heat and allow sauce to cool.

11 Make the mayonnaise. Add the cold onion sauce a little at a time to the mayonnaise then stir in the apricot jam.

12 Lightly fold the whipped cream in to the mayonnaise. Adjust the seasoning, adding a little more lemon juice if necessary. Set aside.

13 Remove the skin from the cold chickens and cut them into joints, using poultry shears. Pull away all flesh from the chicken bones and cut into neat bite-sized pieces.

14 Mix the chicken flesh with the curry sauce. Leave covered in the refrigerator for at least 1½ hours before serving to allow flavours to amalgamate. Just before serving, garnish with sprigs of watercress.

Salad selection

Serve a selection of salads to go with coronation chicken. Do not prepare the salads too far in advance or flavour will be lost. As well as the salads given below, you may also wish to serve large, plain lettuce salads. To serve 18, you will need 3–4 large lettuces. The vinaigrettes may be made a day in advance. Make up about 850 ml [1½] for the potato salad and green salad. Make up about 250 ml [½ pt] of tarragon vinaigrette for the cucumber and tarragon salad. Put it into a bottle with a cork and shake well before dressing the lettuce. Don't be too generous with vinaigrette as the chicken has a sauce.

The salads, of course, can be varied to suit your own preferences and also the saladstuffs that happen to be in season. Whatever you decide on, bear in mind that flavours need to complement the chicken in its light curry sauce.

The three salads given here will serve 18 people.

Fresh potato salad

Scrub and boil 1.6 kg [3½ lb] small new potatoes. Remove the skins when cooked if wished. Slice and divide between two salad bowls. Dress with vinaigrette while still hot and sprinkle liberally with freshly chopped chives. Toss gently. Serve cold.

Cucumber and tarragon salad

Slice 3 large cucumbers. Place in a colander and sprinkle liberally with salt. Leave to drain for 15 minutes then refresh with cold water. Pat dry. Dress with vinaigrette made with tarragon vinegar and sprinkle liberally with freshly chopped tarragon.

Nut crunch salad

Core and finely slice, but do not peel, 6 red-skinned eating apples. Place them in salad bowls with a little lemon juice and toss until the slices are covered (this prevents the apples browning). Scrub and chop two large heads of celery. Place in salad bowls with 100 g [¼ lb] chopped walnuts. Toss in vinaigrette.

Raspberry and almond tart

Three of these tarts will be ample to serve 18. Do not complete the tart more than 4 hours in advance or the meringue may turn tough. If you wish, make the sweet richcrust pastry in advance and chill until needed.

MAKES 3 TARTS,
EACH SERVING 6
500 g [1 lb 2 oz] richcrust pastry
1.1 kg [2¼ lb] fresh raspberries
30 ml [2 tablespoons] cornflour
9 large egg whites
pinch of salt
500 g [1 lb 2 oz] caster sugar
250 g [9 oz] ground almonds
175 g [6 oz] blanched, flaked almonds

1 Set the oven to 200°C [400°F] gas mark 6.

2 Roll out the pastry and use to line three 20 cm [8"] fluted flan tins. Prick the pastry base and bake blind for 15 minutes.

3 Toss the raspberries in cornflour to absorb juice during cooking and place them in the flan tins.

4 Place the egg whites in your largest, clean bowl. Add the salt and stir. Whisk until they stand in stiff peaks.

5 Whisk half the caster sugar in, a spoonful at a time. Fold in the remaining sugar in two batches.

6 Fold the ground almonds into the meringue and spread or pipe over the raspberries. Sprinkle blanched almonds over the top.

7 Bake at 180°C [350°F] gas mark 4 for 15 minutes. Leave to shrink away from the side of the tin for 2 minutes, then remove from tin. Leave on the metal base to make cutting easier. Serve cold.

Garden barbecue for 12

With the onset of long, warm summer evenings, even the most devoted television and armchair addicts begin to feel the call of the great outdoors. Now is the time to take your entertaining out of the dining-room and into the garden. Build a barbecue, light your fire, cook the simple and delicious dishes given here and there'll be outdoor fun for grown ups and children alike.

Menu

❀

Hamburgers
Tray of burger
relishes
Boy scout sausages
Baked potatoes

━━◆❉◆━━

Fresh fruit tartlets
Toasted
marshmallows
Baked bananas
Baked apples

━━◆❉◆━━

To drink: beer, cider, shandy,
ginger beer, lager and lime or
squash.

Somehow, food always tastes better in the open air. And better still if the cooking is done over an open fire. If you have the fire in your garden there is no long and weary trail home afterwards to spoil the day and small fry can retire indoors when they get tired, leaving older guests to stay out as late as they please.

One of the advantages of having an outdoor party is that there is no lack of willing helpers; so it is a great opportunity for you to relax and let others get on with the cooking. There are no problems about everything being ready at the same time—barbecues work on a principle of first come, first served, as the food comes sizzling hot from the fire.

An outdoor party is essentially a free and easy affair so don't invite someone you want to impress. Close friends and their children, in whose company you will be able to relax and enjoy yourself, are the perfect guests.

BUILDING THE FIRE

Your first consideration is an outdoor cooker and where to put it. If you are already the proud owner of a purpose-built barbecue, there are no problems. But if not, don't think you have to rush out and spend considerable sums of money buying one. An arrangement of domestic bricks with a charcoal fire in the middle is perfectly adequate. You might even be able to manage with a simple wood bonfire and no bricks, but that sort of blaze is unreliable and it is hard to maintain a steady fierce glow for cooking. Food tends to end up black on the outside and raw within.

Before you start building your fire, pick a patch of the garden or patio that won't be badly damaged by scorching. If there is no such patch available, invest in an asbestos sheet (available from ironmongers).

To build your barbecue, you need 15 whole bricks and one half. Arrange seven of these bricks in a square and put the half brick in the bottom row on the side the wind is coming from, leaving a gap. This will encourage a draught and helps your fire to burn better. Then make a square on top of these bricks with the other eight bricks. If you wish, you can add a few more bricks and make the side walls higher to save bending.

Two 1.5 kg [3½ lb] bags of charcoal briquettes will be enough fuel; one bag to start the fire and the other to keep it going as the evening progresses. Place the charcoal in the middle of the fire and add a couple of fire-lighters—it is impossible to get charcoal going just with matches.

Lighting up time

You need to light your fire at least an hour before you start cooking (more if you are cooking baked potatoes) to give the charcoal time to become red and glowing. Light the fire-lighters and fan the flames with bellows or a thickly folded newspaper. Never, never use paraffin or petrol to encourage the fire to burn. It may save time, but it can be extremely dangerous.

When the charcoal starts to go grey on the surface, drop in a few fresh bits to keep the fire going.

To provide a cooking platform over your fire, you need a grid. Two old oven shelves (often available cheap from second-hand shops) or two drain gratings (from demolition sites) laid side by side with the ends

Countdown timetable

THE DAY BEFORE
Do the shopping.
Fresh fruit tartlets: make pastry and bake cases—steps 1-8. Leave to cool— step 9.

ON THE DAY
In the morning
Hamburgers: prepare and store—steps 1-11.
Baked potatoes: scrub and dry, prick.
Baked apples: core, stuff and wrap in foil.
Relishes: make and put in bowls. Cover with cling film.

3 hours before
Build the fire and light.
Set up trestle table. Take out cutlery, china and night-lights if using. Take out baking tray for cooking burgers, and skewers for sausages and marshmallows.

1½ hours before
Bury scrubbed and pricked baked potatoes in hot charcoal.

½ hour before
Take out the food, arrange on the trestle table and cover.

resting on the bricks would be suitable.

SPECIAL EQUIPMENT

To cook the hamburgers, you need an old baking sheet. As this is liable to become very hot, you also need several thick cloths for the cooks to use.

The hamburgers and their buns have to be brought out of the house and into the garden. A large plastic container with a clip-on lid will keep the hamburgers cool and fresh while they are waiting to be cooked. The buns should be split in readiness and placed on a tray. Cover with kitchen paper. To turn the burgers while they are cooking, you need a pair of tongs or a fish slice. Special tools are sold for barbecues and these have extra long handles to keep your hands away from the heat.

Put the relishes into bowls which are attractive but not particularly prized, then it will not matter so much if one of them is broken. To serve the relishes, provide spoons. Once again, choose those whose loss will not be too important. The same goes for the bowl containing whipped cream for the tartlets.

Barbecue food is inclined to be greasy and messy and also rather too hot to handle. Provide paper napkins or double-thick squares of kitchen paper, and paper plates, knives and forks for awkward-to-eat items like baked potatoes. If you are serving baked apples, provide spoons. For the drinks, choose plain, cheap glasses or even tin mugs. It is also a nice idea to provide a damp cloth or some cologne wipes to clean messy or greasy hands.

To cook the sausages and marshmallows provide long skewers or toasting forks or encourage the kids to take to the woods and find some thin willow twigs. Peeled, these make ideal toasting forks, as every good scout knows.

The fruit tartlets can be arranged on a large tray. Once again have plenty of kitchen paper available to cover them.

To provide a place to put the food, rig up a trestle table. Two dustbins and an old door covered with a pretty paper cloth are easy, functional and cheaper than wrought-iron garden furniture. You can put butter, salt, relishes, plates, glasses, tartlets and cutlery at one end and the food to be cooked at the other. Be sure to situate your table somewhere near the fire so that you are not galloping up and down the garden in search of sausages and burgers.

With so many paper napkins about, it is wise to provide a large empty box or bin for litter, otherwise your garden will be a mess. More to the point, the rubbish might blow into neighbours' gardens which would make you most unpopular.

Finally, just in case there should be a rain shower, have a metal dustbin-lid handy. This can be used to cover the fire and keep it burning until the weather improves.

Night lighting

If you are having your barbecue in the evening, lighting will be required. Night-lights standing in saucers of water or in jam jars hung from trees are pretty and inexpensive. Night flyers are attracted by light so, to keep them away, invest in some mosquito repellent coils. These make attractive lights and, when lit, emit a repellent which keeps the mosquitoes and moths at bay.

SHOPPING CHECKLIST

All the food featured in this menu is simple, so shopping should not present problems. The only difficulty is to remember it all. Children are likely to take it badly if you have promised toasted marshmallows and then forget to buy any.

The best time to do the shopping is the day before the party, so that you have plenty of time to prepare things.

At the butcher, buy steak for the hamburger mince. It is much better to buy rump steak and mince it yourself just before making the hamburgers, as it is much tastier and fresher then. Also buy sausages, allowing one sausage per person (a fair approximation, as some people won't want them and hungry guests can then have two); you will need about 1 kg [2 lb] for twelve people.

At the greengrocer, buy the vegetables for the relishes. If there is no fresh sweetcorn available to make mid-western relish, frozen or canned sweetcorn kernels may be used. Buy also bananas and apples, if you plan to bake them, and the filling for the fresh fruit tarts. If there are no fresh apricots or strawberries available, use any other soft fruit or in the case of apricots, canned. Alternatively use canned pie fillings.

At the ironmongers, buy the charcoal, fire-lighters, night-lights, mosquito coils and an asbestos sheet if you need it.

Hamburgers are traditionally eaten inside a bun, so buy two dozen soft-crusted rolls. Sesame seed buns go very well with hamburgers. Do not buy crusty rolls as these are difficult to eat when you are standing up.

At the supermarket, stock up on paper towels and foil. Also buy chutney and mustard if necessary, apricot jam and redcurrant jelly for the tart glazes, oil and vinegar if needed for mayonnaise and don't forget the marshmallows.

DRINKS

Long, cool drinks, not too alcoholic in content, are best for an outdoor party. For children, provide ginger beer or fruit squash, for the adults, cider, lager and lime, beer or shandy. If the beer is in cans, keep it cool by standing the cans in a washing-up bowl full of water and ice. Bottled squash (dilute it first) can be kept cool in a similar way. Ice can often be bought in large quantities from hotels and bars.

Hamburgers

If you use the very best mince available and season it really well, there should be no criticisms of home-made hamburgers. It is best to buy rump steak whole and mince it yourself on the day you plan to make the burgers; mince twice for really good results. If cooking hamburgers indoors, it is best to grill them under a very hot grill, as this extracts excess fat. Cook the burgers under fierce heat for one minute each side. Then reduce heat or lower grill pan and cook for a further two minutes each side for rare meat, three minutes each side for medium-rare and four minutes each side for well-done.

If you do not cook all 24 hamburgers, the excess may be frozen. Interleave them with greaseproof paper so that they don't freeze together in a mass. Hamburgers will keep in the freezer for six months.

MAKES 24
1.4 kg [3 lb] rump steak
350 g [¾ lb] onions
6 thick slices white bread
20 ml [4 teaspoons] mixed freshly chopped parsley, chives and marjoram or 15 ml [3 teaspoons] dried mixed herbs
10 ml [2 teaspoons] salt
freshly ground black pepper
3 medium-sized eggs
50 g [2 oz] dripping or lard
50 g [2 oz] plain flour
24 buns, baps, or soft-crusted rolls

1 Cut the steak into cubes and mince.

2 Peel the onions. Cut into chunks. Mince the steak again, adding the onions to the mincer.

3 Cut the crusts off the bread. Reduce to crumbs using either the large holes on your cheese grater or a liquidizer.

4 Add the breadcrumbs, herbs and seasonings to the mince and onion mixture. Mix well.

5 Break the eggs into a jug and beat with a fork.

6 Pour the beaten egg into the mince mixture and mix well until the mince is clinging together.

7 Lightly flour a board.

8 Take 45 ml [3 tablespoons] of the mixture out of the bowl and place on the board.

9 Form into a round cake about 6 mm [¼"] thick with your hands.

10 Make the rest of the mince mixture into burgers in this way, re-flouring the board as necessary.

11 If preparing in advance, pile into a plastic box, placing a sheet of greaseproof between each layer. Cover and chill until required.

12 To cook, spread the dripping over the baking tray and place on the barbecue.

13 When the fat is smoking slightly, place 4-6 burgers (or however many can be comfortably accommodated) on the tray.

14 Cook the burgers for 3 minutes each side for rare meat, 4 minutes for medium-rare and 5 minutes for well-done, turning once.

15 Split the buns. These may be toasted, if wished, on skewers or by placing on the grid. Place a burger in each bun and let the guests help themselves to relishes. The buns are optional and the burgers are just as nice without.

Burger relishes

Anyone who has ever eaten in an American-style hamburger restaurant will know the fascination of the relish tray. Here are a few simple relishes to give your home-made hamburgers that authentic touch. Each of the recipes given below provides enough to accompany 24 hamburgers and 12 sausages. Leftovers go well with baked potatoes.

Mid-west relish
Mix together 175 g [6 oz] cooked sweetcorn kernels, half a finely chopped red pepper, 30 ml [2 tablespoons] French or German mustard and 60 ml [4 tablespoons] mayonnaise.

Russian relish
Dice a cucumber, removing seeds if wished. Mix with 250 ml [½ pt] sour cream or natural yoghurt and a finely chopped onion.

Horseradish relish
Older guests enjoy the combination of horseradish and beef. Simply add 20 ml [4 teaspoons] freshly grated horseradish or 30 ml [2 tablespoons] horseradish sauce to 250 ml [½ pt] mayonnaise.

Other accompaniments
As well as these relishes, provide chutney, mustard (several different kinds if you have it), crumbled blue cheese and lots of finely chopped raw onion.

Other fire food

As well as the food for which recipes are given, cook sausages, bake potatoes, bananas and apples, toast marshmallows on your fire, according to your guests' appetites.

Boy scout sausages
Sausages cooked on an open fire so that they are charred almost black on the outside but juicy and tender within are a treat worth tasting. Plump pork sausages are best as they have enough fat not to dry out over the fire. When the fire is red and glowing, spear your sausage on a peeled willow twig, skewer or a toasting fork and hold over the coals. Turn from time to time. When the sausages are dark brown (about eight minutes) they are cooked.

Alternatively, fry your sausages on the tray used for burgers or cook them on a grid over the fire.

Baked potatoes
Large, floury potatoes are best for this. Scrub the outsides well, dry them and prick with a fork to prevent the skins bursting while cooking. Do not coat the potatoes with fat, this causes flaring. Bury them in the charcoal embers just outside the hottest red part of the fire. Leave for about two hours depending on size, then serve split in napkins with plenty of butter and salt.

Toasted marshmallows
When toasted, marshmallows turn brown and crunchy on the outside and stickily liquid within. They are a great favourite with children. Spear the marshmallows, three or four at a time, on a stick or skewer and cook over the fire until the outsides are golden. This will take about four to five minutes. Never cook marshmallows on a grid—they will stick and drip through on to the fire.

Baked bananas
Slightly under-ripe bananas are best for baking in this way. Bury the banana, still in its skin, in the fire. Leave for about 10 minutes, until the skin is charred. Remove from the fire, peel a strip of skin (using a paper napkin so you won't burn yourself) and eat the banana with a spoon.

Baked apples
Cooking apples, cored and filled with brown sugar, butter and raisins or other dried fruits and chopped nuts, can be baked in the embers. Stuff the apples, wrap them in foil, bury in the embers and leave for 1 hour. Open up the foil, using it as a plate and eat the apple with a spoon.

Fresh fruit tartlets

⊠⊠ *These attractive fresh fruit tartlets are served cold and may be prepared well in advance. Because the tartlets have an uncooked filling they must be baked blind. Allow the pastry cases to cool well before filling. It is more economical to bake all 24 pastry cases at once. If, however, you do not own two 12-cup tart tins, they will have to be baked in two batches. Be sure that the tin is clean and cold before putting in the second batch of pastry.*

Serve with a large bowl of whipped cream for a touch of luxury.

MAKES 24
275 g [10 oz] shortcrust pastry
6 fresh apricots or 12 canned apricot halves
30 ml [2 tablespoons] apricot jam
250 g [½ lb] fresh strawberries
30 ml [2 tablespoons] redcurrant jelly

1 Heat the oven to 220°C [425°F] gas mark 7.

2 On a lightly floured board, roll out the pastry until it is 6 mm [¼"] thick. Using a 7.5 cm [3"] scone cutter, cut as many rounds as you can from the pastry.

3 Pile the trimmings one on top of each other and reroll. Cut further rounds until you have 24.

4 Using the scone cutter as a guide, draw a 7.5 cm [3"] circle on a sheet of greaseproof paper. Cut out and use as a pattern to cut another 23 greaseproof circles.

5 Place one pastry circle in each tartlet mould in two 12-cup tart tins. Press so the pastry is moulded to the tin.

6 Place a greaseproof circle in each pastry-lined mould. Weigh down with baking beans.

7 Cook just above the centre of the oven for 10 minutes.

8 Remove from oven. Remove baking beans and greaseproof. Return to the oven for 5 minutes, then cool.

9 Using a round-bladed knife, gently lever the pastry shells out of the tin. Stand on a tray and leave until quite cold.

10 If using fresh apricots, skin, stone and halve. If using canned, drain thoroughly.

11 Place half an apricot in 12 of the pastry shells rounded side up.

12 Sieve the apricot jam into a heavy-based pan. Heat gently until melted. When melted, remove from the heat.

13 Using a pastry brush, brush the apricot jam over each apricot half.

14 Rinse, dry and hull the strawberries. Place 3 small berries in each of the remaining cases. Where strawberries are very large, cut in half. Arrange the strawberries with the pointed side up.

15 Place the redcurrant jelly in a heavy-based pan and heat gently. When liquid, glaze the strawberries in the same way as the apricots.

16 Leave in a cool place for at least 2½ hours to allow the glaze to set.

GLOSSARY

BAIN-MARIE
(or double-boiler): Cooking vessel usually used for dishes best cooked away from direct heat. Pâtés are often cooked in a bain-marie and it is a great aid in keeping dishes hot without risk of over-cooking. To use, half-fill with hot or boiling water and insert the dish to be cooked into the bain-marie. The temperature of water in the bain-marie should be kept near boiling point throughout cooking.

BARD: To cover breast of poultry or game with strips of bacon fat to keep it moist during roasting. The bacon should be removed twenty minutes before the end of cooking time to allow the meat to brown. If you have no bacon, rub butter generously over the breast of the bird before roasting, and baste frequently. Duck and goose do not need barding as they are fatty birds.

BLANCH: Literally, to whiten, but usually now means to boil vigorously in water for one to two minutes. Some foods (such as gammon, brussel sprouts, kippers and onions) are blanched to cleanse and harden them, and to remove strong taste. Vegetables, fruits and nuts (almonds in particular) are blanched or scalded with boiling water to make them easier to peel.

BOMBES: Fancy, moulded ice-cream puddings. They are traditionally shaped as a dome in a special mould or small pudding bowl. The outer layer of bombes is always of ice-cream (and there is a hidden layer, which may be of ice-cream, or water-ice or sorbet) and a special custard-like bombe mixture may fill the centre. A bombe is usually made up of three parts ice-cream to one part bombe mixture. To make 150 ml [¼ pt] bombe mixture use 40 g [1½ oz] caster sugar and 2 large egg yolks. Optional extras are flavourings, 1 egg white, stiffly whisked, and 30 ml [2 tablespoons] lightly whipped cream. Put 150 ml [¼ pt] cold water into pan, add sugar and stir until completely dissolved. Then bring quickly to boil. Simmer for three minutes. Remove pan from heat and cool in bowl of water and ice cubes. Whisk egg yolks in double-boiler over very low heat until thick, light and creamy. Whisk cooling syrup into eggs, adding very little at a time, and whisking between each addition. Continue whisking until mixture is doubled in bulk—about fifteen minutes. Plunge pan into iced water. Go on whisking until mixture is thick and completely cold before use. Fold in flavouring and/or whipped cream or whisked egg white just before using mixture.

BOUQUET GARNI: A faggot or bunch of herbs usually made up from sprigs of thyme, parsley and bayleaf. Marjoram can be added. It is used to flavour stews and stocks.

CALORIE: Unit of heat used in measuring the fuel (energy) value of food, or technically the amount of heat required to raise 1 kilogram of water 1°C. Every adult needs so many calories daily to maintain strength. High energy foods will not help you get things done and must be eaten in combination with other foods to give you a balanced diet for energy and vitality.

CANAPES: Small rounds of fried or toasted bread, shortcrust pastry, or biscuits, covered with a savoury mixture or meat. Served hot or cold.

CARBOHYDRATES: A group of foods essential to a balanced diet, including starches, sugars and cellulose, and containing carbon, hydrogen and oxygen. Sugars and alcohol provide 'empty' calories—there is nothing in them which is important to your health, so cutting down on them is a good idea. Foods with a high starch content, on the other hand, often provide a wider range of vitamins than any other foods. Bread, for example, provides protein, calcium and vitamin B, as well as some iron. Wholemeal and granary bread have the advantage of supplying roughage or fibre. Potatoes are quite a good source of vitamin C.

CHAMBRE: A term used to describe red wine at room temperature. If red wine is kept at cellar temperature it will be too cold to give off its full bouquet so it should be left in a warm room for several hours until it is brought to room temperature.

COCOTTES: Small china, earthenware or metal dishes for cooking mousses, soufflés or eggs in, usually with two side-handles and a lid.

CRUDITE: Crudité means 'raw' in French and in culinary terms describes the raw vegetables that are served as an aperitif course with a creamy dip.

FATS: Fat is an essential part of the diet, needed to help make up new living cells and to convey certain vitamins, particularly vitamins A and D. All fats, whether hard or soft, animal or vegetable, provide the same amount of energy. It is a good idea to avoid eating too much fat and it is easy to eat more than you realize—in the form of salad dressings, fried foods and so on.

GALANTINE: Boned poultry, veal or pork stuffed with savoury stuffings, simmered in stock and, when cold, coated with aspic glaze. See, for example, Turkey and tongue galantine in Recipe index.

MACERATE: To soak fruit in liqueur or syrup.

MARINATE: To souse or soak. Applied to meat or game soaked in wine and oil with herbs and vegetables to flavour, before cooking. The object is to make the meat more tender, moist and well-flavoured.

MINERALS: There are about ten mineral elements to be derived from daily food. The chief ones are calcium (found in cheese, herrings, watercress, eggs, etc.), phosphorus (found in sweetbreads, cheese, fish, meat, eggs, bread, milk, etc.) and iron (found in kidney, liver, beef, herrings, watercress, spinach, celery, cabbage, raisins, etc.).

MOUSSELINES: Various preparations which are mousse-like. Mousselines consist of a forcemeat made of chicken, meat or fish, stiffened with whites of egg and lightened and enriched with cream. They can be poached or cooked in a mould in a bain-marie.

PASTRY:

CHOUX PASTRY: Sweet French pastry used for making cakes such as éclairs. To make 16 éclairs, 12 choux buns, 30 profiteroles or 3 rings, sift 65 g [2½ oz] plain flour on to a piece of greaseproof paper. Place 2 eggs in a basin and whisk together. Then put 50 g [2 oz] butter, pinch of salt and 150 ml [¼ pt] water into a saucepan and place over a moderate heat. Bring slowly to the boil, stirring. Take the pan off the heat and quickly tip in the flour and beat with a wooden spoon until smooth. Return pan to a low heat and beat vigorously for 1–2 minutes until the mixture forms a smooth ball. Draw pan off heat and allow to cool for 2 minutes. Beat in eggs a little at a time until incorporated. Then add a few drops of vanilla extract and spoon or pipe the mixture on to a prepared baking sheet. The finished paste should be smooth and shiny and hold its shape.

DANISH PASTRIES: These are made from a soft yeast dough which is lightly rolled and folded with softened butter. They are made in shapes such as envelopes, crescents, pinwheels, etc., and filled with creamy custards, spicy, buttery mixtures or rich nut pastes. To make 16 pastries use 15 g [½ oz] fresh yeast or 10 ml [2 teaspoons] dried yeast plus 2.5 ml [½ teaspoon] sugar plus 75 ml [5 tablespoons] cold water; 225 g [½ lb] plain flour; pinch of salt; 15 ml [1 tablespoon] caster sugar; 25 g [1 oz] lard; 1 egg; 150 g [5 oz] butter. Prepare yeast liquid. Sift flour and salt into large bowl. Cut and rub in lard. Stir in caster sugar. Beat egg and add to yeast liquid. Pour on to dry ingredients and mix with wooden spoon. Knead with fingers on lightly floured surface until smooth. Place in lightly greased polythene bag and rest in cold place for ten minutes. Beat butter until soft and shape with palette knife to a rectangle 23 × 7.5 cm [9 × 3"]. Chill briefly in refrigerator. Roll out dough to a 25 cm [10"] square. Place butter in centre, and fold unbuttered sides of dough over butter to overlap by 1 cm [½"]. Seal top and bottom edges. Lightly roll out dough to rectangle 45 × 15 cm [18 × 6"] and fold over evenly in three. Return dough to polythene bag and rest for 10 minutes in cold place. Repeat rolling, folding and resting twice more. Rest dough for 10 minutes and then dough is ready for filling and shaping.

FLAKY PASTRY: A pastry made in such a way that air and fat are trapped between layers. For 225 g [½ lb] flaky pastry, use 225 g [½ lb] plain flour; 2.5 ml [½ teaspoon] salt; 75 g [3 oz] lard; 75 g [3 oz] butter or margarine; 10 ml [2 teaspoons] lemon juice; and approximately 75 ml [7 tablespoons] chilled water. Divide each fat into four equal pieces and place one portion of each on four plates and chill. Sift flour and salt into mixing bowl. Dice quarter of fats and rub pieces into flour. Add lemon juice and water to make a soft pliable dough. Knead lightly on floured surface and pat into a rectangular shape. Roll out dough to an oblong. Lightly mark dough into three equal sections. Cut another quarter of fats into small pieces and dot alternately over top of two marked sections of dough. Fold fatless section of dough across centre section, making sure edges of dough are straight. Fold top section over centre section. Lightly seal the three raw edges with a rolling pin and press dough at intervals to distribute air. Relax in refrigerator. Repeat process twice more with the remaining quarters of fats. Fold and roll to seal. Cover dough loosely in a polythene bag and place in the refrigerator for a minimum of 30 minutes to firm and relax before use. This resting period gives a more flaky texture.

HOT WATER CRUST: Essentially an English pastry which is both strong and pliable and used for making raised pies. To make 450 g [1 lb] use 450 g [1 lb] strong plain flour; pinch of salt; 100 g [¼ lb] lard; 200 ml [¼ pt + 4 tablespoons] water. Sift flour and salt into bowl. Make a well in centre. Put lard and liquid in a small, heavy-based pan. Heat gently until lard has melted into water. Bring to boil. Take off heat as soon as boiling point is reached. Pour into well in centre of flour. Mix to a dough, working very quickly. Remove on to a floured surface. Using one hand, pinch and knead dough until it is smooth and silky in texture. Wrap dough in film and then in a damp tea-towel. Rest at room temperature for twenty minutes before using.

PATE SUCREE: French sugared pastry, often referred to as French flan pastry and containing both eggs and sugar. It is used for lining sweet tarts of all types. To make 100 g [¼ lb] pâte sucrée, use: 100 g [¼ lb] plain flour; pinch of salt; 50 g [2 oz] unsalted butter; 50 g [2 oz] caster or icing sugar; 2 drops of vanilla extract; 2 egg yolks. Sift flour and salt on to marble slab or pastry board. Spread flour into circle and make well in centre. Place chopped butter in centre. Add sugar. Mix yolks with vanilla extract and add. Draw together the butter, sugar and egg yolks, using the fingertips of one hand. Do not pull in the flour yet. Work flour a little at a time into paste in the centre of the well. Scrape down your hand with palette knife if it becomes sticky. When all flour is incorporated, smooth by pressing down with the heel of your hand, lifting away smartly. Wrap the pastry in polythene or greaseproof paper and then place in refrigerator for 1 hour until pastry is firm.

ROUGH PUFF PASTRY:

Like flaky pastry, rough puff rises in layers of flakes when cooked, but is easier and quicker to make than flaky pastry. Rough puff will hold its shape with ease when cooked and is therefore suitable for intricate decorations. It is never kneaded. To make 225 g [½ lb] of rough puff pastry, use 75 g [3 oz] lard; 75 g [3 oz] margarine; 225 g [½ lb] plain flour; 2.5 ml [½ teaspoon] salt; 90 ml [6 tablespoons] chilled water and 10 ml [2 teaspoons] lemon juice. Cut fats into small pieces and keep chilled in refrigerator. Sift flour and salt into chilled bowl. Add fats and toss lightly with palette or round-bladed knife to coat fats in flour. Add water and lemon juice and carefully gather mixture together with fingertips to form soft, pliable dough. Shape dough on lightly floured board or surface with fingertips. Do not knead. Roll to a rectangle, and lightly mark three equal sections with back of knife. Fold and seal dough. Roll pastry to its original size and repeat folding and sealing process. Place pastry on plate, cover with polythene bag and place in refrigerator for 30 minutes. Repeat rolling, folding and sealing twice more. Rough puff can be used where flaky pastry is specified.

SUETCRUST PASTRY:

Light, spongy pastry, used with both sweet and savoury fillings. To make 225 g [½ lb] suet pastry, use 225 g [½ lb] self-raising flour or 225 g [½ lb] plain flour and 15 ml [1 tablespoon] baking powder; 2.5 ml [½ teaspoon] salt; 100 g [¼ lb] shredded or grated suet; 150 ml [¼ pt] water. Sieve flour and salt (plus baking powder if using plain flour) into mixing bowl, add shredded or grated suet and mix together lightly. Make a well and pour water into this, then stir and cut through mixture until the water is absorbed and mixture is well blended. Form dough into a ball with your hands. Sprinkle a little sieved flour on to a working surface and turn ball of dough on to it. Knead by drawing outer edges of dough lightly into centre with your fingertips for one minute until surface of dough is smooth and free from cracks.

PROTEINS:

Any of a class of nitrogenous substances consisting of a complex union of amino acids. Proteins occur in all animal and vegetable matter and are essential to the diet. They are body-builders and energy producers. They are necessary for repair and replacement in the body.

STIR-FRYING and STIR-BRAISING:

Chinese methods of fast cooking vegetables and/or meat and fish in a little oil or fat and a small amount of liquid. The ingredients must first be chopped, sliced and shredded into small even-sized pieces before placing in the hot, flavoured oil. After initial frying, a small quantity of liquid is usually added to pan. In stir-frying, this is brought to the boil and allowed to reduce rapidly. In stir-braising a little more liquid is added and the ingredients are covered and allowed to soften in the pan. Both are best done in a wok, a Chinese cooking vessel with sloping sides, which ensures even cooking.

VITAMINS:

Organic substances found variously in most foods and essential, in small amounts, for the normal functioning of the body. The principal known vitamins include: *Vitamin A:* found in fish-liver oil, eggs, milk, butter etc. and in carrots and other vegetables; Vitamin B complex includes *Vitamin B₁* (thiamine, aneurine): found in eggs, liver, beans and vegetables, *Vitamin B₂* (riboflavine): found in yeast, milk, liver, green vegetables and cheese, *Nicotinamide:* found in liver, milk, wholemeal bread and yeast, *Folic acid:* found in green vegetables, yeast and liver, and *Vitamin B₁₂:* found in meat, milk and eggs; *Vitamin C:* found in citrus fruits, tomatoes and various vegetables; *Vitamin D:* found in fish liver oils, milk, eggs, cheese etc; *Vitamin E:* found in whole wheat, lettuce, black treacle etc; *Vitamin K:* found in leafy green vegetables, fish meal, hempseed, cabbage, etc.

INDEX

Picture Credits